Calligraphy

HOW I FELL IN, OUT, AND IN LOVE AGAIN

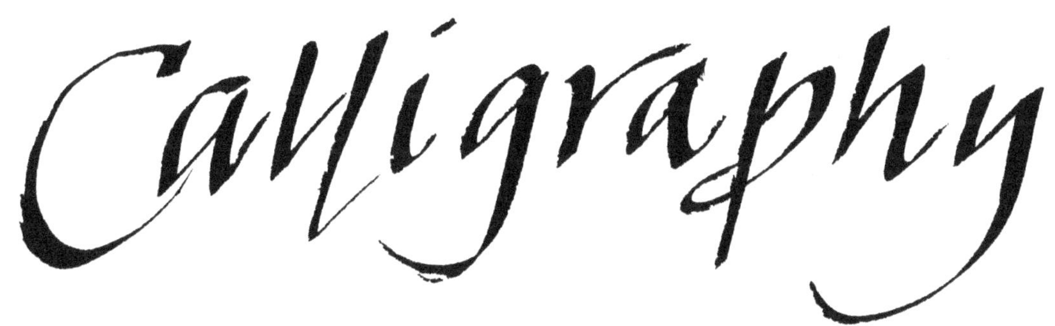Calligraphy

HOW I FELL IN, OUT, AND IN LOVE AGAIN

SUSAN KAPUSCINSKI GAYLORD

ISBN: 978-0-9891642-5-2

Book Design: Susan Kapuscinski Gaylord
Cover Design: Susan Kapuscinski Gaylord and Brendan Gaylord
Typeface: Centaur
Centaur is a typeface designed by Bruce Rogers for the Metropolitan Museum of Art's 1915 limited edition of poet Maurice de Guérin's book *The Centaur*. Based on the Renaissance period printing of Nicolas Jenson (c.1420–1480), it is paired with italic designed by Frederic Warde and based on the calligraphy and printing of Ludovico Vicentino degli Arrighi (1475–1527).

Photo Credits:
Page 15: Jim Higgins
Pages 66–71: Kevin Harkins
Page 90: Jeanne McMenemy
Page 127: Tom Robinson-Cox
Author Photo: Kendra Gaylord

susangaylord.com
Newburyport, Massachusetts

To my husband

Charlie

who has been by my side
and in my corner
every step of the way

I owe the deepest gratitude to my family—my parents, Alfred (Kap) and Helen Kapuscinski, whose faith in me gave me faith in myself, my husband Charlie who has supported me in every way through our forty-five years of marriage, and my children Brendan and Kendra who have guided me into the twenty-first century with kindness and grace.

Special thanks for this project go to: Paul Marion for his vision of the forty blog posts becoming a book and his keen editorial eye; Joan Ross for her design expertise, patience, and good company as the visual structure of the book took shape; Brendan Gaylord for his Photoshop skills and guidance through the publishing process; Kendra Gaylord for her patient listening and sage advice; Cathy Cuffe, Sandra Kavanaugh, Rosemary Noon for their help and support.

IN THE FALL OF 1978, I WAS an unemployed English literature major who had spent the past four years teaching swimming for the Boston School Department. I had taken courses in chemistry to prepare for studying nutrition, education to become a special education teacher, and children's literature because I wanted to open a children's bookstore. I don't know that I could have verbalized it at the time, but I wanted more than a job or a career; somewhere deep inside I was seeking a life's work.

The invitation came in humble package—a request from a high school friend for lettering a page in a wedding album for a friend of hers. My "yes" led me from occasional dabbling to serious independent study of calligraphy, which opened up door after door into the world of art. This book is my story, originally told in forty blog posts in the closing months of 2018. It is about more than learning how to hold a pen and form letters; it is about growing up and growing older. While I experienced much frustration on the path, I know how incredibly lucky I am to have spent the past forty years in the arts and be able to look forward to a future of continued creative work.

I have not done it alone. I have always had the support of my family—my parents, my husband, and my children. I have had teachers who came to me through their books and in person. I have had friends who shared the journey. And I have had Jenny Hunter Groat. She ended the first letter in our correspondence, which I initiated, with the words: "Please keep your soul your own." I have tried.

GIFT

You tell me that silence
is nearer to peace than poems
but if for my gift
I brought you silence
(for I know silence)
you would say
          This is not silence
this is another poem
and you would hand it back to me.

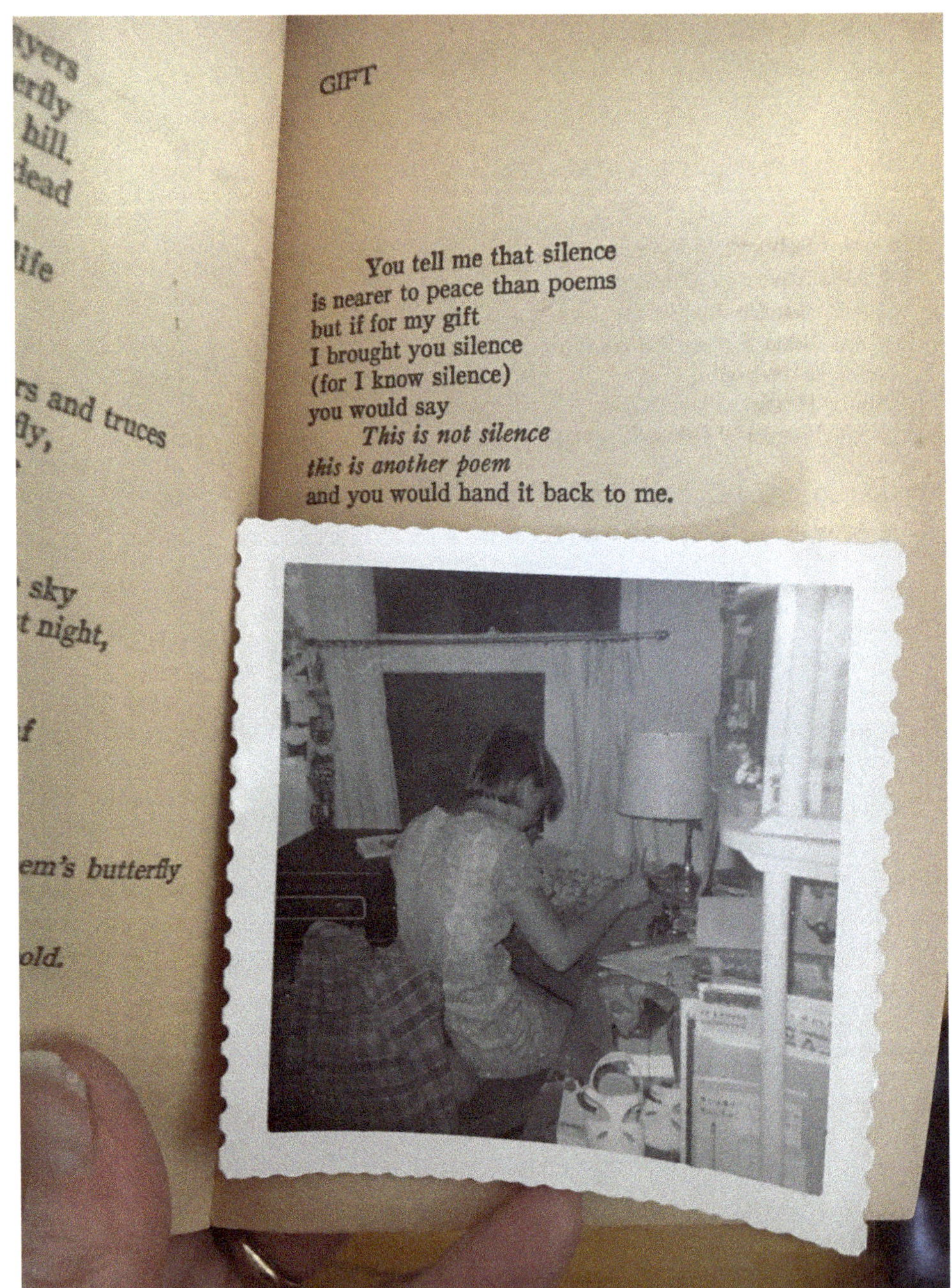

I FIRST ENCOUNTERED CALLIGRAPHY IN HIGH school. I had a friend who learned it in art class, and he in turn introduced it to me. He gave me the small instructional *Speedball Textbook*, a pale aqua pen holder that I still have, a set of Speedball C nibs, and a bottle of ink. From the beginning, the connection to words and writing drew me in. The picture on the opposite page was probably taken in 1969. I am writing the poem "The Gift" from Leonard Cohen's book *The Spice-Box of the Earth*. You can see the paperback book on top of the phonograph to my left. To my right are two bottles of ink.

My favorite hand was the *Speedball Textbook*'s Engrosser's "Old English" Text Alphabet which is frequently used for diplomas. At the time, I didn't give a thought to whether the style of the lettering matched the meaning of the words. It looks like I am using some version of my handwriting in the photograph. Below is a line from an early rendering of Walt Whitman's poem "Out of the Rolling Ocean the Crowd."

Behold the great rondure,
the cohesion of all,

From what I know now, I wouldn't use the word "learn" to describe my early experience with calligraphy. I looked at letters in a book and copied them, but I understood nothing.

> *Books are the quietest and most constant of friends; they are the most accessible and wisest of counselors, and the most patient of teachers.*
>
> Charles W. Eliot

MY HIGH SCHOOL FRIEND KATHRYN TRACY'S request for lettering for a friend couldn't have come at a better time. Since I was collecting unemployment, I could spend my days at the dining room table with my rudimentary supplies. I can't remember whether I looked for a class in the local area and didn't find one or just decided that I would learn from books. For several years, they were my only teachers. While the *Textbook* had a lot of styles, it didn't have as much explanation and direction as I wanted. Access to information was very different in the pre-internet world of 1978. Far fewer books on the subject were available than today. Finding books meant going to libraries (before inter-library loans were common) and bookstores (which had small or non-existent selections of calligraphy books) or somehow finding out about a book and ordering it by mail from the publisher.

The first book I tracked down was the workbook, *The Italic Way to Beautiful Handwriting: Cursive and Calligraphic* by Fred Eager. I liked the idea that it could be part of my everyday handwriting as well as something apart and special. I diligently worked through the book, which included his directions to write a Weekly Alphabet. I would write the letters of the alphabet on a sheet of paper—a through e on Monday, f through j on Tuesday, and on through the week. In the directions, Fred Eager wrote: "The weekly alphabet provides the simplest method of detecting any misunderstandings of the basic structure of the letters or any manual difficulty encountered." How kindly put—misunderstandings, not mistakes! He does use the word fault in the next sentence, but says the Weekly Alphabet makes it easy "to analyze and remove."

The Weekly Alphabet brings up the two key elements of learning calligraphy— learning to see and learning to do. Although we call it handwriting, it is first and foremost about training the eye. We need our eye to help guide our hand as we write and then to analyze the letters we have made to achieve a more correct form.

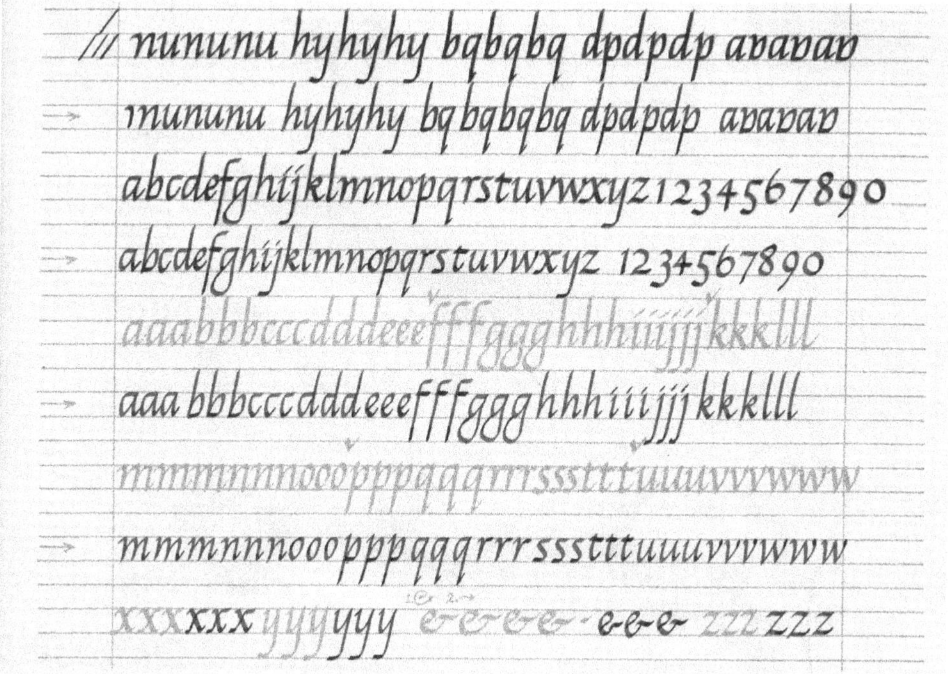

Calligraphy is not arbitrary. Neither is it "fancy," as in "Ooh, you have such fancy handwriting." Traditional calligraphy is based on principles and on consistency. A well-executed page is like a beautifully woven piece of cloth where the tension is even and there are no gaps or loose threads. In the beginning it was all about learning the basics and making my letters as close to the ones in the exemplars as I could. Adding personality to my letters came later.

For me, the absolute magic of calligraphy was, and still is, the fact that the thicks and thins of the letters are created by the placement of the edged pen at a consistent angle to the writing line. Nothing extra is done to change the line from thick to thin. It just happens. Now, at the beginning, it is not easy to keep the pen at that angle but the rewards for understanding and following the rule are substantial.

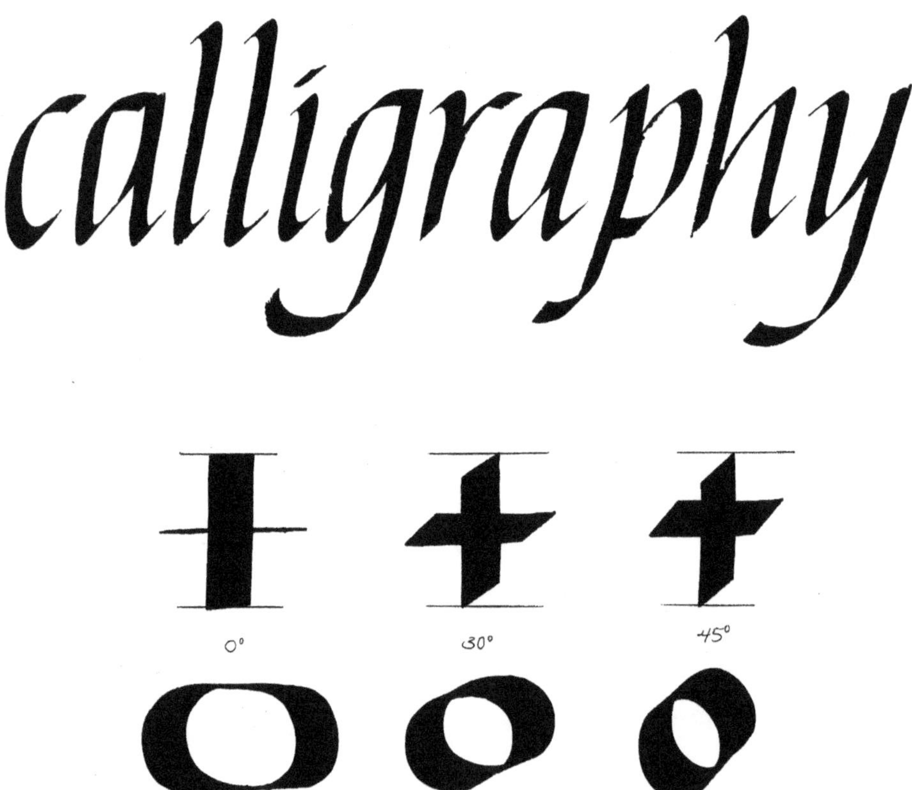

One of my favorite books was, and still is, *Written Letters* by Jaki Svaren. I love the variety of alphabets (22 in my 1981 edition), the beauty of the black-and-red pages with their combination of history and instruction, and especially Jaki's gentle notes for each letter.

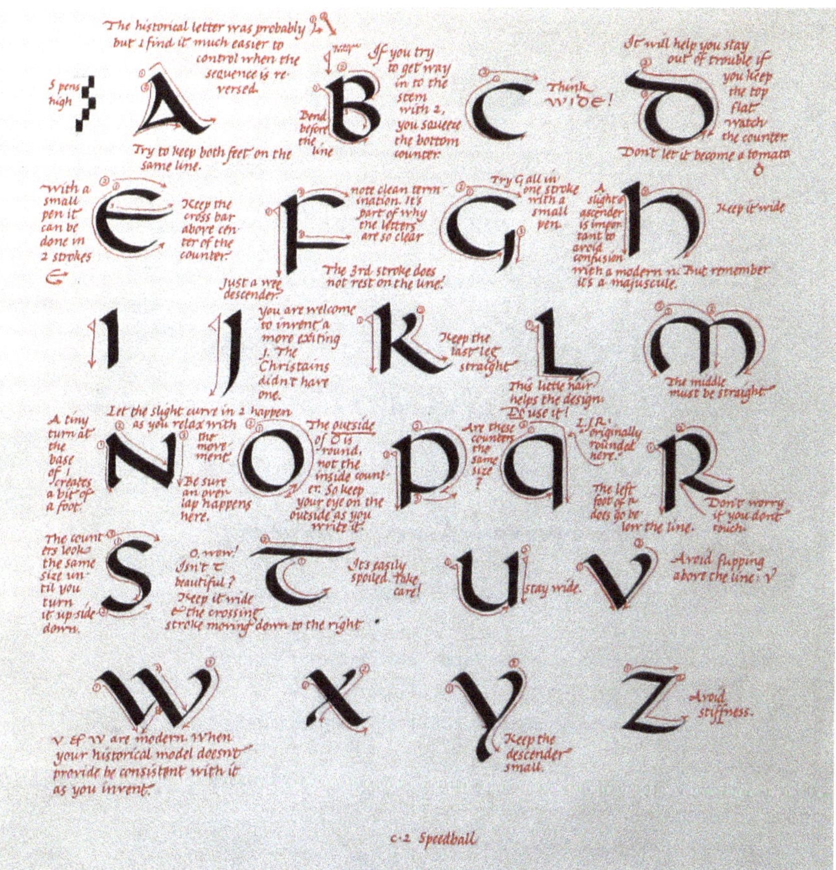

The Mystic Art of Written Forms by Friedrich Neugebauer was a later addition to my library. While I didn't really use any of the models in the book, I responded to his philosophy and feelings about lettering:

Personal lettering is the subtlest detector of one's substance and character; and lettering is the scribe's confession, the score composed of his states of being, his impulses and emotions—all the things that move him at the moment of communication. . . . Thus is lettering: royal and humble, vulgar and noble, muddled or freely structured and self-evident. A grand procession of all human conditions, bound together by the rhythm of a significant act.

Learning
Calligraphy
suited me.
It serves a
certain kind
of impatience
and needs
a certain kind
of patience.

Calligraphy wasn't the first creative endeavor I tried. In pottery class I didn't have the patience for preparing the clay or the continual struggle to center it on the wheel. I loved taking pictures but didn't have the patience for the darkroom. Getting started in calligraphy was immediate. Find a piece of paper, dip a pen in ink, make a letter. Instantly there is something to react to on the page. The journey begins.

But there is also patience. When I taught calligraphy at Rivier College (now University) in Nashua, New Hampshire, I would tell students that learning calligraphy was more like learning how to play an instrument than learning how to draw. Repetition and practice are necessary. You have to love, or learn to love, the twenty-six letters to keep going, to put in the time (hours, days, weeks, months, years) to make them your own.

I was prepared for that. I had been a competitive swimmer. Back and forth in the pool—a mile or two a day for ten summers. Each movement required attention: Is my elbow coming out of the water at the correct angle? Is my kick consistent? It was the same with calligraphy. So many questions to ask for each letter. How am I gripping the pen—lightly or am I squeezing it? Is the nib at the correct angle in relation to the line? Is the "m" arching properly? In the study of calligraphy, you can look at a blank page as an invitation to boredom or an offering of opportunities for fresh encounters with the twenty-six letters. I chose the latter.

What initially drew me into calligraphy was spending time with words I loved in a very different way than I had as an English literature major at Boston University. By graduation time in 1973, I was tired of analyzing. Writing ten pages on a fourteen-line sonnet meant getting very, very picky.

I've had a habit throughout my life of getting so caught up in my current passion that I don't see or credit how much of what I have done in the past is influencing the present. When I started doing calligraphy, I thought I was working in complete opposition to my study of literature. On reflection, I see that I had transferred the analytical skills from the words to the letters. The red pen of correction that I thought I had left behind was now critically evaluating each stroke I made and letter I wrote. I'm not sure if I could have made the progress I did working on my own if it hadn't been for those years of study that I was trying to get away from.

On the day of the dead, when the year too dies,
Must the youngest open the oldest hills
Through the door of the birds, where the breeze breaks.
There fire shall fly from the raven boy,
And the silver eyes that see the wind,
And the Light shall have the harp of gold.

By the pleasant lake the Sleepers lie,
On Cadfan's Way where the kestrels call;
Though grim from the Grey King shadows fall,
Yet singing the golden harp shall guide
To break their sleep and bid them ride.

When light from the lost land shall return,
Six Sleepers shall ride, six Signs shall burn,
And where the midsummer tree grows tall
By Pendragon's sword the Dark shall fall.

from The Dark Is Rising by Susan Cooper

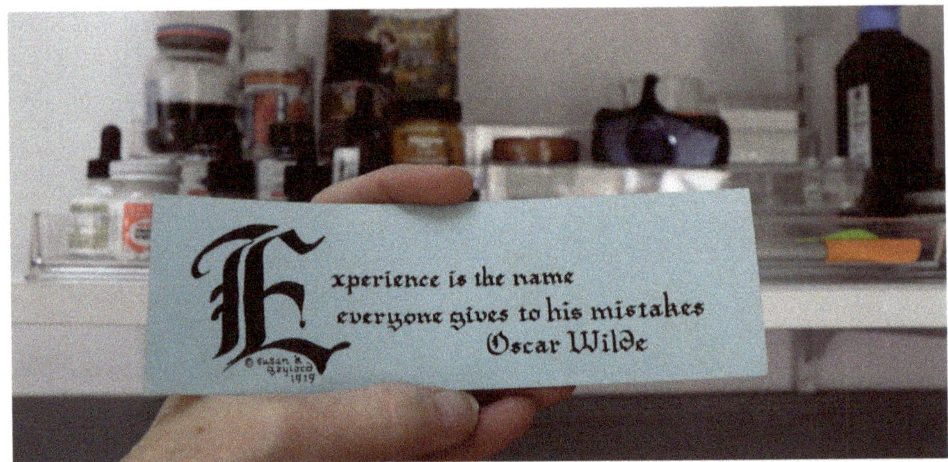

ALTHOUGH THERE WAS SOMETHING SO PEACEFUL about those early days at the dining room table, I didn't stay in that bubble for long. Because I was unemployed and spending all my time doing calligraphy, I thought I should try to make money at it. After all, the person for whom I had lettered the wedding album page sent me a check for $10. After I had written out a poem for a friend, I received a package of goodies at Christmas. I was sufficiently encouraged to have a table at an art and culture gathering at the Lowell Memorial Auditorium in Lowell, Massachusetts the following spring.

I threw myself on the unsuspecting and largely ignorant (of the finer points of calligraphy) public with a combination of outward enthusiasm and inward insecurity. You might think my insecurity lessened as I went on but the opposite was true. As my calligraphy got better, so did my critical skills. I could see flaws that I didn't know existed the year before. Instead of abating, my insecurity grew. A year later, I wrote these two passages in my journal:

Ann Schecter's (art critic for the Lowell Sun and later a good friend) column in the Sunday Sun—met her Friday night—she said nice things about me, very nice, in relation to exhibit at the Medical Associates (a medical building that exhibited the work of local artists)—called my script "exquisite and moving," which of course from my eyes isn't true at all. From this end it's awkward and static, and I know my opinion is based on greater knowledge, and so I feel like a sham, a fake, and while I will say it has renewed my desire to work hard, etc., it has also contributed to my ache in the stomach.

Am feeling discouraged about my work—my skill is improving but also has a long way to go and I wonder if with my fear and stubbornness and pride I will ever get to be as good as I could/should be. I have such a difficult time bringing myself to take a lesson or do probably very constructive things for myself instead of plodding along in the dark—my good points are that I am able to be self-critical, self-disciplined—usually—and that I set high standards for myself, but I wonder if this is enough. Can I get by with just that or will I be less because of it? I keep thinking I'd like to be a little better—get to that certain stage before I venture out. Will I ever get to that stage, or know it when I do, or know it but still be too afraid?

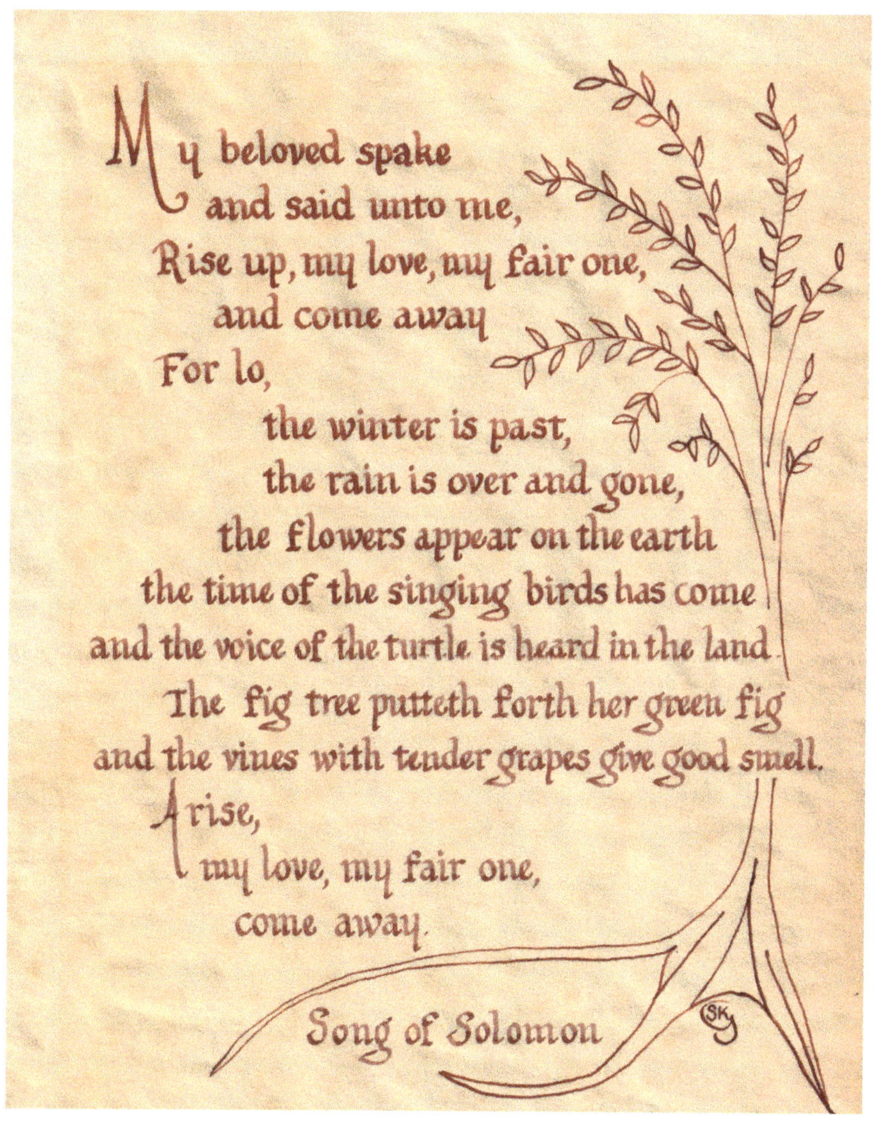

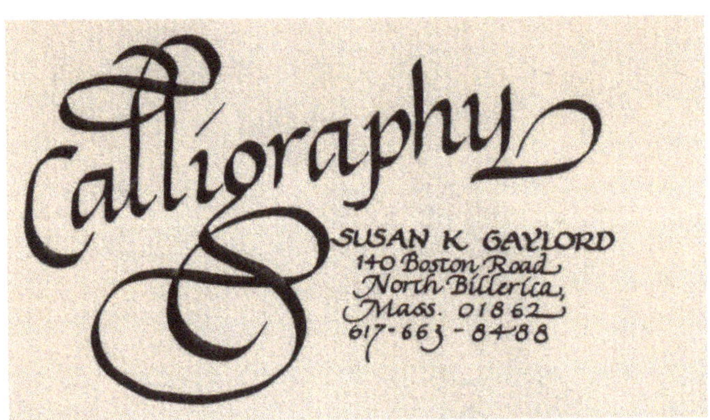

FROM THE START, MY WORK WAS DIVIDED into two basic categories: commercial calligraphy and calligraphy for exhibition. I did calligraphy for hire from 1979 to 1988. I discovered early on that there was a lot to learn in addition to letters and spacing. I wrote this in 1980:

As if worrying about the craft of my work is not enough, there is that wonderful business end of the whole matter. I've had a couple of discouraging encounters—I just plain old don't charge enough—I don't have the right business spirit—part of the problem is that I am basically a cheap person who doesn't spend large amounts of money for anything and I can't get it through my head that other people do. But I don't want to be an asshole so I want to strike a balance and get what I should be paid but not change myself. I'm wondering if I should take an assertiveness training or something like that.

I never took assertiveness training and I never charged enough. I always underestimated the time it would take, a characteristic I have carried forward to this day. I used to say that I either needed a personality transplant or another line of work which is what I chose. I eventually replaced the calligraphy with teaching bookmaking workshops in schools. One of the advantages of the teaching was that the money part was simple. I charged by the day and everyone paid the same rate.

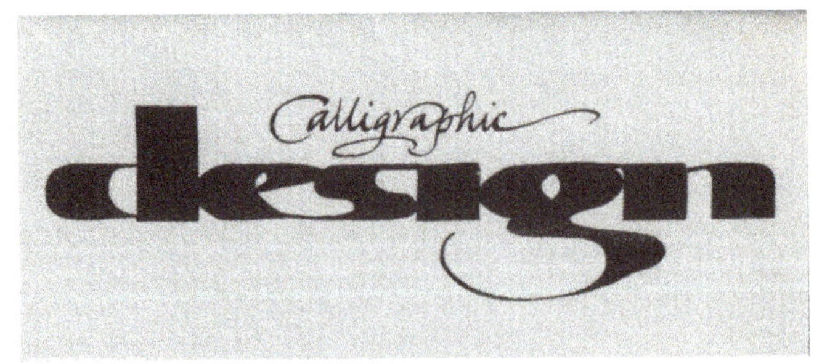

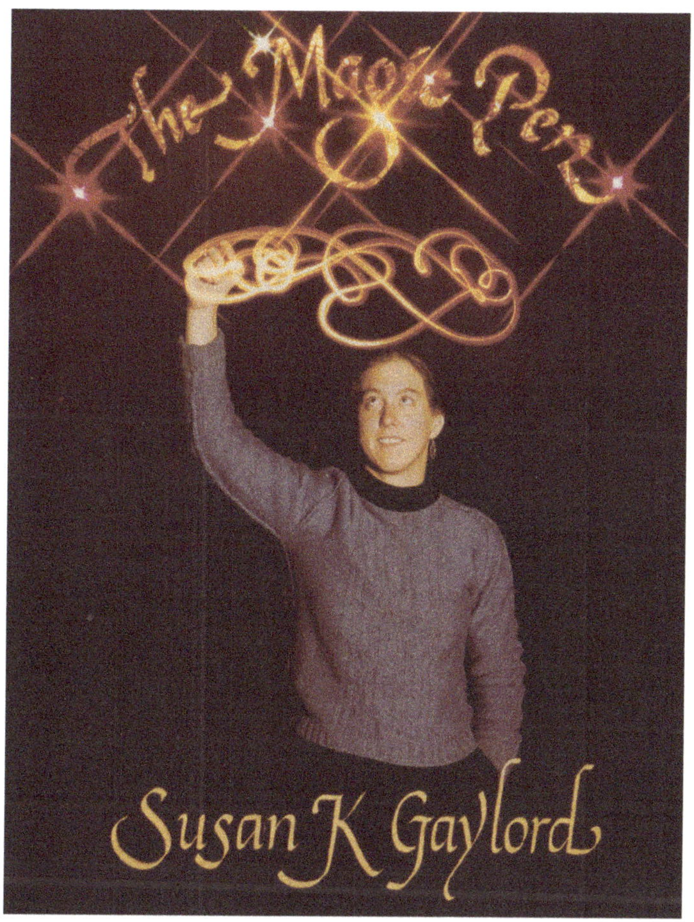

I initially called my business "The Magic Pen" but as I started to do more work for exhibition, I felt that it was clearer to do everything under my name. The hardest thing about changing the name was that this amazing photograph by Jim Higgins of Higgins & Ross Design became a historical piece instead of a current promotional image.

Jim conceived of the idea of photographing me writing in the air with what I assume was a small flashlight. We did it outside on a cool fall night. I prepared for the weather by wearing a sweater. If you look closely, you will notice that it is inside out. I was so caught up with worrying about what I needed to do that I didn't think about how I would look at all. Jim was a master in the darkroom and spent hours and hours putting this image together with my lettering. It speaks to how fortunate I have been to get to know creative people who were interested in working together.

A lot of my work was filling in names on certificates and diplomas. Sometimes I would design certificates that were then printed or copied. Occasionally I did one-of-a-kind awards for a particular person. They were for universities, non-profits, and businesses of all kinds including manufacturing plants and convenience stores. Occasionally they were for me.

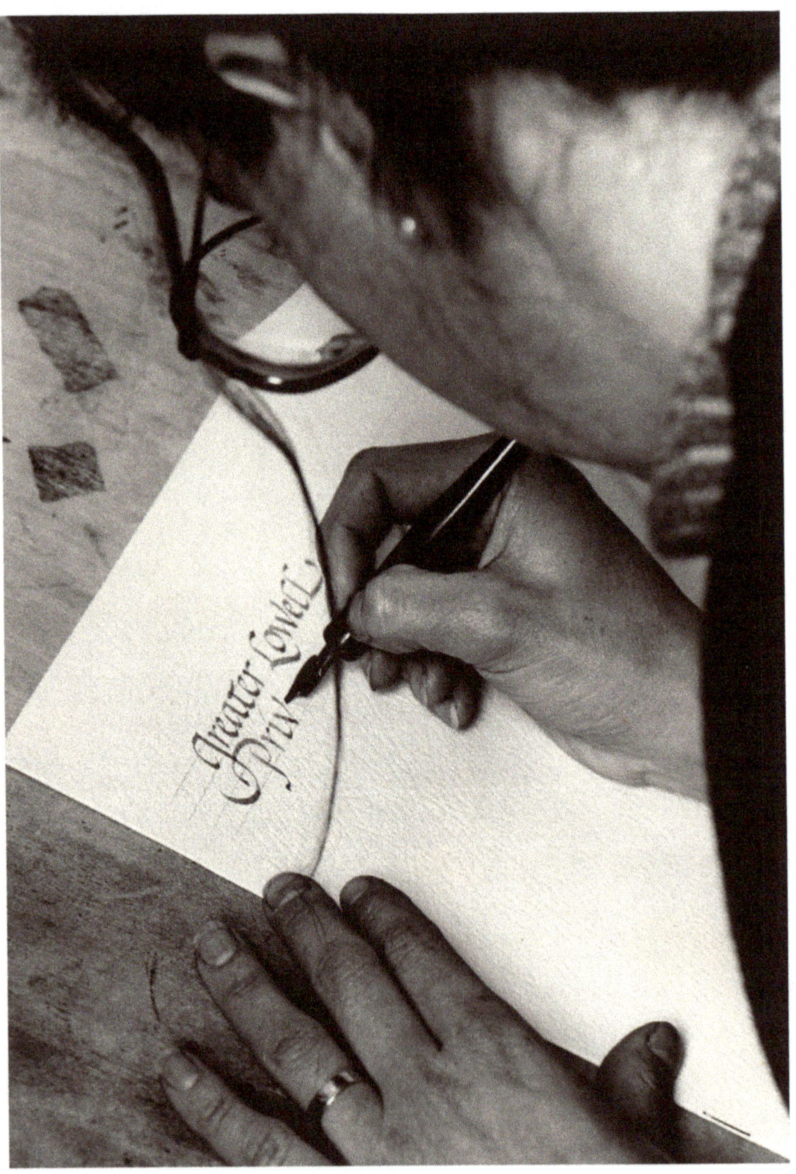

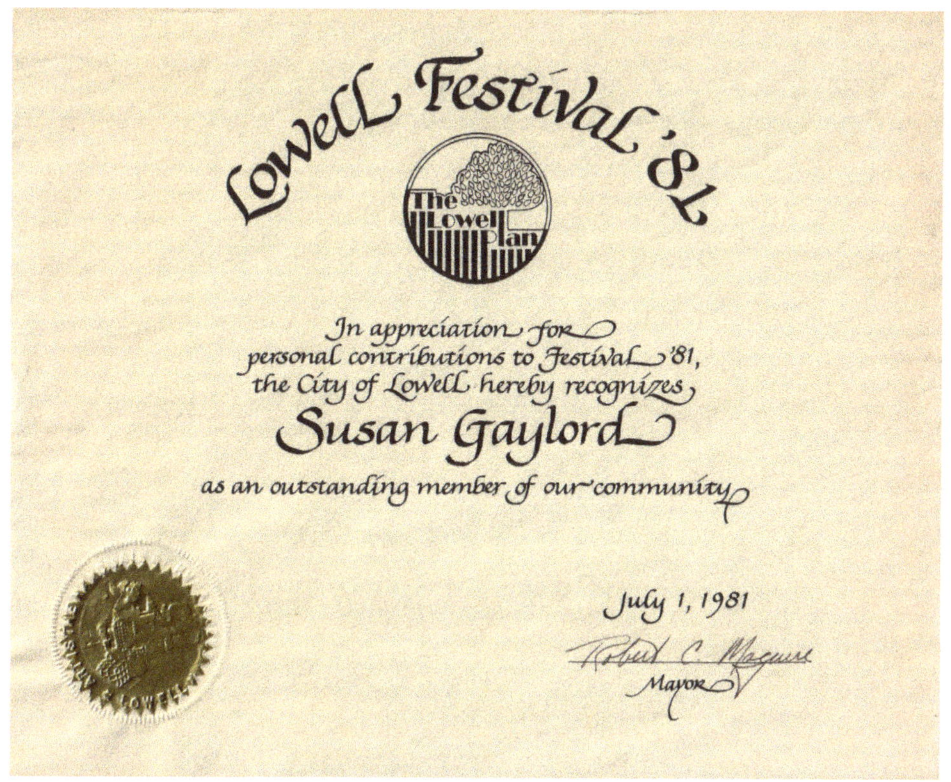
Lowell Festival '81
The Lowell Plan
In appreciation for
personal contributions to Festival '81,
the City of Lowell hereby recognizes
Susan Gaylord
as an outstanding member of our community
July 1, 1981
Mayor

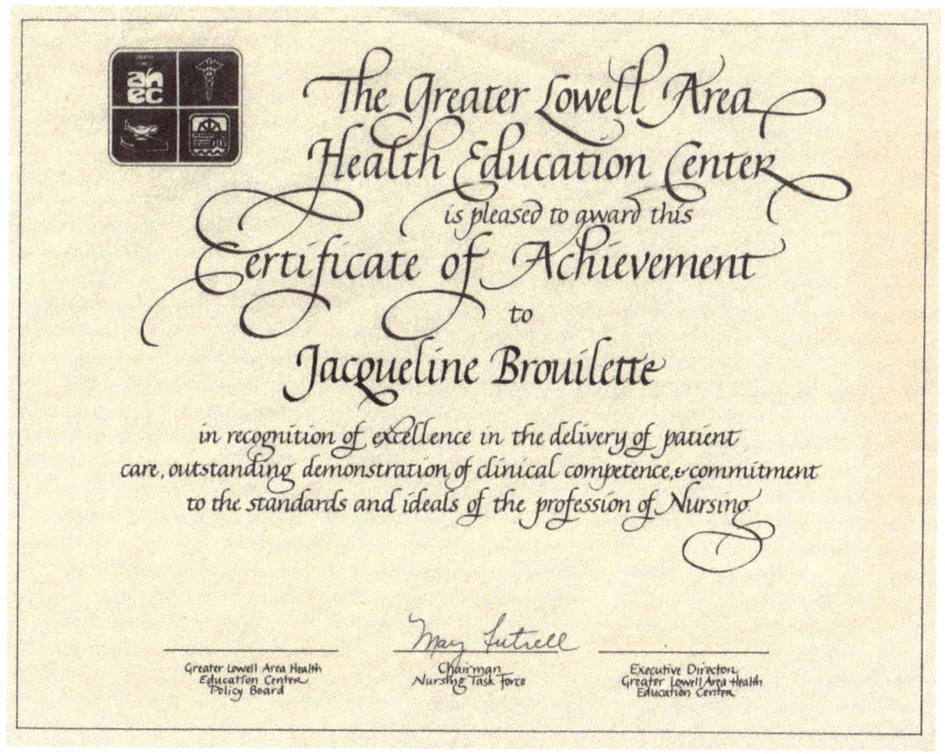
The Greater Lowell Area
Health Education Center
is pleased to award this
Certificate of Achievement
to
Jacqueline Brouilette
in recognition of excellence in the delivery of patient
care, outstanding demonstration of clinical competence, & commitment
to the standards and ideals of the profession of Nursing
Greater Lowell Area Health
Education Center
Policy Board
Chairman
Nursing Task Force
Executive Director
Greater Lowell Area Health
Education Center

Invitations—for weddings as well as business and civic events—were a staple. Below is the first one I did and the beginning of a long relationship with the Greater Lowell Chamber of Commerce. The local newspaper, *The Lowell Sun,* hired me to letter the invitation on the opposite page for their dinner before the Golden Gloves boxing finals.

The Northern Middlesex
Chamber of Commerce and Industry
cordially invites you to a
special preview of a documentary film project
"Revolution and Renaissance" Lowell, Massachusetts
to be held at
Anastas Advertising Associates
45 Merrimack Street
Suite 229
Lowell, Massachusetts

November 19, 1979   5 - 6:30 p.m.
R.S.V.P. 454-5633   Cocktails will be served

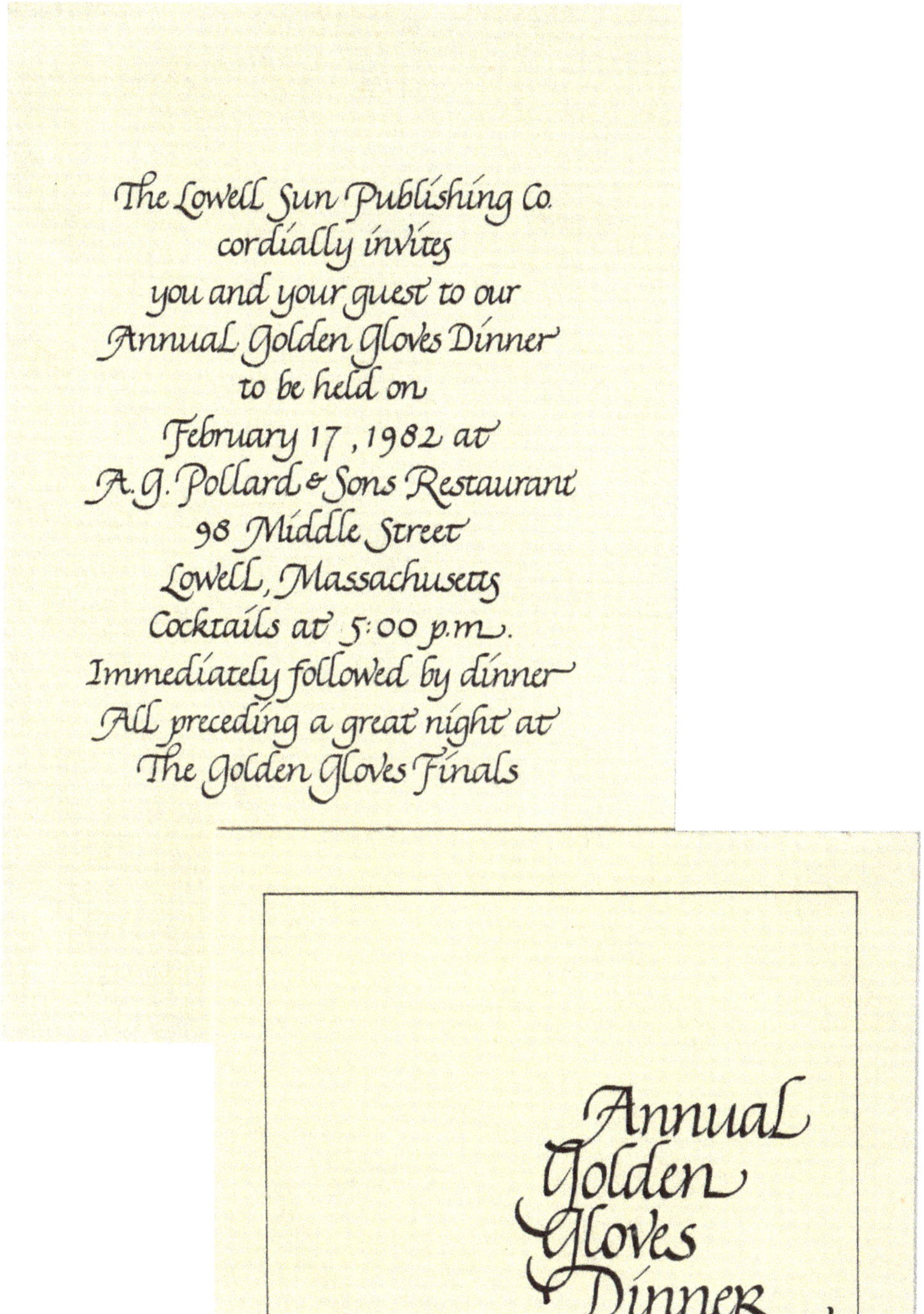

The Lowell Sun Publishing Co.
cordially invites
you and your guest to our
Annual Golden Gloves Dinner
to be held on
February 17, 1982 at
A.G. Pollard & Sons Restaurant
98 Middle Street
Lowell, Massachusetts
Cocktails at 5:00 p.m.
Immediately followed by dinner
All preceding a great night at
The Golden Gloves Finals

Annual
Golden
Gloves
Dinner

I made signs for local shops. The ones below were a few of many made for a British shop and included food from a freezer case and a line of toiletries.

Price List

Pork, Beef, & Sliced Sausage 1 LB. PKG $3.29
Scottish-Style Steak Pie SERVES 4 $9.69
Pork Pies, Meat Pies,
    Bridies, & Sausage Rolls FOR 1 DOZ $9.69
Potato Scones FOR 1/2 DOZ $1.49
Bacon PER POUND $4.50

Floris

Britain's most
Exclusive Line of Toiletries

I did a lot of restaurant menus. I worked for a printer who printed for an upscale restaurant group whose menus changed seasonally. They also changed their minds a lot so working for them was often a challenge.

I occasionally did work supplying lettering to designers for their projects. Below are two I did for Catherine M. Bucciarelli of The Ink Spot in Lowell. I was excited to get the commission for lettering for the book cover on the opposite page. I thought I did a particularly good job of matching the lettering to the image. They didn't like my lettering but happily, they used it anyway.

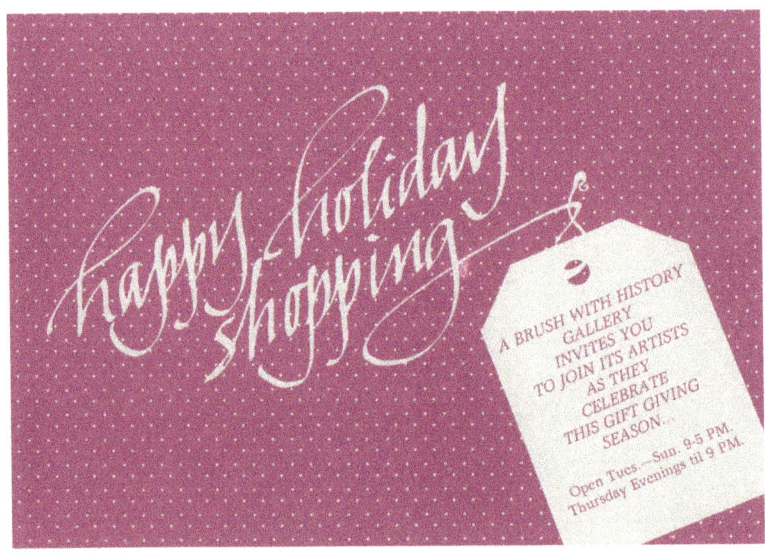

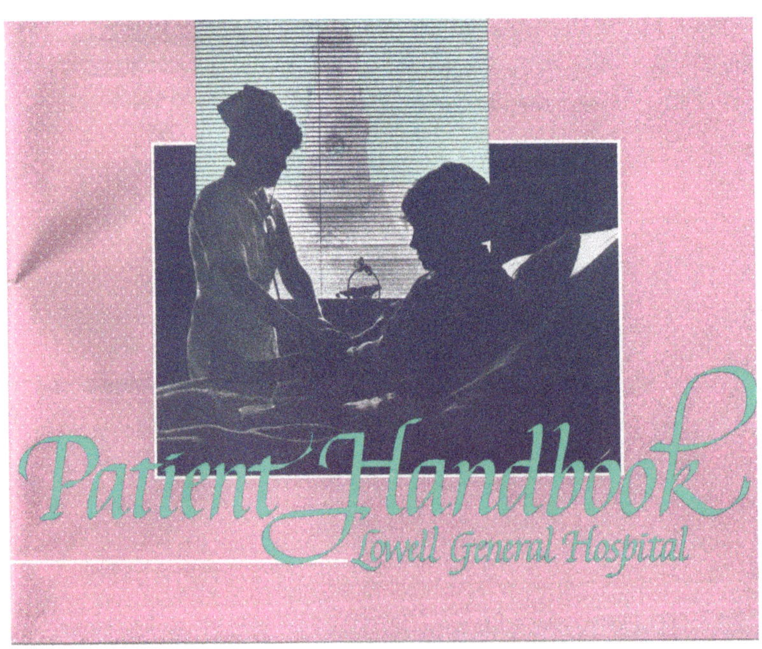

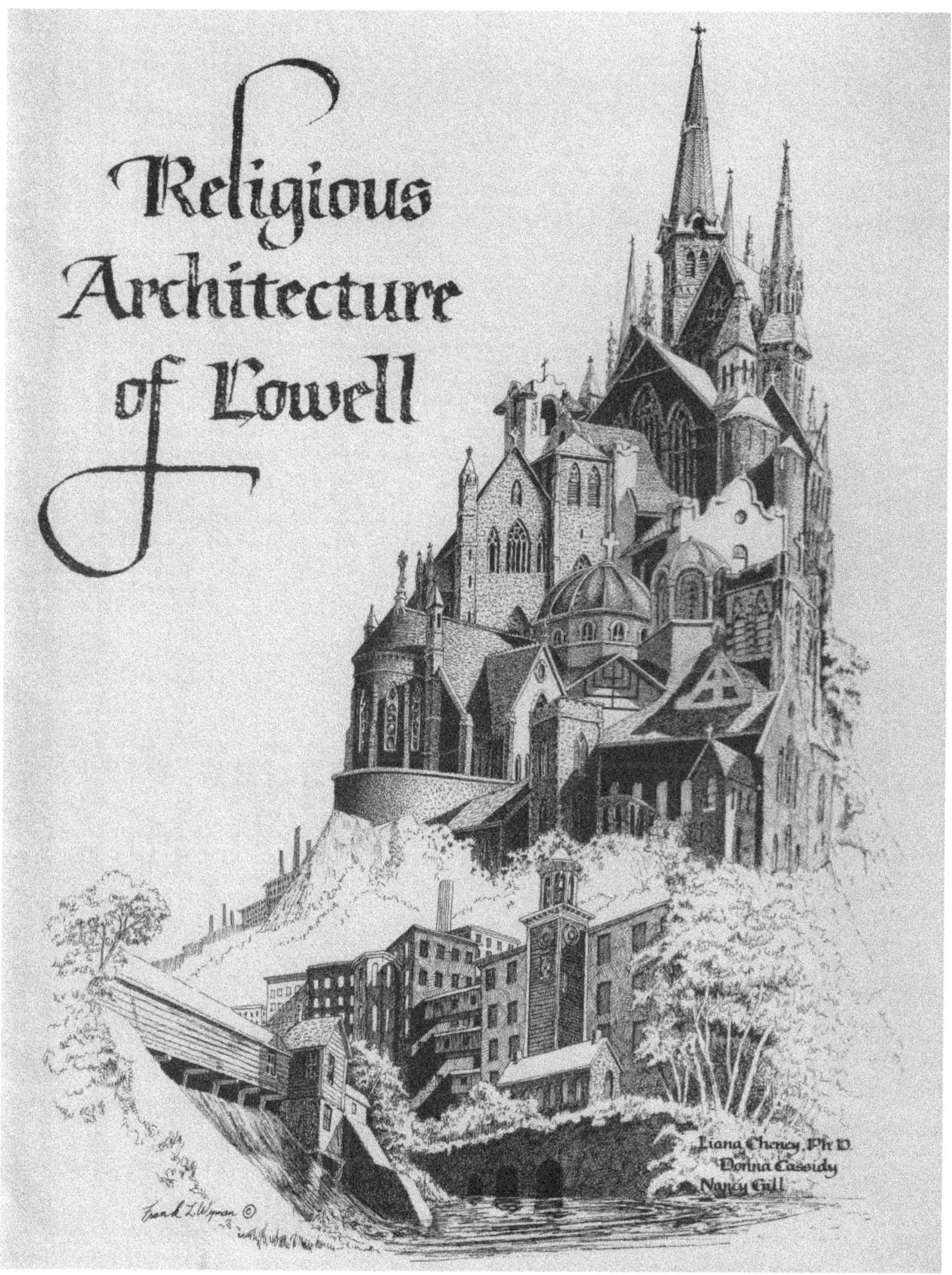
Religious
Architecture
of Lowell
Liana Cheney, Ph.D.
Donna Cassidy
Nancy Gill
Frank L. Wyman ©

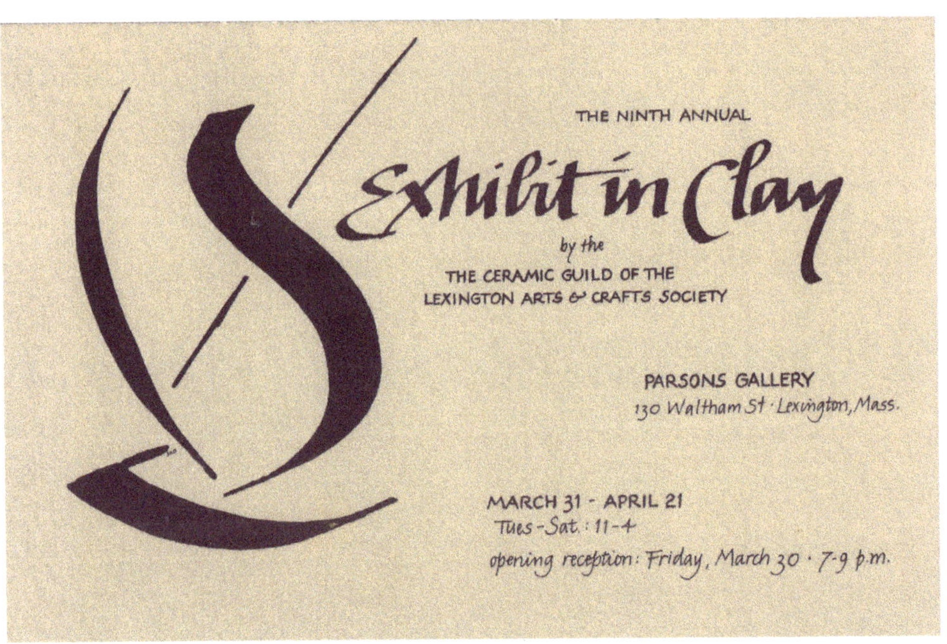

My favorite work was designing invitations for the art exhibits of friends and colleagues. In the days before computers and desktop publishing, it was cheaper, quicker, and easier for me to hand-letter the whole thing.

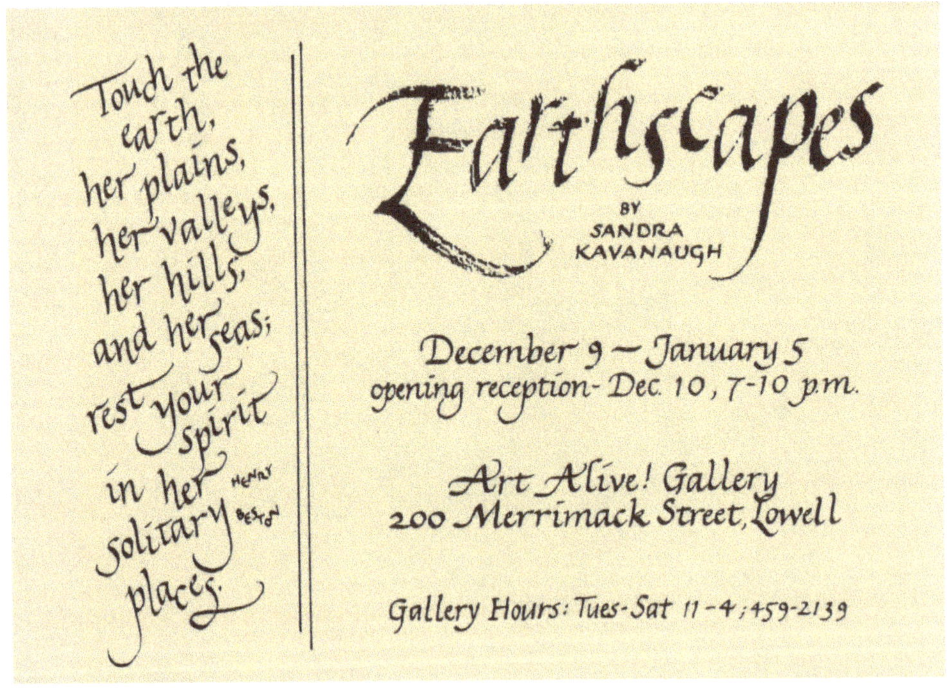

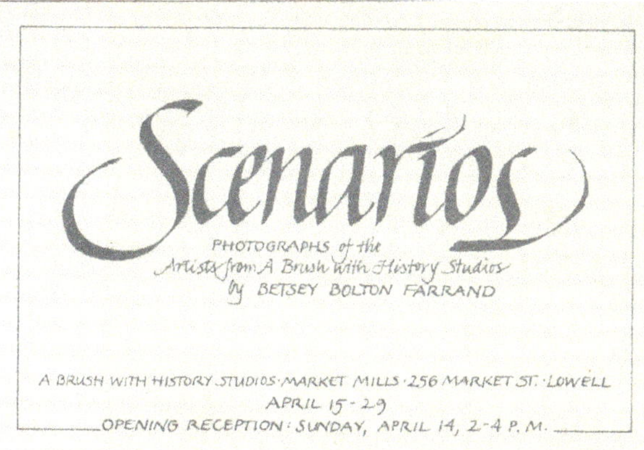
Scenarios
PHOTOGRAPHS of the
Artists from A Brush With History Studios
by BETSEY BOLTON FARRAND
A BRUSH WITH HISTORY STUDIOS · MARKET MILLS · 256 MARKET ST. · LOWELL
APRIL 15 - 29
OPENING RECEPTION : SUNDAY, APRIL 14, 2-4 P. M.

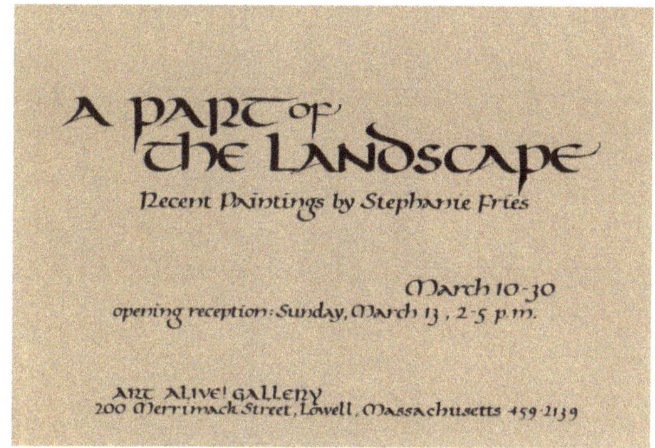
A PART OF
THE LANDSCAPE
Recent Paintings by Stephanie Fries
March 10-30
opening reception: Sunday, March 13 , 2-5 p.m.
ART ALIVE! GALLERY
200 Merrimack Street, Lowell, Massachusetts 459-2139

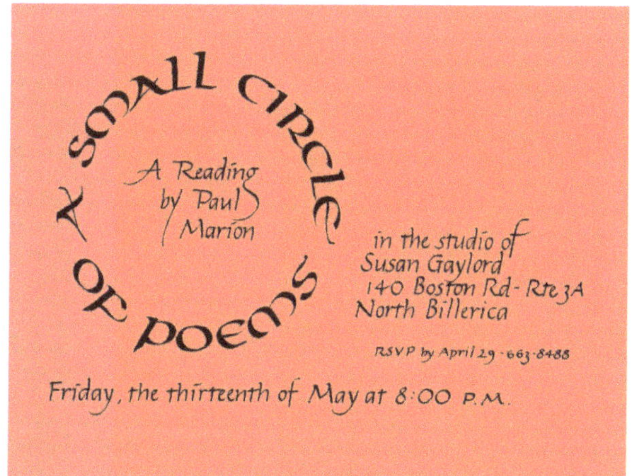
A SMALL CIRCLE
OF POEMS
A Reading
by Paul
Marion
in the studio of
Susan Gaylord
140 Boston Rd - Rte 3A
North Billerica
RSVP by April 29 · 663-8488
Friday, the thirteenth of May at 8:00 P.M.

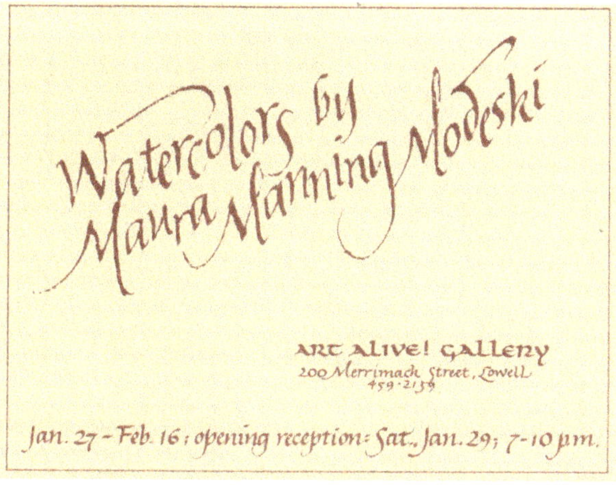
Watercolors by
Maura Manning Modeski
ART ALIVE! GALLERY
200 Merrimack street, Lowell
459-2139
Jan. 27 - Feb. 16 ; opening reception : Sat., Jan. 29 ; 7-10 pm.

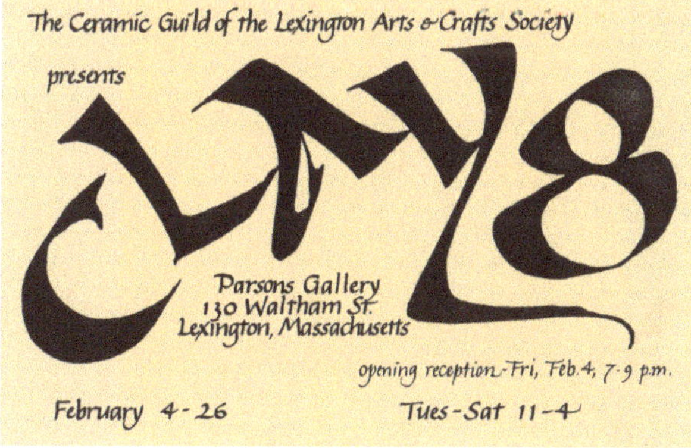
The Ceramic Guild of the Lexington Arts & Crafts Society
presents
CLAY 8
Parsons Gallery
130 Waltham St.
Lexington, Massachusetts
opening reception - Fri. Feb. 4, 7-9 p.m.
February 4 - 26
Tues - Sat 11 - 4

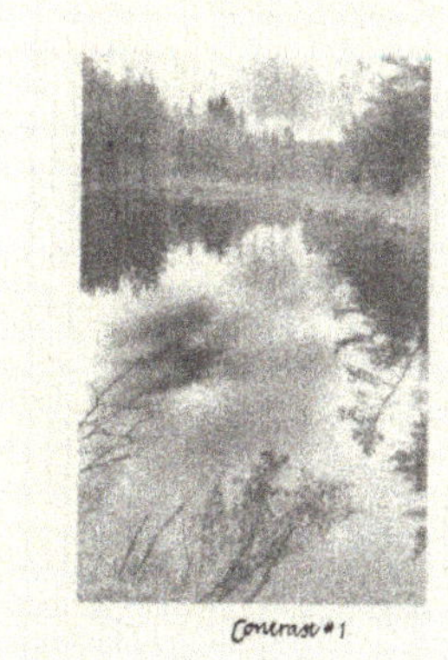
Contrast #1

Photographic
Landscapes by
TOM BELKAKIS
Art Alive! Gallery
200 Merrimack St.
Lowell, MA 459-2139
Dec. 17 ~ Jan. 5
OPENING RECEPTION
Dec. 19 , 6-9 pm.

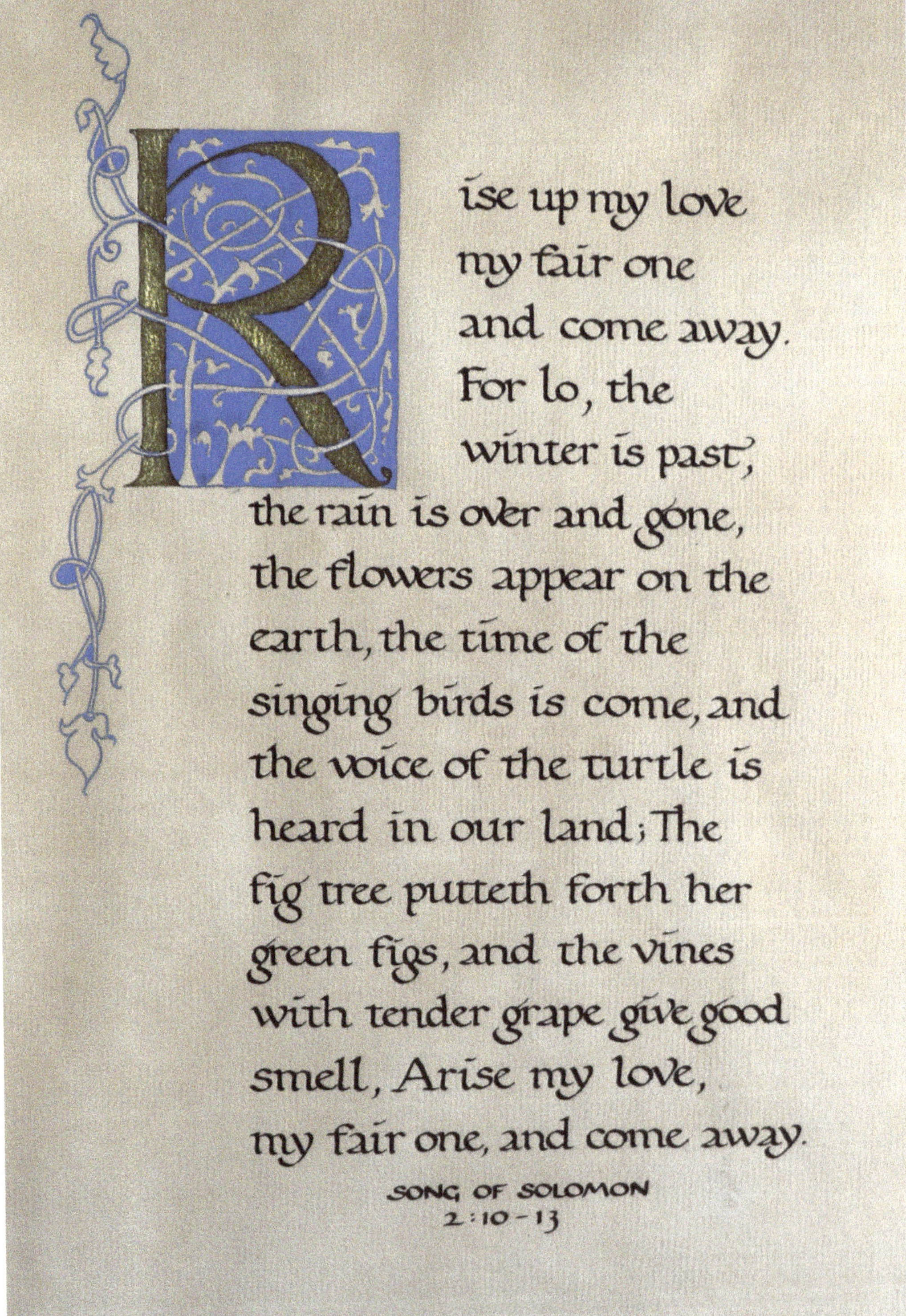
Rise up my love
my fair one
and come away.
For lo, the
winter is past,
the rain is over and gone,
the flowers appear on the
earth, the time of the
singing birds is come, and
the voice of the turtle is
heard in our land; The
fig tree putteth forth her
green figs, and the vines
with tender grape give good
smell, Arise my love,
my fair one, and come away.
SONG OF SOLOMON
2:10-13

FROM THE BEGINNING, I WAS INTERESTED IN doing work that could be framed and hung on the wall. My earliest pieces were inspired by calligraphy of the past. I spent a lot of time looking at, and copying, pictures of old manuscript pages. *Two Thousand Years of Calligraphy*, a catalog from a 1965 exhibition given to me by William Cladek, a calligrapher from my hometown of Rahway, New Jersey, was the source for the white vine initial in the 1981 rendition of a passage from the "Song of Solomon" on the opposite page and the border in the Elizabeth Barrett Browning sonnet below. Both were from fifteenth-century Italian books.

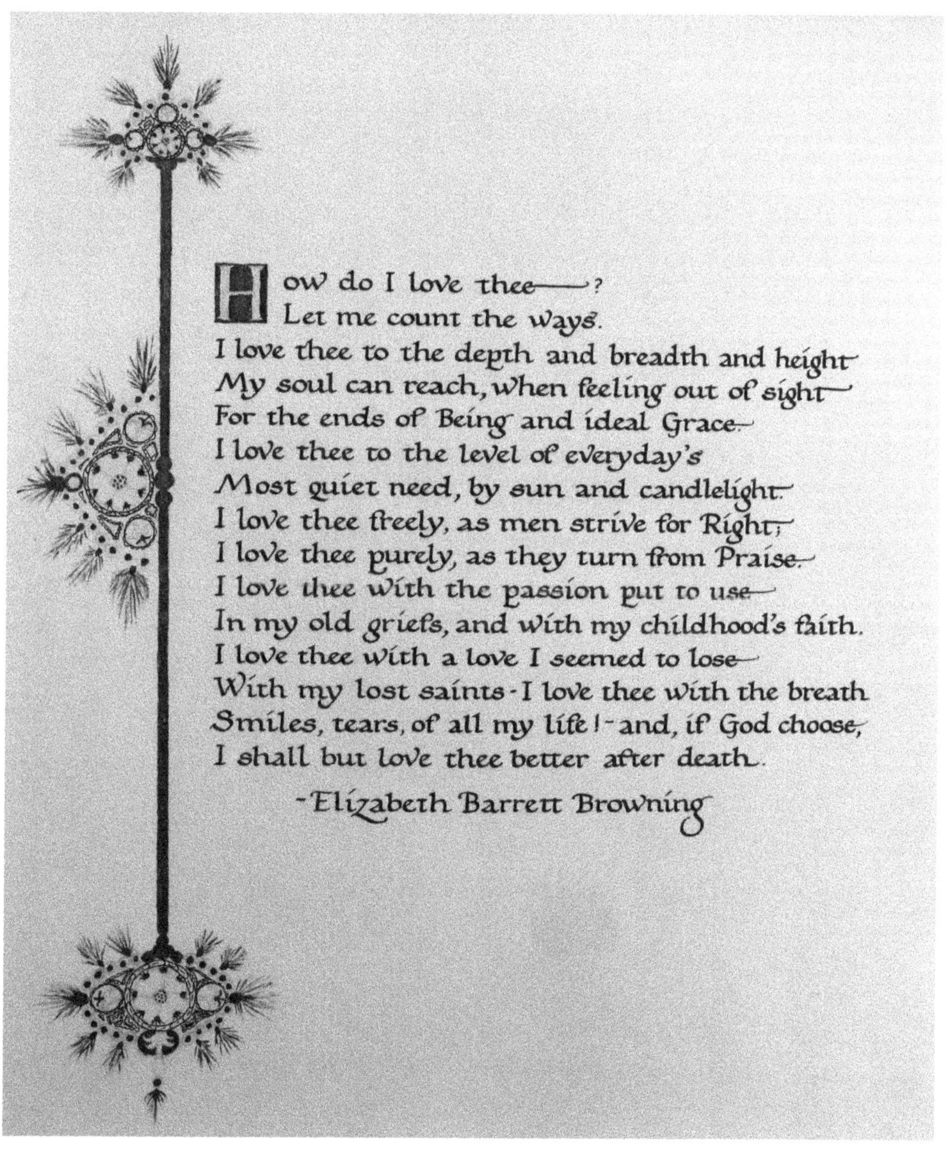

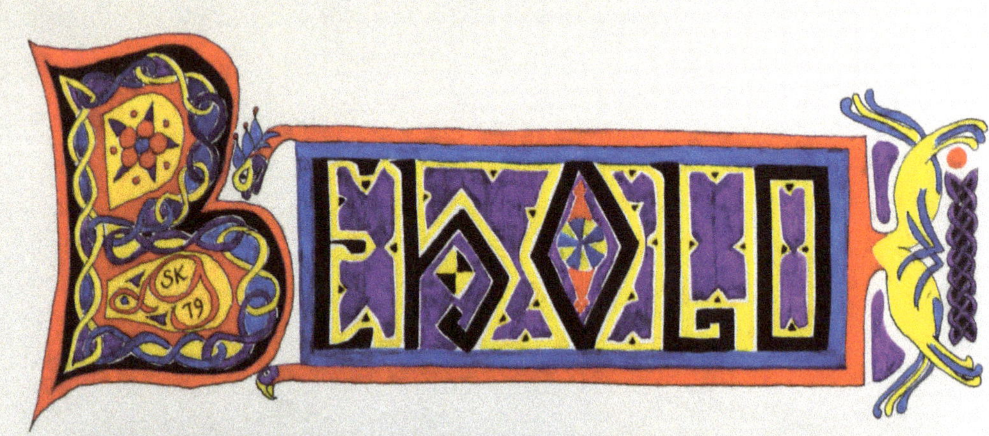

which shall be to all people For unto you is born this day in the city of david a Saviour, which is Christ the lord. And this shall be a sign unto you; ye shall find the babe wrapped in swaddling clothes, lying in a manger And suddenly there was with the angel a multitude of the heavenly host praising God, and saying,

Glory to God in the highest, and on earth peace, good will toward men. Luke 2:10-14

The passage from the Gospel According to St. Luke on the opposite page was inspired by the Lindisfarne Gospels created in England in about 698. The borders in the piece below was probably a pretty direct lift (except for the little drawings of the peacock feather, dove, fleur-de-lis, pomegranate, and gold and silver grapes that go with the poem) from William Morris, best know for wallpapers and interior design but also a creator and publisher of books through his Kelmscott Press.

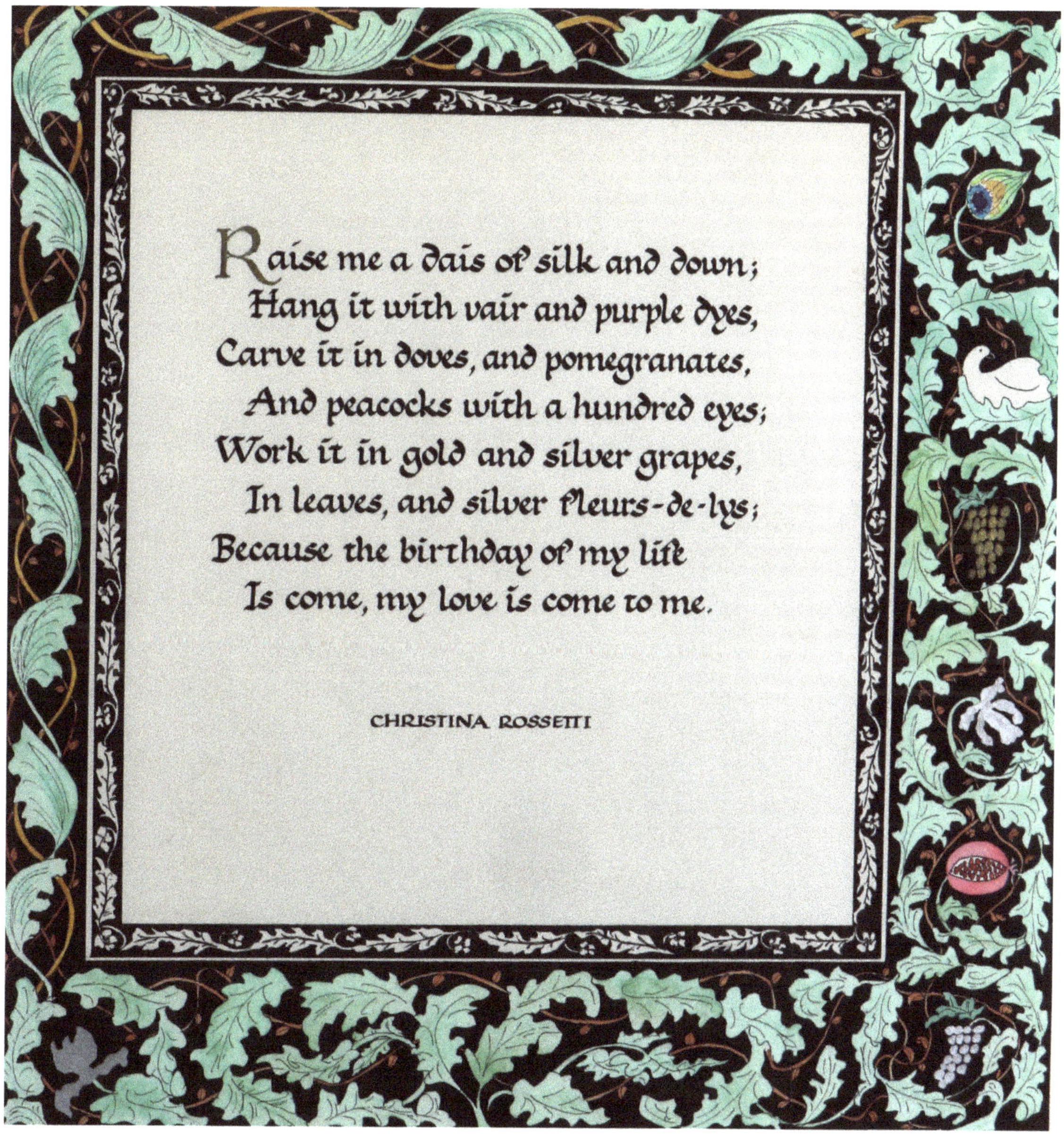

Zucchini Recipes

(4) Pocket Sandwiches
Sauté 1 chopped clove of garlic and 1 chopped small onion in oil. Add abt. 3 cups bite-size pieces of zucchini & sauté until translucent. Add 2 cups chopped tomatoes & cook 2 minutes. Sprinkle with salt & parmesan cheese. Fill toasted, halved Syrian bread pockets & eat.

Spaghetti Sauce
for 4-6 ~ In a large pan, sauté 2-3 cloves of minced garlic, 2 chopped medium-size onions, & 2 chopped peppers in oil. Add a little more oil and sauté abt. 6 cups of cut-up zucchini until translucent. This recipe is especially good with larger zucchini, just remove seeds & soft center. Add 2 cans tomato puree, ½ tsp. dried basil, ½ tsp. dried oregano, ½ tsp. salt. Cover and cook for one half hour to 45 minutes. Serve with spaghetti and lots of parmesan cheese.

makes 2 **Zucchini Quiche**
Make 2 9" pie crusts ~ Try it with wholewheat flour and lard - delicious! For filling ~ saute 2 sliced onions in oil. Add 3 cups zucchini, cut in bite-size pieces, and sauté til translucent. Bake pie crust in 450° oven for 5-10 minutes. Remove. Put zucchini & onions in pie shells. Add ½ pound grated Swiss or Gruyère cheese. Mix 4 eggs lightly beaten, 2 cups light cream, & grated nutmeg. Pour in shell. Bake 10 minutes at 450°, reduce heat to 325°, and bake til firm - about 20 minutes. Serve hot or cold.

Stir-Fried Zucchini with Pork or Chicken
Use tender, young zucchini - 2 to 3 per person and one thin porkchop or chicken breast (boned) per person. Slice zucchini & meat into thin slices, making the cuts on an angle. Heat 2 tbs. oil (vegetable or peanut) in a wok or skillet. Add 2 thin slices of fresh ginger, sizzle ½ minute & remove. Add sliced meat and stir-fry (keep it moving) for 3 minutes. Add zucchini and stir-fry for 2-3 minutes. Add master sauce and cook, stirring, for 1 minute, or until thickened. Serve immediately with rice

*** Master Sauce** for 2 servings
2 tbs. cornstarch dissolved in ¼ cup of water
2 tbs. spoons soy sauce
1 tbs. rice wine or sherry
½ tsp. sugar

to Freeze
Freeze only young zucchini with small seeds. Wash & slice, discarding ends. Blanch for 3 minutes in boiling water. Cool immediately in ice water. Pack in container, leaving ½" headroom. Seal and freeze

SUSAN K. GAYLORD

After my table at the Lowell Memorial Auditorium, I eased into showing my work at low stakes events like the Lowell Farmers Market along the canal at Lucy Larcom Park. I sat amongst farmers and beekeepers. I made the zucchini recipe sheet on the opposite page to sell there. The lettering leaves a lot to be desired, but I do think it has a certain charm. I'd be a lot more careful with the recipes today. I'm sure I didn't test them. I'm hoping I at least made them.

I wrote out names for people on pre-printed pages with outlined floral borders that could be colored in. I charged $1.00, and found it a good way to offset the table fees—and to make a more personal connection to people. Another thing I would do differently today: I'd wear a top with a back.

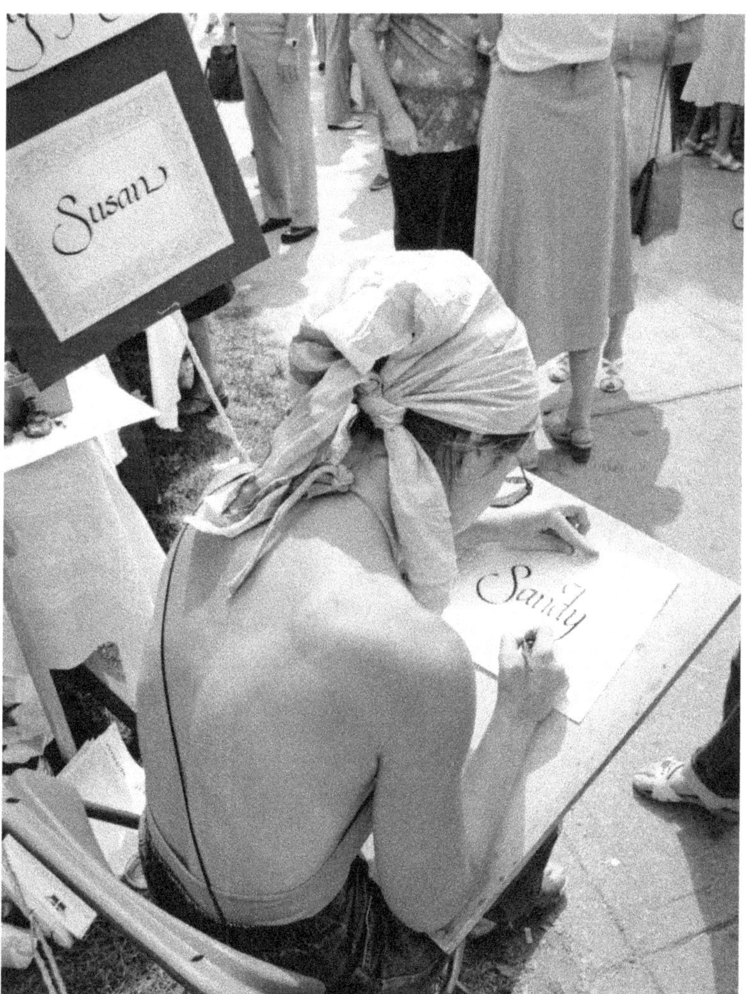

Over the years I did a lot of art and craft shows. I'd have some framed pieces, my name sheets, and lots of small matted quotes that I chose for their message (happiness was a frequent theme) and humor (Erma Bombeck was a favorite). I'd have them photocopied in black and white and add the color by hand. The shows were exciting at first, but I eventually found the process grueling—packing up to go, setting up, sitting there talking to people all day or waiting for someone to come by, then packing up to go home and unpacking. Now, I never go to an art or craft show without being grateful that I am not the one sitting behind the table or standing in the booth.

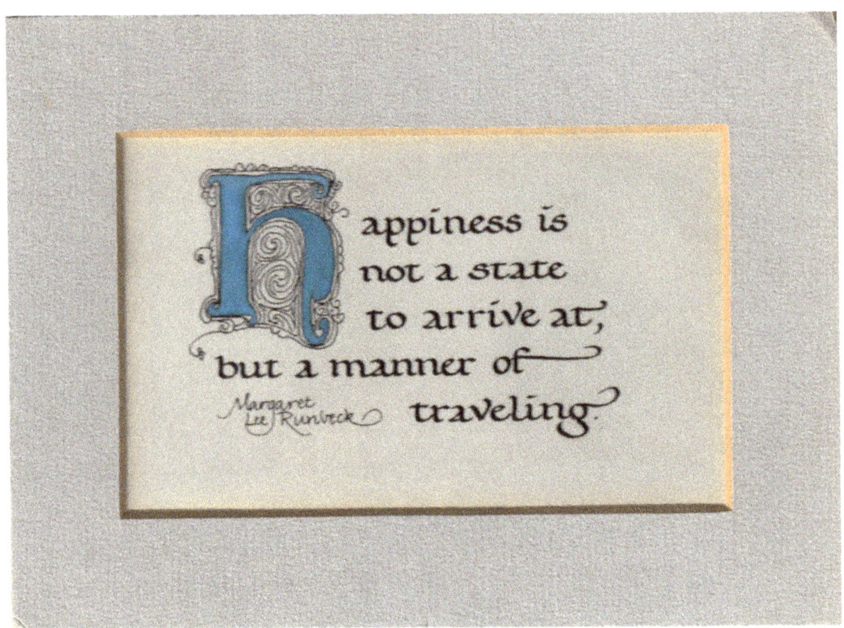

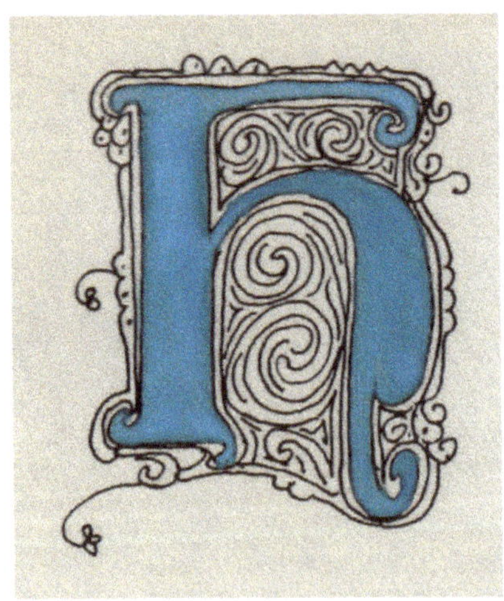

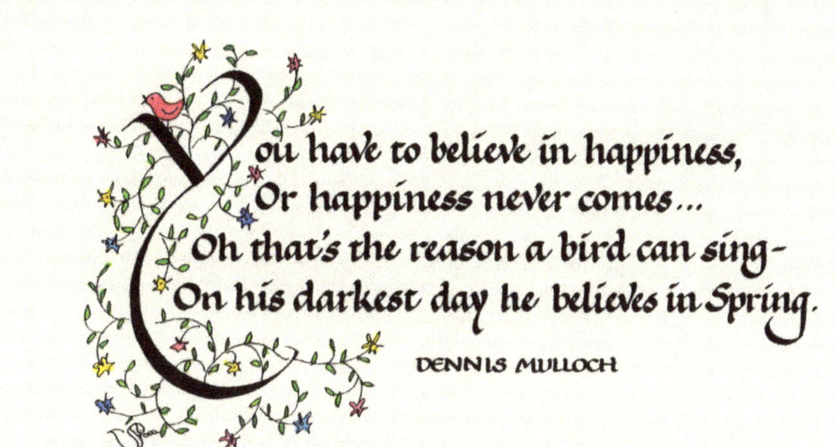
You have to believe in happiness,
Or happiness never comes...
Oh that's the reason a bird can sing-
On his darkest day he believes in Spring.
DENNIS MULLOCH

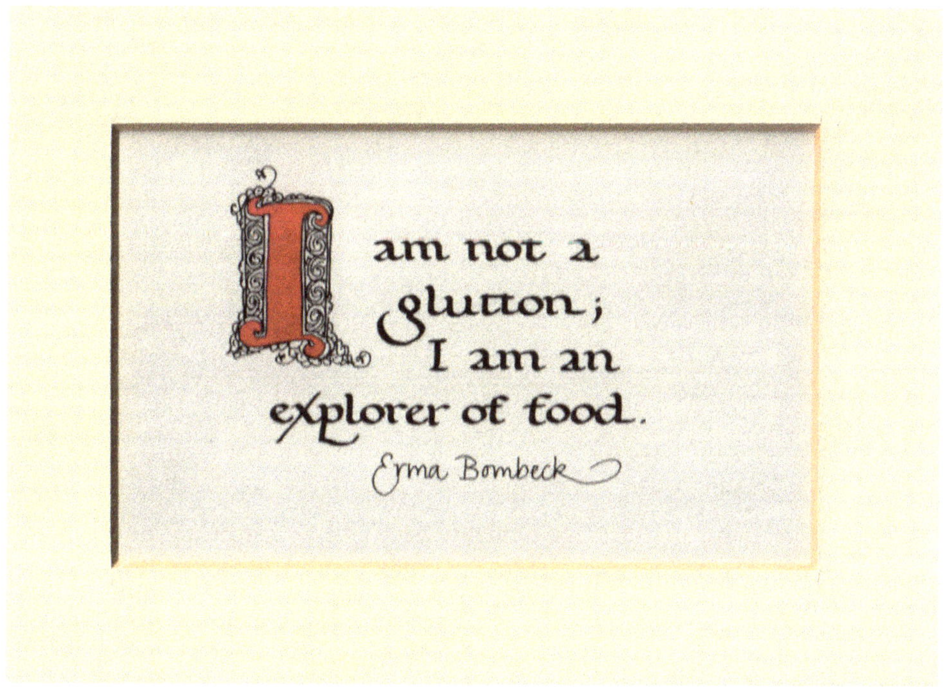
I am not a
glutton;
I am an
explorer of food.
Erma Bombeck

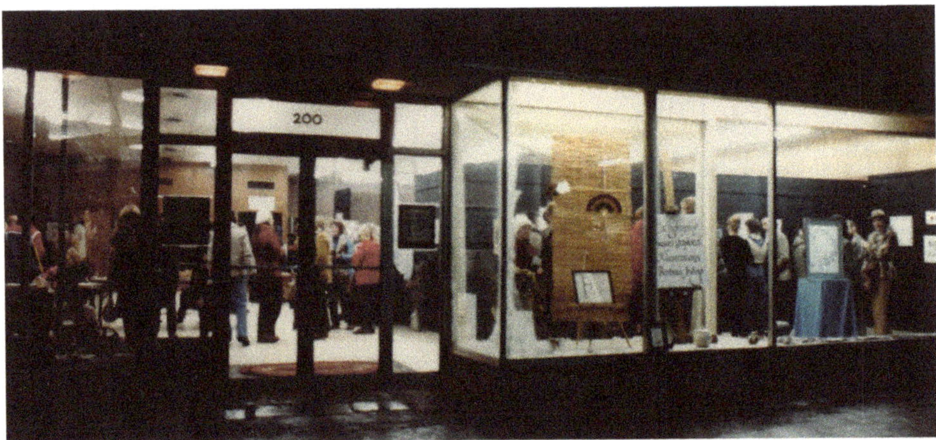

Exhibition at Art Alive!

At the arts event at the Lowell Memorial Auditorium, I met some of the artists who were forming a group that came to be called Art Alive! The Greater Lowell Art Co-op. I was deeply involved from its beginning in November 1979 until I moved from the area in 1985. We saw ourselves as an alternative to the older Lowell Art Association, established in 1878. We were generously given gallery space downtown by the newly created Lowell National Historical Park, which had purchased the Solomon's Fabrics building at 200 Merrimack Street and did not yet have a use for it. We shared the space with a local non-profit organization, Human Services Corporation. Once the word got out, we drew members from a thirty-plus-mile radius. While there was an age range, most of us were in our late twenties to mid-forties. Some had been to art school; many had not. Some were experienced artists with resumés of exhibitions; many had never exhibited before.

We forged close bonds. We had monthly exhibits where we could exhibit one or two pieces and opportunities for solo and shared shows. To have a place to regularly exhibit with the support of friends was such a great starting point. I shared the struggles and joys of making art with like-minded people. I learned about framing, presentation, meeting deadlines, publicizing work, and pushing ahead. Again, maybe too soon, but it made me work harder and get comfortable with the public part of being an artist.

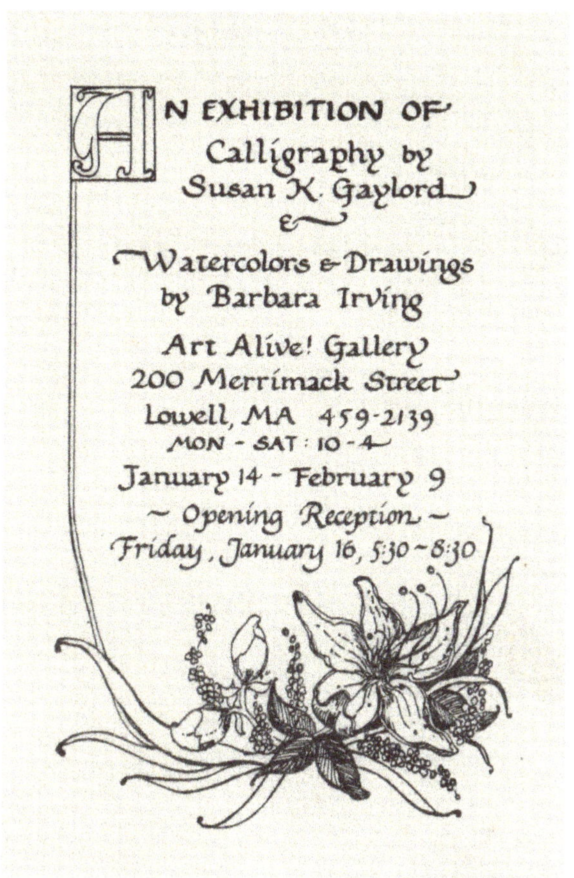

I had my first exhibit in 1981, a two-person show with Barbara Irving (now Barbara Levesque), one of the founders and the first president of the organization. We had the good fortune to have a member and friend, Stephanie Fries, who was a framer with a business called the Underground Framer. We did not work with standard sizes. Steph cut the mats for us. We ordered the frames (by phone or mail, no online shopping then), bought the glass at a local glass company, and assembled the frames ourselves. I spent the opening reception avoiding handshakes as I had cut my right hand on the glass while finishing up the framing that morning.

I learned that having an exhibit was stressful and a ton of work, but that I could do it. The satisfaction of seeing a collection of one's work on the wall and sharing it with others was worth it.

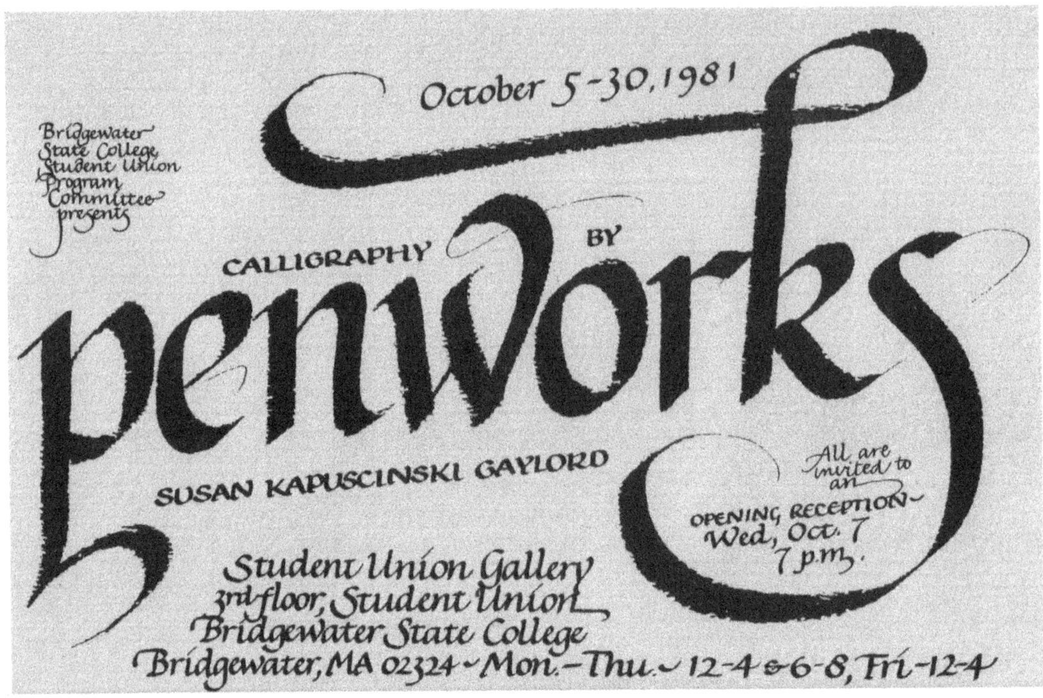

My first solo exhibition was Penworks at Bridgewater State College (now University) in Bridgewater, Massachusetts. Very much about interpreting texts, the collection was eclectic.

Susan Kapuscinski Gaylord follows the maxim of the French philosopher, Michel Montaigne, "I quote others to better express myself." A graduate of Boston University with a degree in English, she attempts to interpret the written word through the visual art of calligraphy. The works exhibited range from the romantic poetry of John Keats to the cryptic prose of Gertrude Stein to the powerful voice of Jack Kerouac.

Susan has a studio in her home in North Billerica, Massachusetts and has exhibited and been actively involved in the arts in the Greater Lowell area.

Office of the Director
Student Union
Bridgewater State College
Bridgewater, Massachusetts 02324

There were nineteen pieces in the show. The photos aren't great but I am happy to have a record. One piece in the exhibition sold—Catsup is a vegetable—which was a classification for the school lunch program by the USDA under Ronald Reagan.

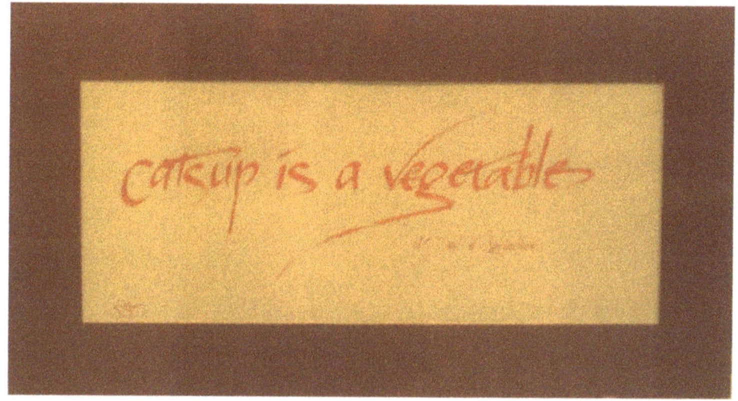

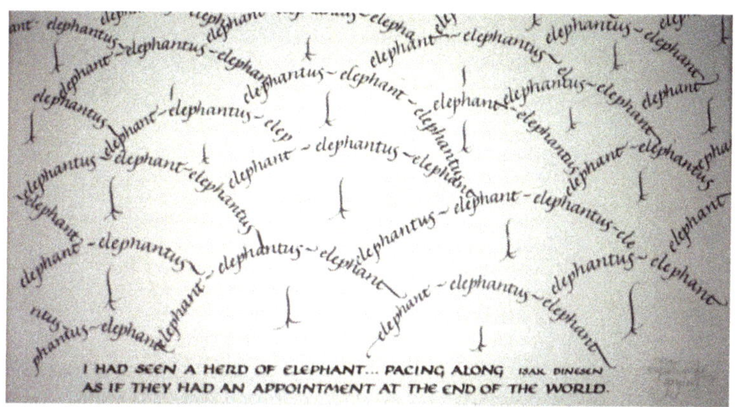

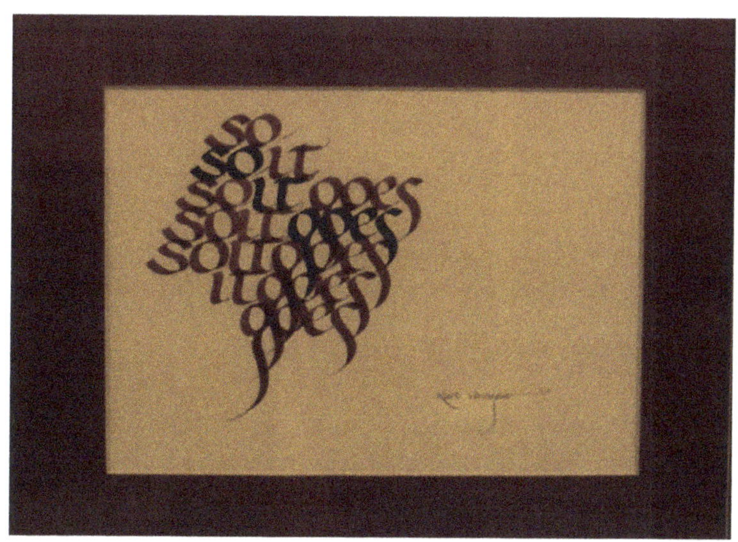

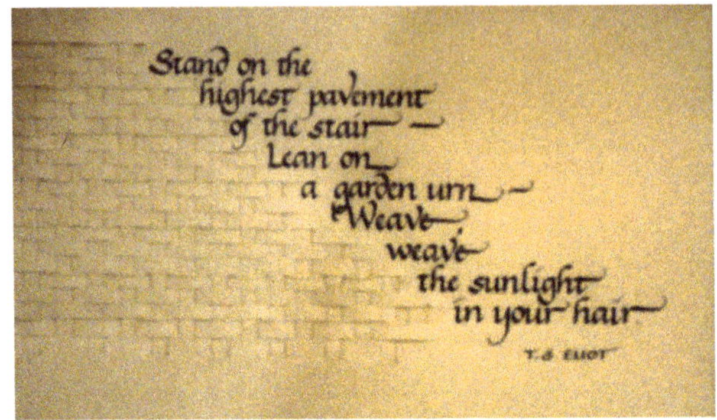

Stand on the
highest pavement
of the stair —
Lean on
a garden urn —
Weave
weave
the sunlight
in your hair —
T. S. ELIOT

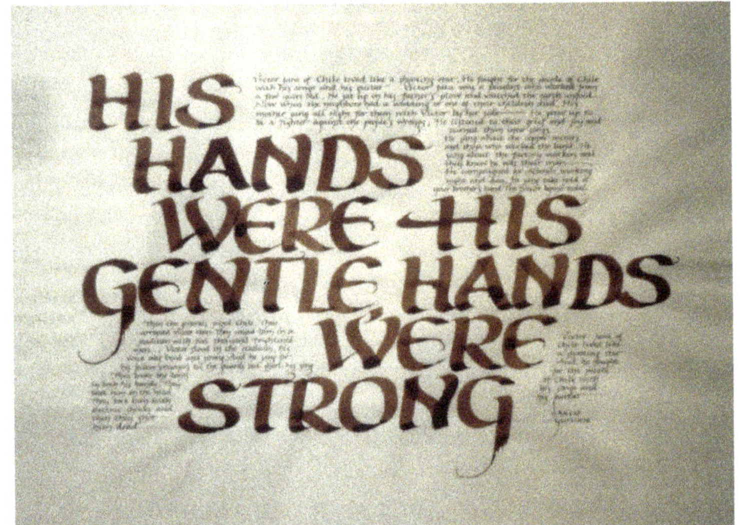

HIS
HANDS
WERE HIS
GENTLE HANDS
WERE
STRONG

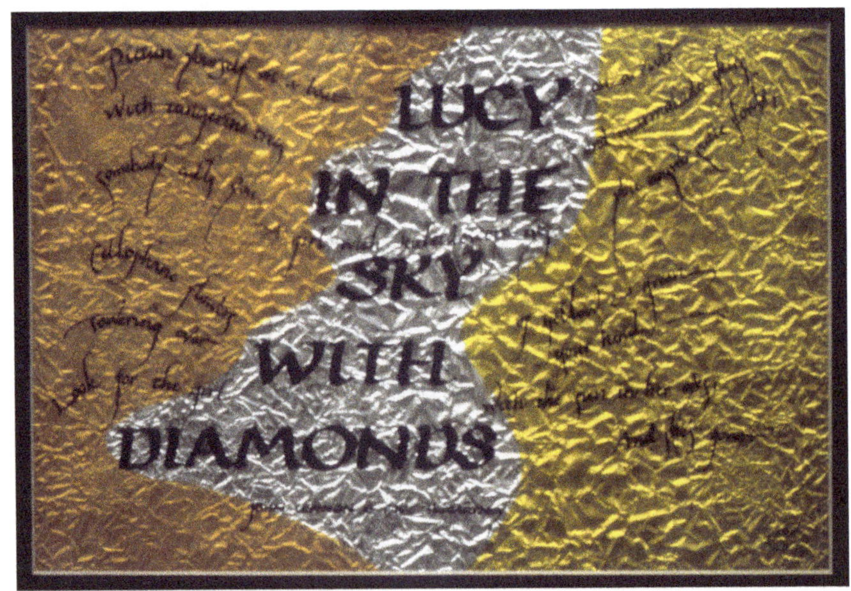

LUCY
IN THE
SKY
WITH
DIAMONDS

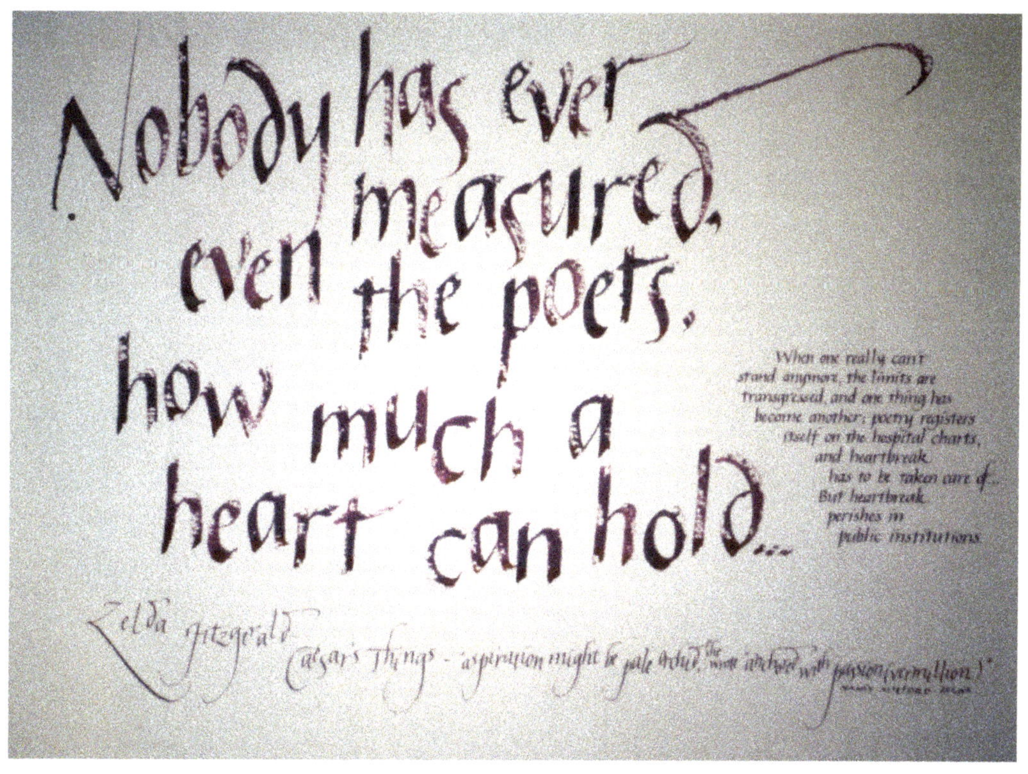

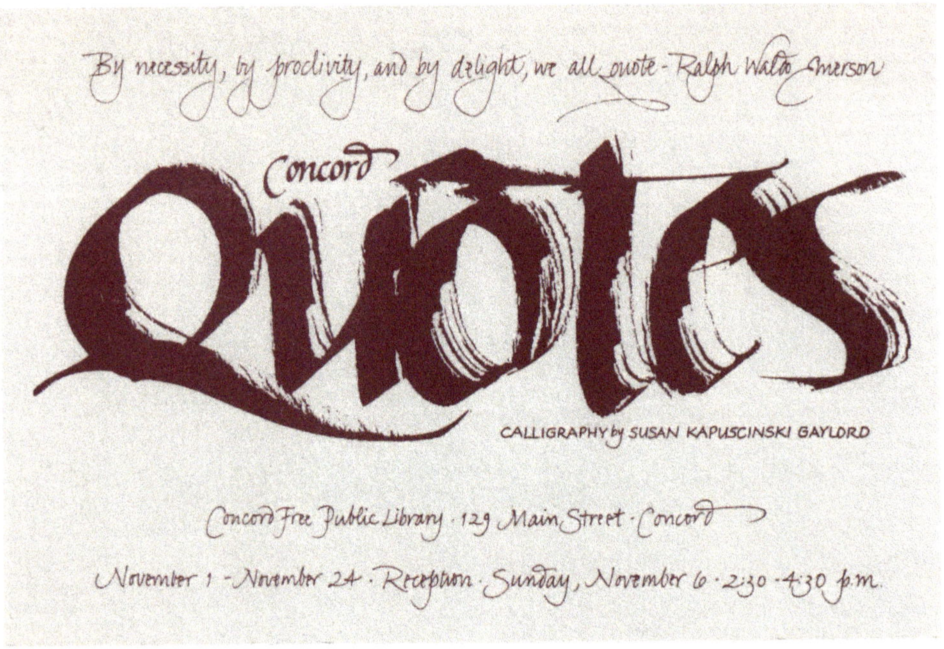

While it didn't seem like it at the time, this 1983 exhibit was in a way the high point of my calligraphic work before I moved on to books in 1988. At the time, I thought it was the beginning of a new chapter of working in series—doing calligraphic pieces with texts that fit together in some way. For the exhibit at the Concord Free Public Library, I chose quotes from Concord writers—Louisa May Alcott, Henry David Thoreau, Ralph Waldo Emerson, and Margaret Fuller. Everything I did was in service of the words. I used lettering style, paper, color, and design to put forward my interpretation of the text. As time went on, my ambitions changed. I no longer wanted to be the interpreter; I wanted to the creator.

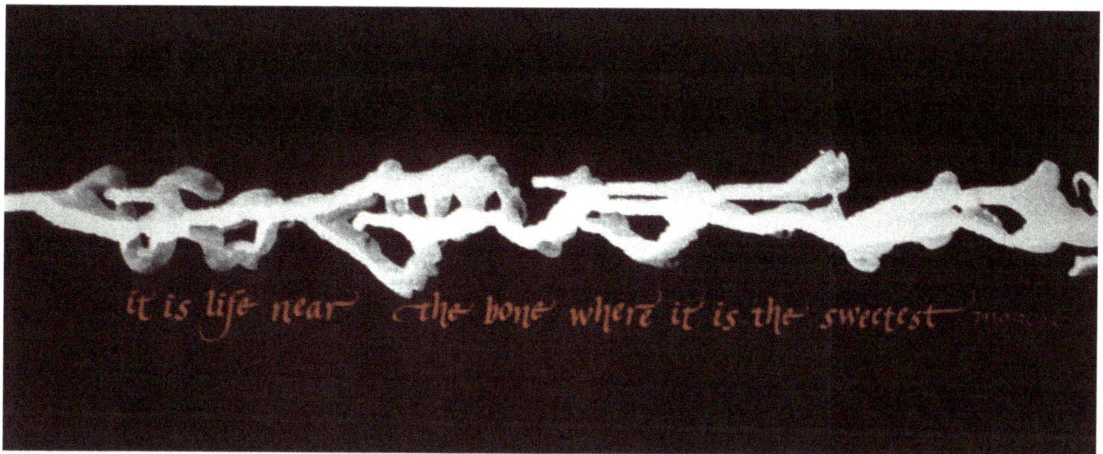

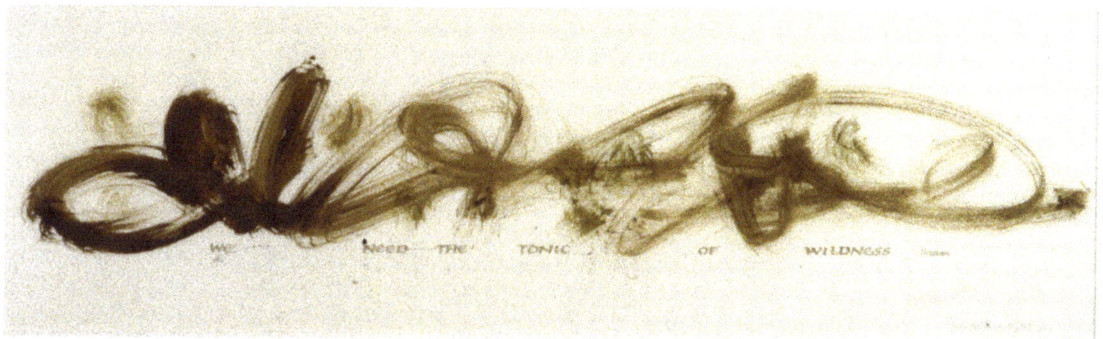

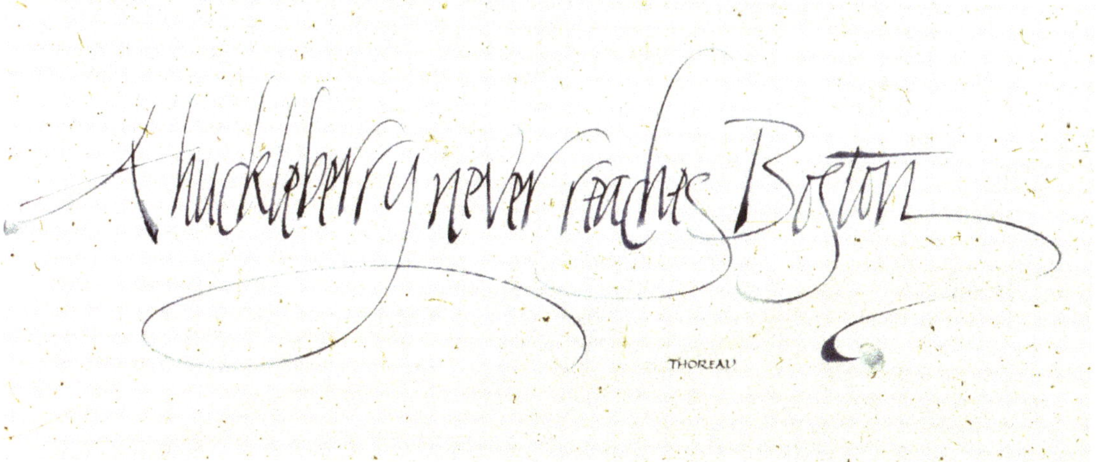

Above: Bone design made by dripping white-out from a bottle, lettering in red gouache. Middle: Abstract design made with reed and gouache, lettering done with pen and gouache. Below: Lettering with gouache and automatic pen. Dot at the end of the "n" in Boston directly printed from a blueberry.

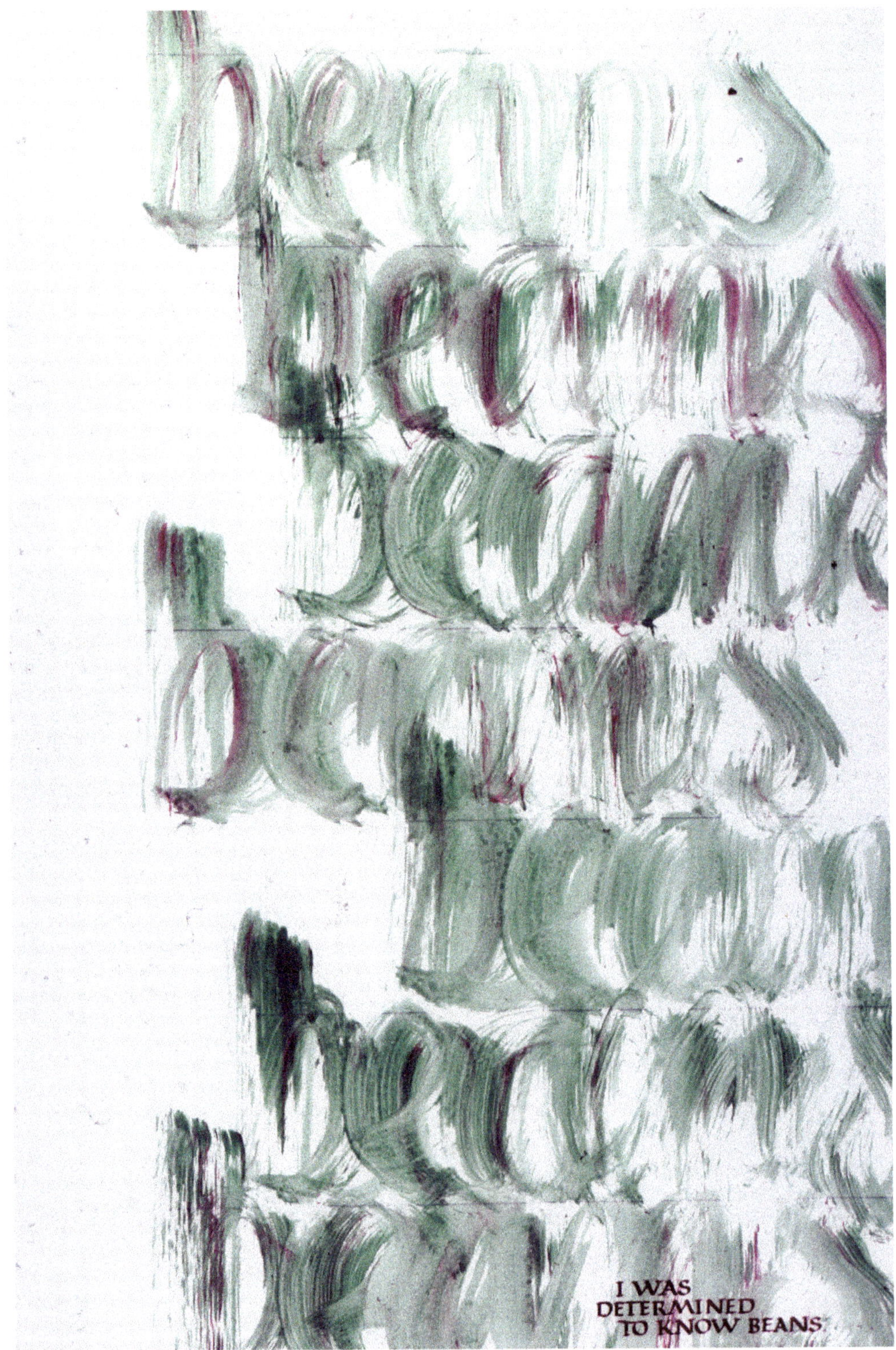

Beans written with acrylic paint using a toothbrush. Lettering done with gouache.

Ought they to smoke like that?
asked Beth, from her perch on the bed.

It's the dampness drying, replied Jo

What a queer smell! It's like burnt feathers,
— observed Amy, smoothing her own pretty curls with a superior air.

There, now I'll take off the papers,
and you'll see a cloud of little ringlets,
said Jo, putting down the tongs
She did take off the papers, but no cloud of ringlets appeared,
for the hair came with the papers, and the horrified hairdresser laid a row
of little scorched bundles on the bureau before her victim.

Louisa May Alcott

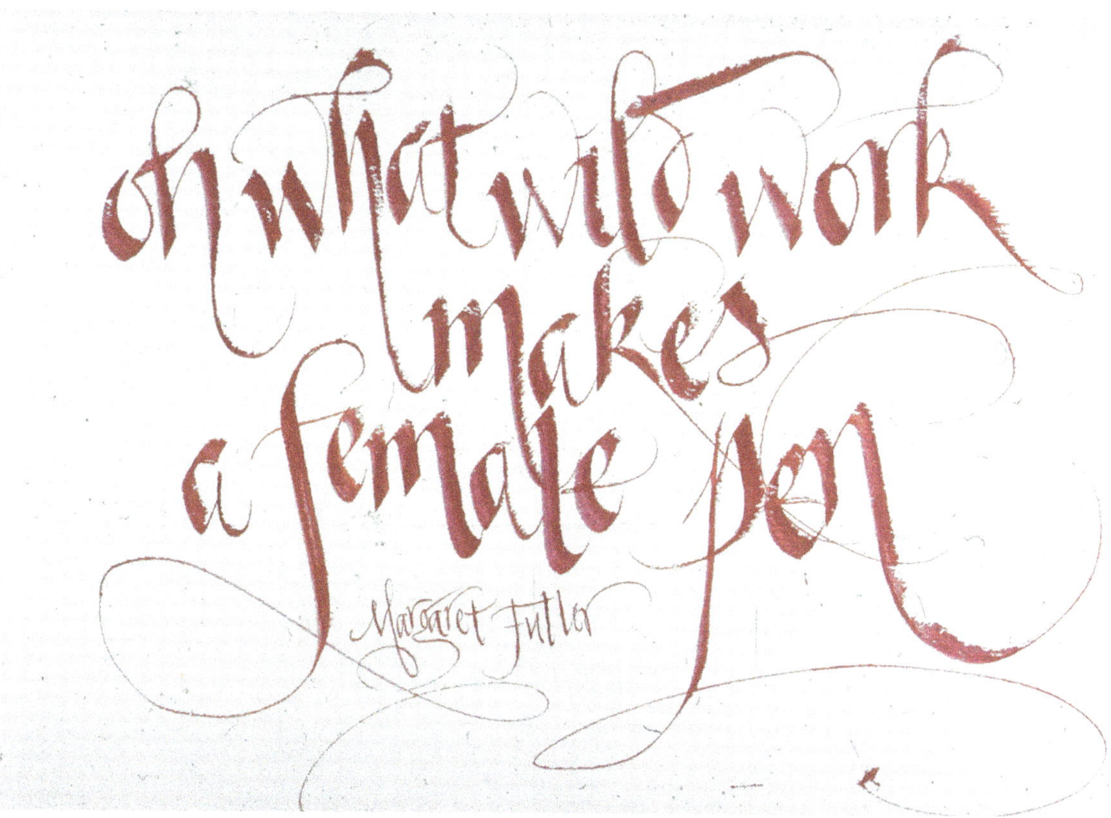

Above: Little Women quote done with gouache and ink. Below: Margaret Fuller quote written with gouache using an automatic pen.

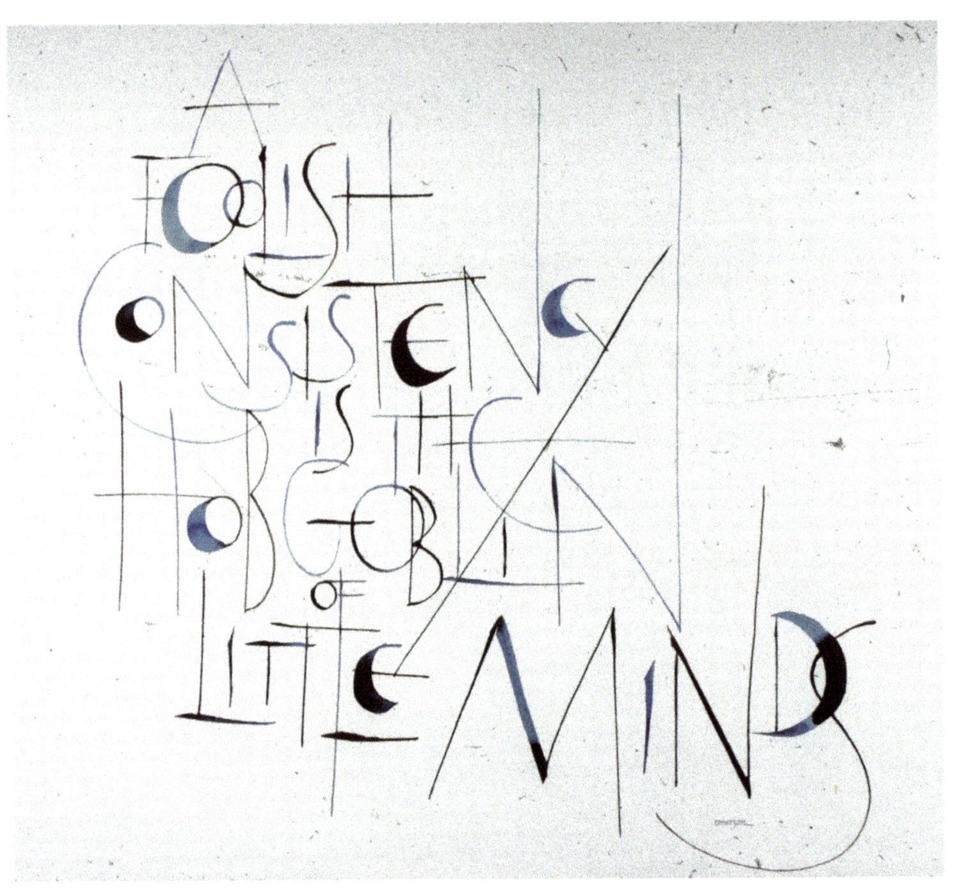

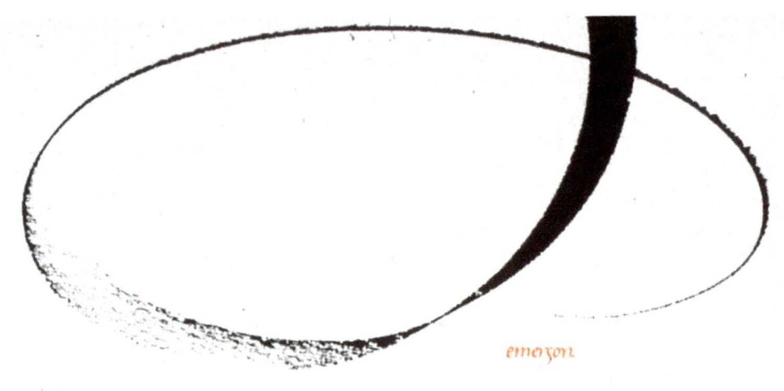

Art is the path of the creator to his work

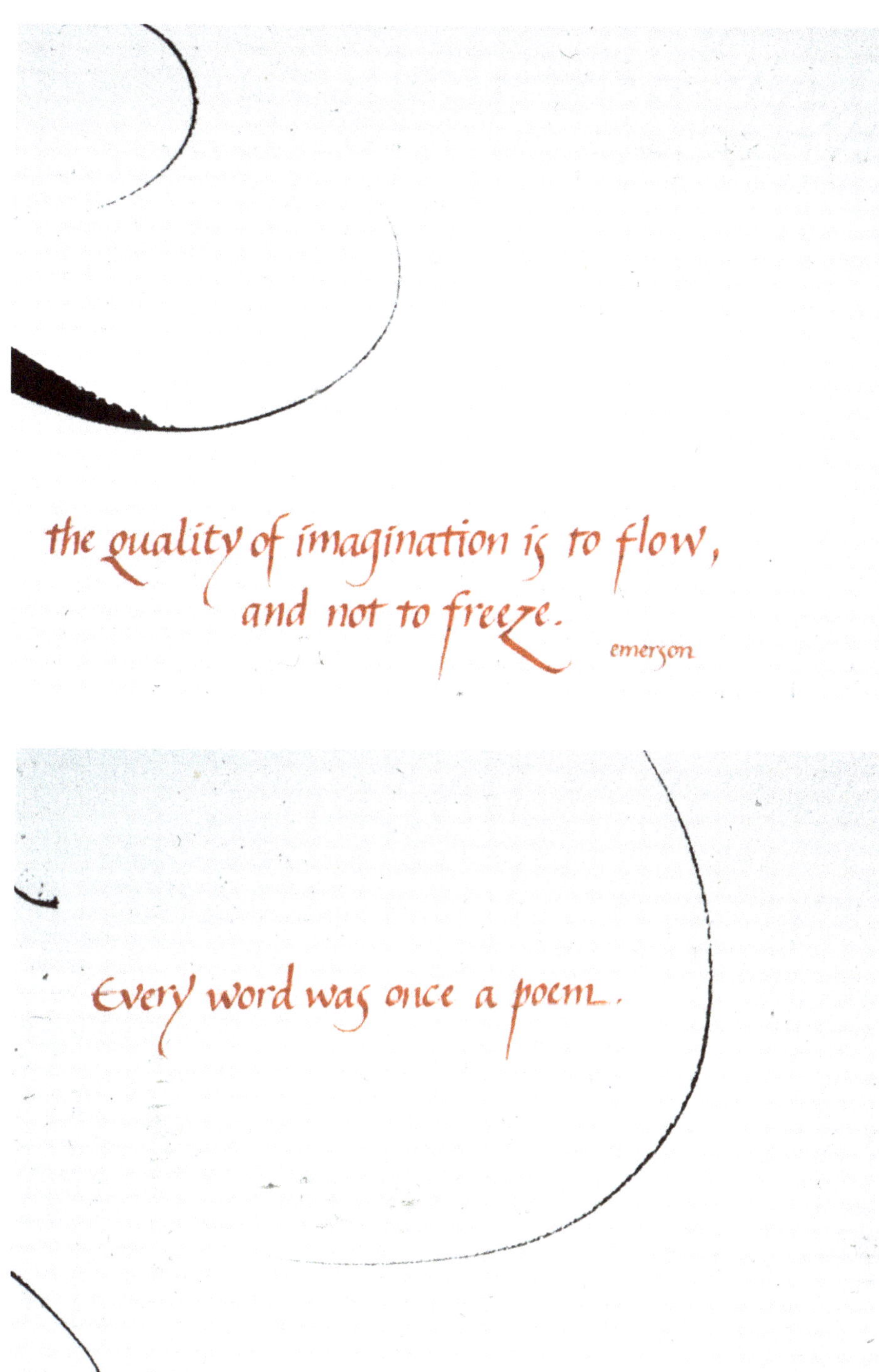

Opposite Page Above: Emerson quote written with brown and aqua inks using an automatic pen. Opposite Page Below and Above: Black gestural marks made with an automatic pen and sumi ink, lettering with red sumi ink.

Salmon Ladders

Spawned in snowy mountains, flushing to the sea,
it ran fat with salmon for Indian camps;
saw brick giants churn its wild rush
to a hydro-science of grinding power.
Though choked with mill crap and heavy with dark water,
the current kept repeating, slugging past the valley,
foaming at the falls, anxious for the salt.
Today's machines filter out muck,
cycling purification to coax back life
as the old wide streamer slaps rhythm in its cold wash.

New ladders will get salmon back schooling
in the Merrimack's rapids and basins.
At sundown the florid water will ripple under its skin
with pink meat, gills, and fins of slippery fish
whose flat eyes look upstream!

Black ink on bristol board. I think I used an Osmiroid fountain pen.

THE FIRST TEXTS I WORKED WITH BY a contemporary writer were the poems of
Paul Marion. I met Paul at the same art festival in the Lowell Memorial Auditorium
where I met the artists who were forming the organization that became Art Alive!
He read his poetry, and I soon after asked him for permission to write out his
poems. I exhibited them at the National Park Service across the street from Art
Alive! on Merrimack Street. "Salmon Ladders" was one of the poems in the exhibit.

I later showed my renderings of Paul's poems at the Whistler House Museum and
Lowell City Hall, and recently as part of a piece called "New England Haiku"
featuring haiku by seven New England poets at the Masscribes exhibit at the John
Joseph Moakley United States Courthouse in Boston.

Green windows in the redbrick mills
Green syllables in a red sentence
Green lights in a dark street
Green mouths in the open air
Green eyes all in a row

Glass windows stained green
from fingerprints of loom fixers,
bobbin boys, mill girls --
fingerprints of former farmers
who that morning walked to work
and bent down by the roadside
to rip up a fistful of grass,

and those green stained hands
wiped dust from mill windows,
smearing green ink onto glass,
leaving a trace that built up
over years as green stained hands
rubbed panes for a clearer look...

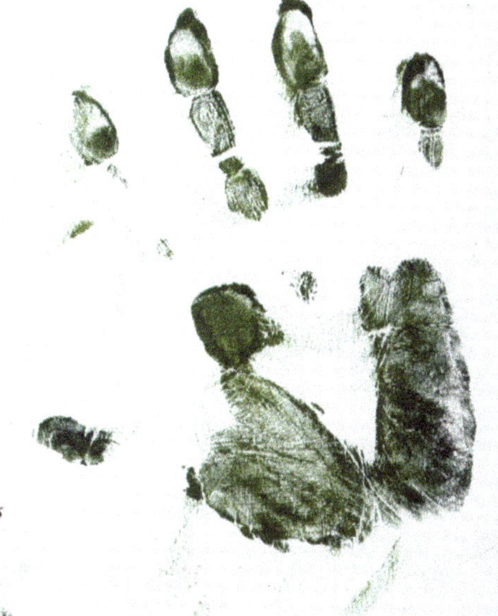

by Paul Marion

Green signs painted by countryfolk
who worked in factories to make a living wage
who signed up for the industrial army
who changed old ways to pay for groceries
who left poor soil for dependable machines
who took inside jobs but left green handprints
on the windows so someone might imagine
those window panes were green
from the grassy dreams shining behind them

GREEN WINDOWS

Hand prints made with acrylic paint. Lettering done with gouache and Brause nibs.

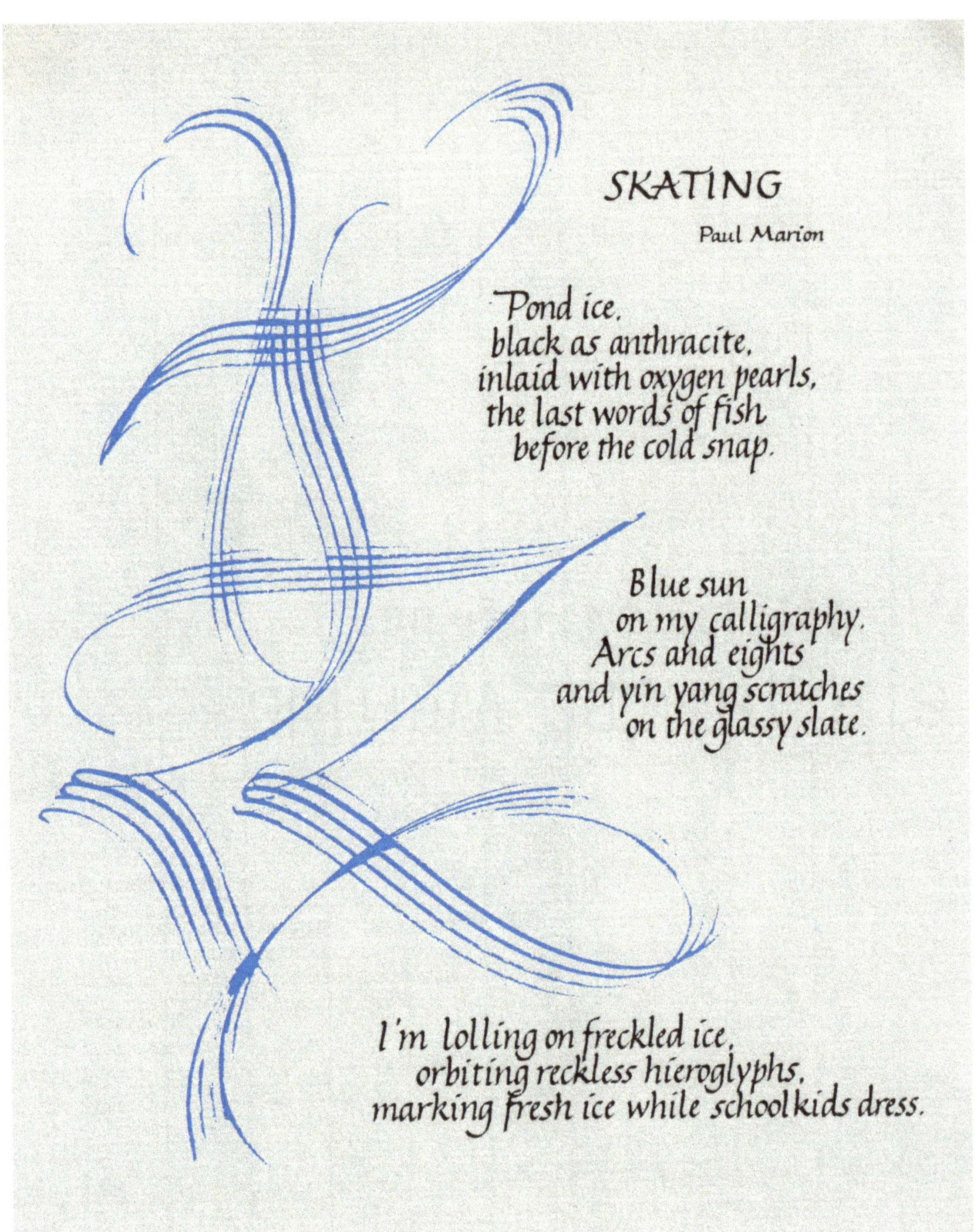

Abstract pattern made with a Coit pen. Lettering done with Brause nibs.

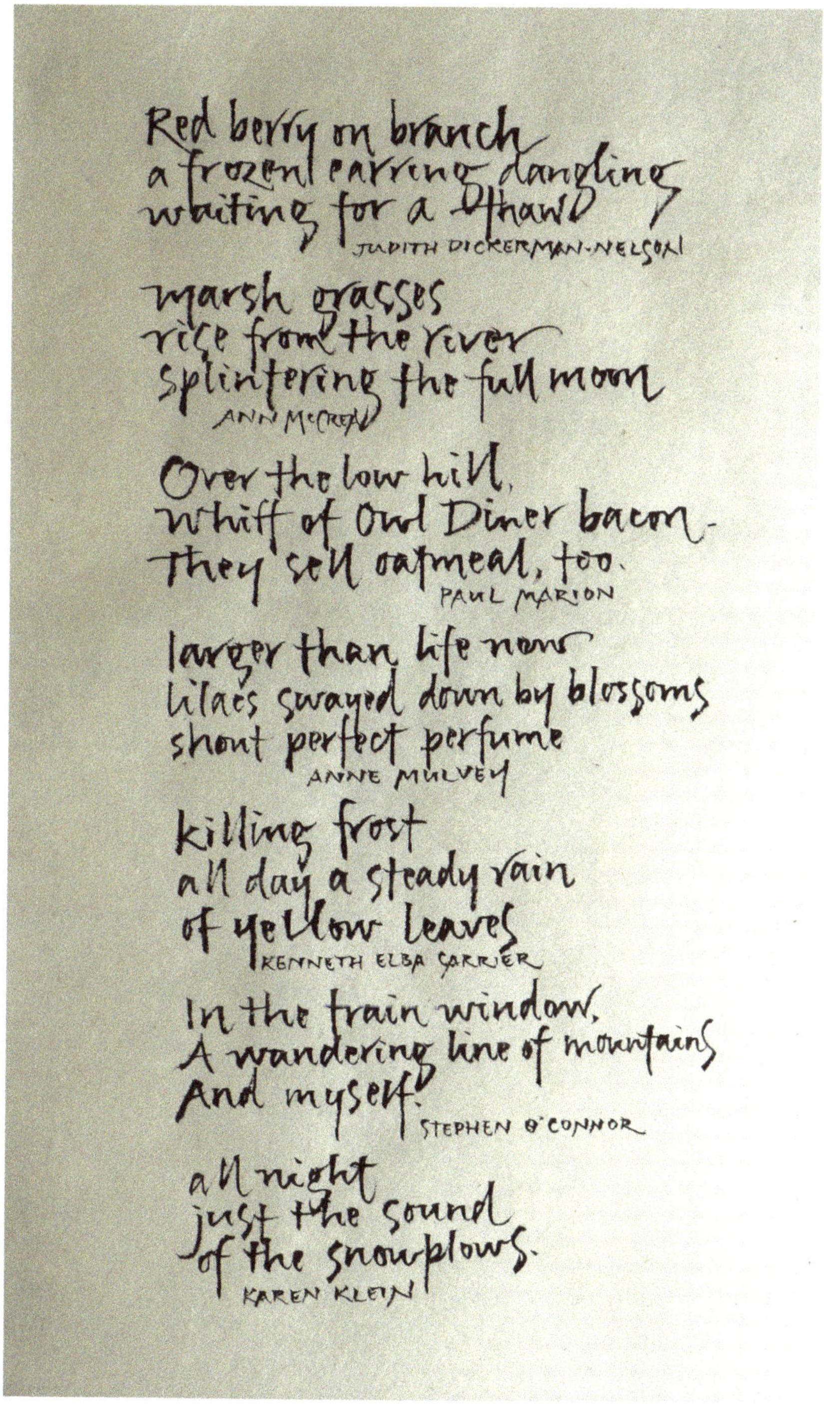

Red berry on branch
a frozen earring dangling
waiting for a thaw
JUDITH DICKERMAN-NELSON

marsh grasses
rise from the river
splintering the full moon
ANN McCREA

Over the low hill,
whiff of Owl Diner bacon—
they sell oatmeal, too.
PAUL MARION

larger than life now
lilacs swayed down by blossoms
shout perfect perfume
ANNE MULVEY

killing frost
all day a steady rain
of yellow leaves
KENNETH ELBA CARRIER

In the train window,
A wandering line of mountains
And myself.
STEPHEN O'CONNOR

all night
just the sound
of the snowplows.
KAREN KLEIN

New England Haiku: Lettering with sumi ink and brush from Korea.

Living in a town next to Lowell, I immersed myself in the writings of Jack Kerouac, especially his Lowell books: *The Town and the City, Maggie Cassidy, Visions of Gerard, Dr. Sax,* and *Vanity of Duluoz.* I could feel his presence as I walked the streets of the city. The passage below is from his last book, *Vanity of Duluoz.*

> But, wifey,
>   I did it all,
>   I wrote the book,
>   I stalked the streets
>   of life,
>   of Manhattan,
>   of Long Island,
>   stalked thru 1,183 pages
> of my first novel, sold the book,
>   got an advance,
>   whooped,
>   hallelujah'd,
>   went on,
>   did everything
> you're supposed to do in life.
>   But nothing
>   ever came of it.
>   No "generation" is "new."
> There's nothing new
>   under the sun."
>   "All is vanity."
> Forget it, wifey.
>   Go to sleep.
>   Tomorrow's
>   another day.
>   Hic calix!
>   Look that up in Latin,
>   it means "Here's the chalice,"
>   and be sure
>   there's wine in it.
>
> jack kerouac

Paul Marion and I organized two Kerouac events at Art Alive! The first, in 1981, was KEROUAC LIVES! (We liked titling things with exclamation points!) It featured a series of speakers including Joy Walsh, editor of the Kerouac journal *Moody Street Irregulars* and an incredible reading of a long poem by a very young George Chigas along with an art exhibit. Kerouac's widow Stella Sampas attended along with about 200 others. My husband and I went out after with Joy and a childhood friend of Kerouac's, Joe Chaput. It was a memorable evening.

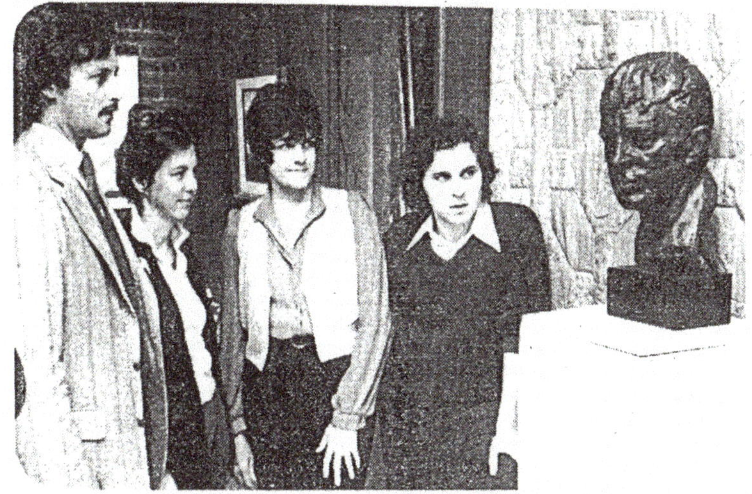

Participants in the 'Kerouac Lives' program at Art Alive! study Mico Kaufman's head of the Lowell-born writer. From left are John McHale, Susan Gaylord, Joy Walsh and Paul Marion.

The next year, we did an event called KEROUAC ALOUD. Members of Art Alive! and the community took turns sitting on a velvet chair on a worn Oriental rug and reading *Dr. Sax* throughout the day and into the evening.

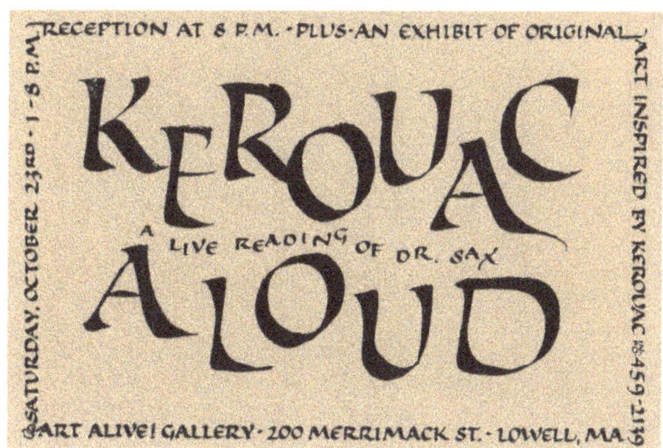

The Kerouac-Lowell connection took us further afield. In 1987, a group of artists from Lowell took part in the "Rencontre Internationale de Jack Kerouac" in Québec City in Canada. We showed work at the Galerie Quatre Saisons. I had two framed pieces, an artist's book, and a sculptural piece in the exhibition.

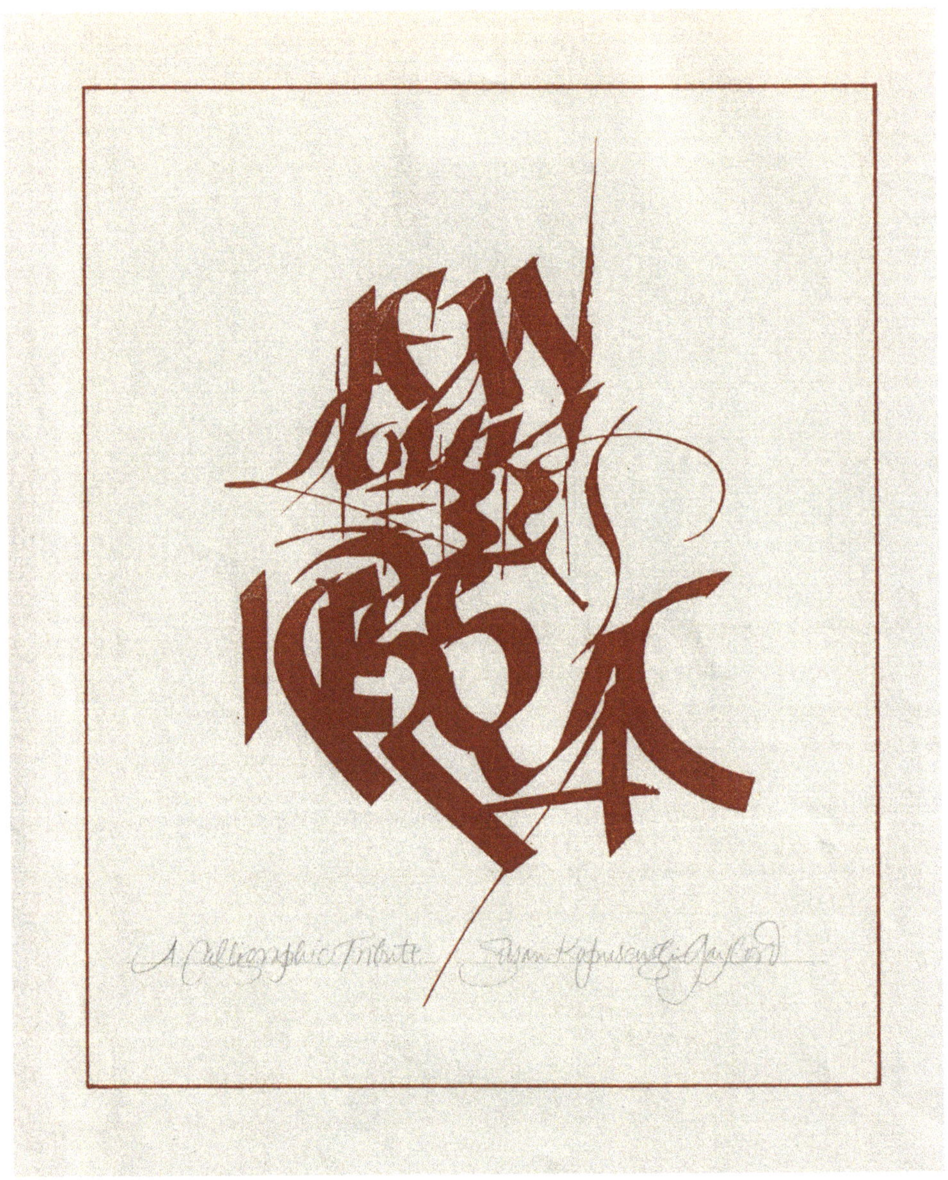

My connection with Joy Walsh and *Moody Street Irregulars* continued as I did some calligraphy that was published in the magazine, including the poem below by Roger Lacerte of Lowell.

Le Pays de
Ti-Jean

Roger Lacerte

Ti-Jean naquit en mons pays,
Connut ses rues, ses gens, leur vie.
Ti-Jean devint, comme il se doit,
Contestataire en Lowellois.

Ti-Jean quitta souvent l'pays,
Courut partout sans vrais amis.
Marié deux fois, jamais heureux,
Ti-Jean chez lui revint sans feu.

Ti-Jean trouva toujours les ponts,
Les tours de Dieu, les quat'saisons,
Surtout maman au coeur en or
Grondant d'amour l'enfant-trésor.

Ti-Jean Bougeotte alla très loin:
Ivre, drogué, la plume en main,
Pondant roman après roman,
Ti-Jean Canuk devint un grand.

"Héros des Beats" l'ont-ils voulu,
Leur roi, leur Jack, leur inconnu.
"Ti-Jean", pour moi, demeurera
L'orgueil des siens qu'il incarna.

Ti-Jean, te v'la rendu au bout.
Villon, Gavroche es-tu pour nous.
Tu nous chantas sur tous les toits
Cherchant en vain ton ciel, ton "toi".

Ti-Jean repose au cimetière
Edson... Les Saints renient sa bière.
L'eau bleue coule encore aujourd'hui
Près de Ti-Jean en mon pays.

I also did calligraphy for Joy's Textile Bridge Press: a broadside of "All-American Girl," a poem by Joy, and the entire book and cover of *The Jungle Book* by Bonnie Johnson shown on the opposite page.

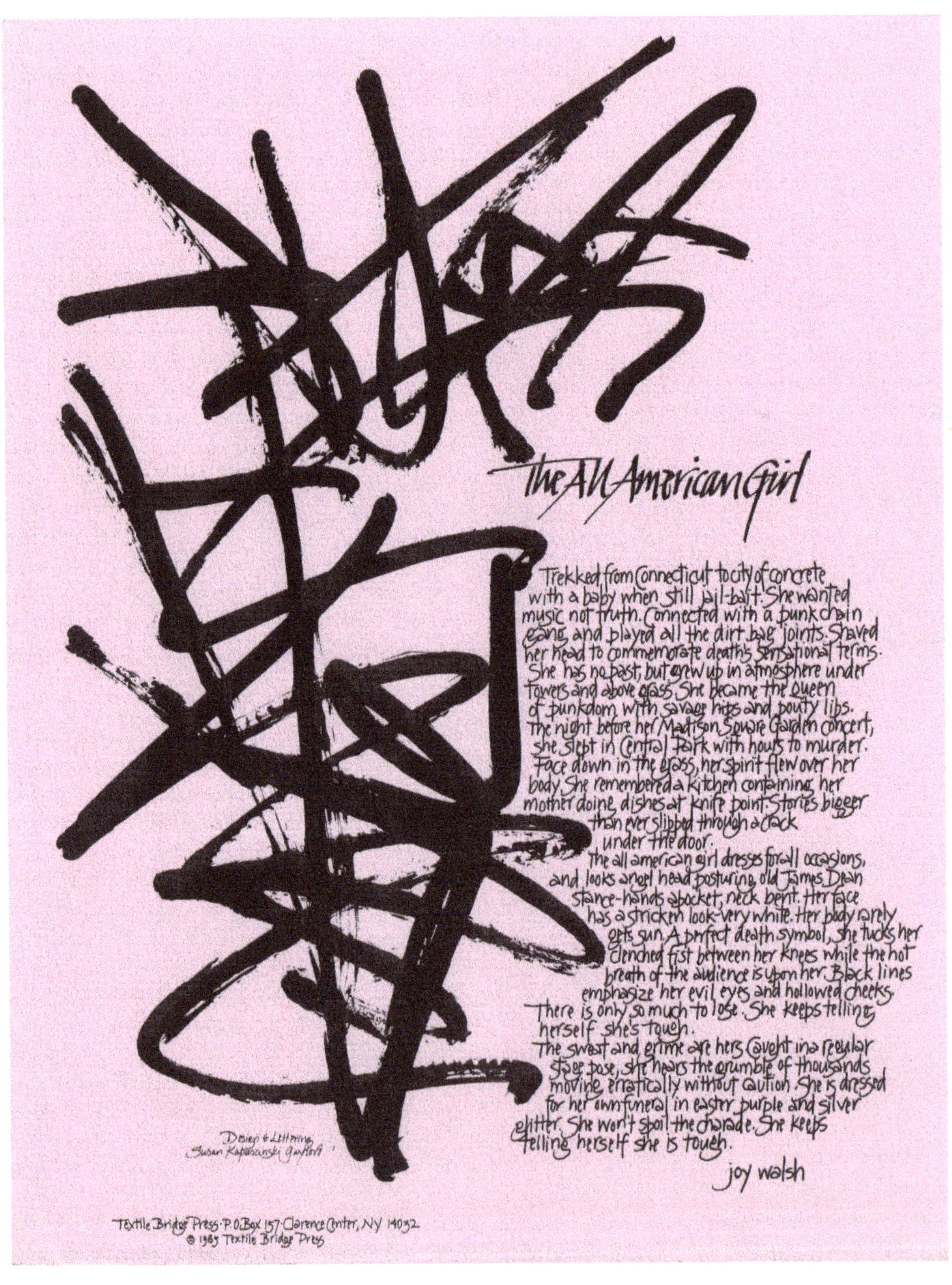

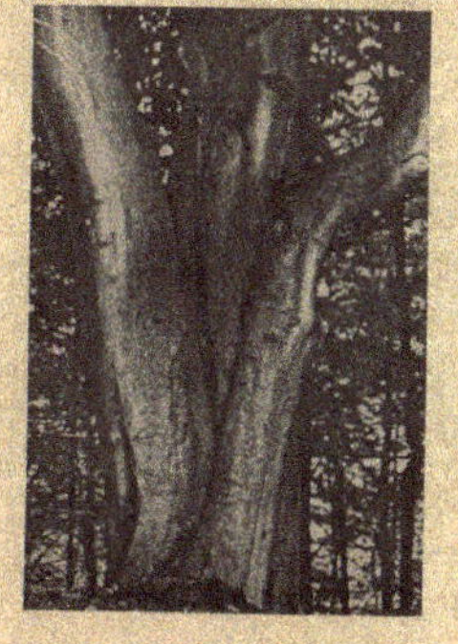

It's no good
complaining about the
state of the back yard unless you're prepared
    to do something about it

when I think of how it
used to be rambling vivid roses blooming
in every corner, joyously overflowing
the walls yes
with thorns yes but
beauty is always paid for in
some coin scratched and bleeding
hands, arms wild with
tangled vines
in the rain rose heads bending
and the green growth everywhere

you complained of the riotous profusion
spoke of pruning, began
to pinch off shoots and
getting braver, chopped
whole bushes not
wisely but well

looking out the window now parched
crackling earth even the weeds
find it difficult to
hold their heads upright
stones grow deeper, wider
soon there will be room only
for baby Krakatoas
live steam
scalding the air

IN 1982, I TOOK MY FIRST CALLIGRAPHY workshop. I traveled to the Philadelphia Conference on the Calligraphic Arts where a couple of hundred calligraphers from around the world gathered for a week of workshops and lectures. I had never been around that many people who did calligraphy before. I kept waiting for someone to come up to me and say, "Who do you think you are? Why do you think you belong here?" It was, of course, a reflection of my self-doubt and had nothing to do with the people who were there.

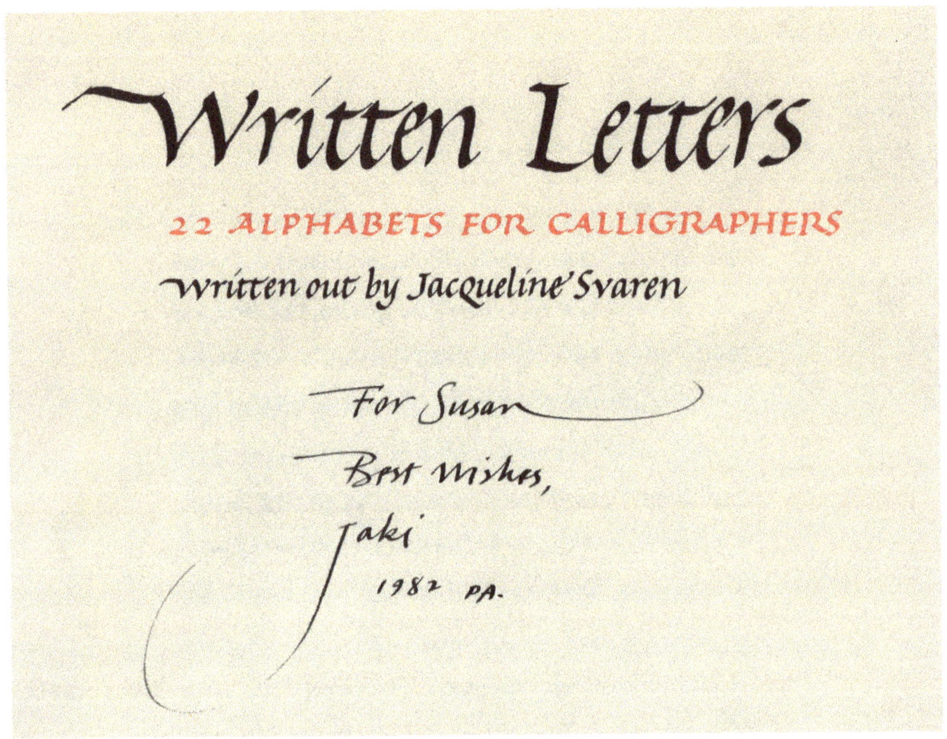

I chose a week of mornings with Jaki Svaren because I loved her book *Written Letters*. She was such a kind and understanding teacher on the page: "Strive for equal amounts of white space between the letters, but delight in your humanity." I thought she would be the perfect person for my introduction into this world, and she was.

Jaki taught us what she called the bone alphabet which involved twisting the pen instead of making straight strokes. We experimented with unusual writing tools including the dental hygiene product Stim-U-Dent. Excellent as the calligraphy instruction was, it was her philosophy shared through stories and especially her love of the book *Zen Mind, Beginner's Mind* by Shunryu Suzuki that really affected me. Jaki urged us to take away value judgments in reference to our lettering. If we make a letter and think it's good, it puts pressure on us as we make the next one. If we look at a letter we have just made and say it's bad, it decreases our confidence and our flow and we don't make the next one with the right attitude. Suzuki wrote: "Good and bad are only in your mind. So we should not say, 'This is good,' or 'This is bad.' Instead of saying bad you should say, 'not-to-do!'"

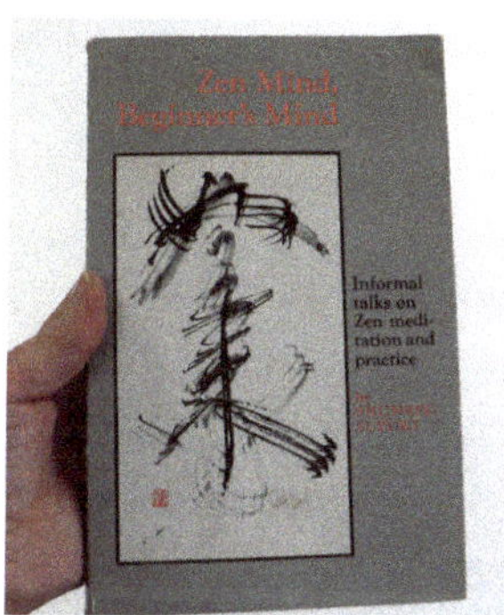

While in Philadelphia, I found a copy of the book in a bookstore. I think it's fair to say that *Zen Mind, Beginner's Mind* changed my life. I tried to extend the suspension of value judgments and resistance to defining things as good or bad to other aspects of my life. I can't say I have always succeeded but it has made a difference. The other passage that really stood out to me was: "Of course some encouragement is necessary, but that encouragement is just encouragement. It is not the true purpose of practice. It is just medicine. When we become discouraged we want some medicine. When we are in good spirits we do not need any medicine. You should not mistake medicine for food." These words were a guide on my path to becoming an artist. The understanding that validation for one's work has to come from within has deepened over the years.

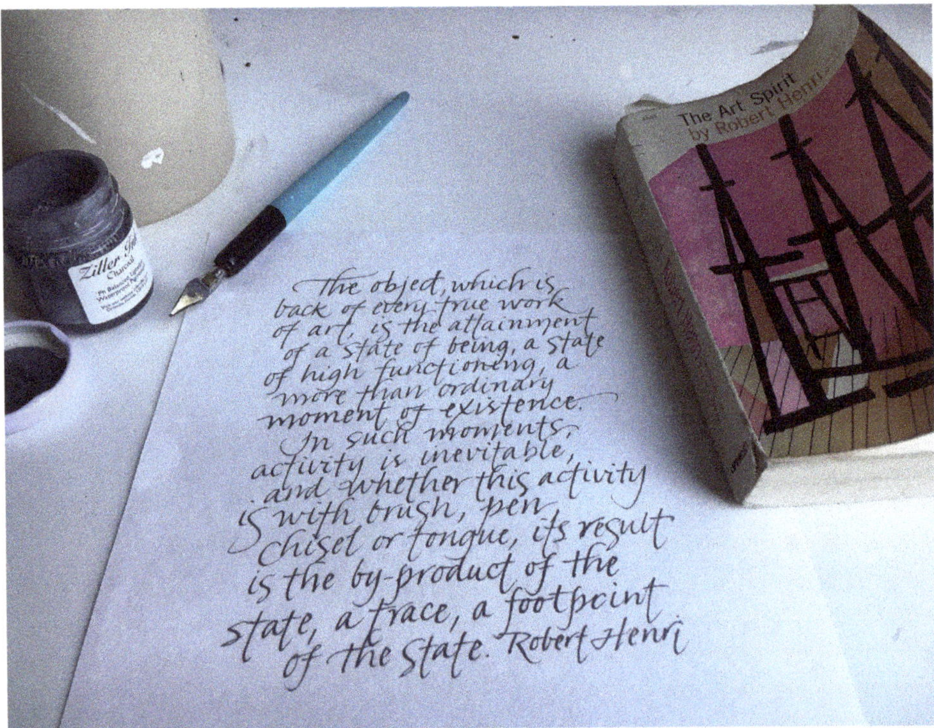

In 1983, I traveled to New York City to attend a week-long workshop with the Welsh calligrapher Ieuan Rees sponsored by the Society of Scribes. Again, as important as the calligraphy was the book he introduced us to—*The Art Spirit* by the early twentieth- century artist and teacher Robert Henri. And, again, I bought the book and pored over it. Henri's focus on the process—the importance of the moment of creation and the state of the artist at that moment—was very much in line with the writings of Shunryu Suzuki. It was the beginning of my thinking more broadly about making art rather than doing calligraphy. On the opposite page is a review I wrote for the *Society of Scribes Newsletter*.

REVIEW
Ieuan Rees Workshop

Intense is the first word that comes to mind to describe the five day workshop with Ieuan Rees. He said he came to this country to share what he could with us, and that he did. There was so much to learn from him on so many levels--from technical things on tools and letterforms to valuable information on design and "seeing," to his approach to his work, his clients, his art, his life.

The workshop began on Monday morning with a review of the letters A which we brought to class (instructions were for as many rough sketches with as much variety as possible). Then we traced some of those letters to get variations, making them longer, shorter, fatter, thinner, looking for the most extreme differences we could.

On Tuesday we took a break from the workshop proper and had a critique of work by members of the class who chose to participate. Ieuan explained that we were not requested to bring work so that we would not be intimidated, but as a result, several out-of-state people missed this valualbe opportunity. The critique led into a group discussion of the meaning of calligraphy, calligrapher, art, beauty, etc. Ieuan read us passages from what I have since found to be a very special book, The Art Spirit by Robert Henri. He told us of his new way of looking at calligraphy, as dressmaking with ink-the important shape being the inside counters and white space which is clothed in ink. What hit home for me was his discussion of uncertainty--stating that it is this which interferes with the production of good work. Make your marks with conviction--know why you're making them and put your whole self into them. (Worthwhile as an approach to life as well.)

The critique itself was done with kindness and thoroughness. He showed us the difference a minor adjustment--an eighth of an inch--can make and how far you can take a critique. It made me realize that I needed to look more critically at my own work, and that developing the ability to analyze and critique your own work can be as important as the technical skills.

On Wednesday, we returned to our projects, loosening up with free exercises, and then choosing, from all the A's we had done, four

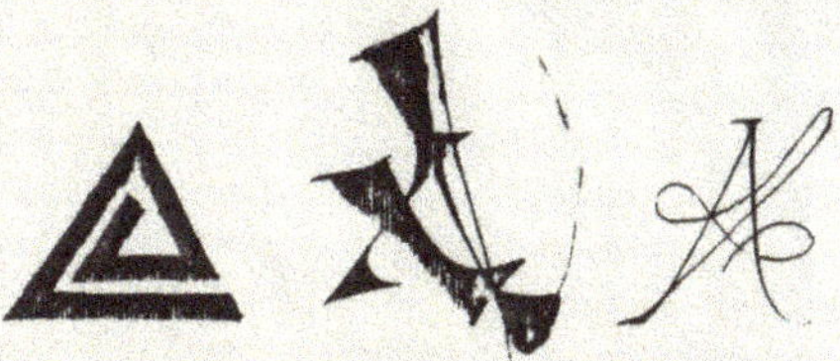

original A's

to work on and refine. Our project was to construct a word for each of the A's, creating the other letters to fit. If it sounds easy, it wasn't. The rest of the workshop was spent working on that problem with individual attention and group explanations by Ieuan. If he encountered an interesting or typical problem with any one person, he would gather everyone around, using it to illustrate his point. Most of us did not get 4 completed words, but only two if we were lucky. A bit rushed at the end, we only had time for a very short critique of the work produced, which was unfortunate as learning to see was what we had been spending our time on during the entire week.

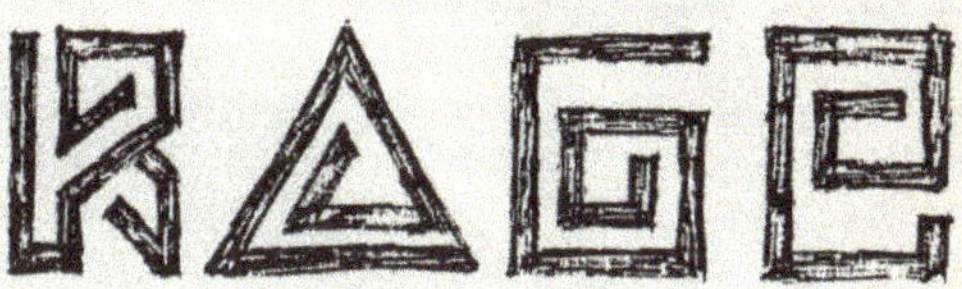

Some additional thoughts and observances from the workshop:

When someone would ask Ieuan, "Will this idea work?" his answer would be "I don't know, the only way to find out is by trying it."

Don't be cheap with paper. Keep experimenting and trying things out.

Everything affects the total picture. So try to make "roughs" as accurate as possible, otherwise you'll have to start all over when you go to do a finished piece. If it is to be a solid letter, make it solid. A line drawing will not tell you what it is going to look like as a solid shape.

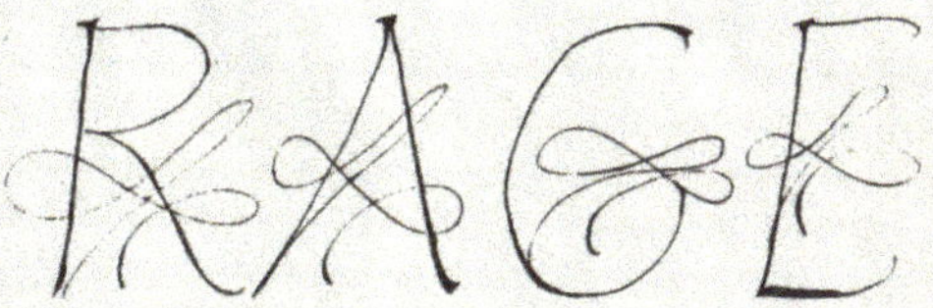

Ieuan described a commission for Open Education in Britain, how he had grand and wonderful ideas for huge sandblasted glass doors, but in the end had to put himself and his desires out of the way and choose a way of handling it that reflected the Open Education system. The overall design and purpose must be the most important.

When Ieuan went to do some careful work, he combed his hair and washed his hands, getting into the proper frame of mind for a particular job.

When Ieuan sat down at my table to help with a problematic letter (unsloved--the R in rage) I could tell he was having a great time. He enjoyed the challenge. I suspect he would have enjoyed some time to himself to try and remedy the problems of that R. He viewed the problems and frustrations with energy and enthusiasm.

In summary, I have just begun to assimilate and use the many things I learned in the workshop. I am more aware, and in fact, am learning to see.

Susan Gaylord

THE ZEN WAY
OF CALLIGRAPHY
IS TO WRITE IN THE
MOST STRAIGHTFORWARD, SIMPLE WAY
AS IF YOU WERE A BEGINNER,
NOT TRYING TO MAKE SOMETHING
SKILLFUL OR BEAUTIFUL,
BUT SIMPLY WRITING
WITH FULL ATTENTION
AS IF YOU WERE DISCOVERING
WHAT YOU WERE WRITING FOR THE FIRST TIME;
THEN YOUR FULL NATURE
WILL BE IN YOUR WRITING.
THIS IS THE WAY
OF PRACTICE
MOMENT AFTER MOMENT.

SHUNRYU SUZUKI
Zen Mind, Beginner's Mind

I taught Art 221: Introduction to Calligraphy at Rivier College for four semesters starting in the fall of 1984. I was recommended by Deborah Partington when she left her position there. Most of the students were studying graphic design. Calligraphy was a required course that preceded typography. I also had some students from the community including an ER nurse looking for relaxation and stress relief and a nun sent by her order to learn calligraphy for making signs. Here's what I wrote in the syllabus:

Calligraphy has been defined by Edward Johnston, who has been called the father of modern calligraphy, as making good letters and arranging them well. This deceptively simple definition describes the work for this course, and indeed, a lifetime if one chooses. Layout and design— arranging them well—will be considered as important as making good letters. And because letters are used to make words, the connection between the meaning of the words and their presentation will be stressed.

The teaching was a challenging experience. While I had taught a couple of Adult Education calligraphy classes, there was a big difference between preparing for two hours of class time for eight weeks (sixteen hours) and five hours for thirteen weeks (sixty-five hours total). I was starting from scratch in many ways. Because I had learned calligraphy from books rather than class instruction, I didn't have a model for what to do, or not do. The Art Department at Rivier was supportive, especially the head of the department Sister Theresa Couture. She had faith in me while I struggled with my new role.

A workshop with Marsha Brady on teaching calligraphy was helpful. She taught a lot about organization and presentation. She insisted that every teacher should be able to do calligraphy with her left or right hand. Practicing with my left hand enabled me to give concrete suggestions for left-handed students and understand their struggles while showing them that it was possible (and that I wouldn't take left-handedness as an excuse for poor work).

My presentation of the material developed over the four semesters. By the end I had
a program that started with cutting Roman capitals from black paper. I felt it was
helpful to grasp letter form and spacing before introducing the pen. We then learned
basic Roman caps with a round Speedball B nib so we could focus on the letters
without having to worry about the pen angle. The edged pen was introduced with
Uncial, followed by Foundational Hand. I also shared some of the philosophy from
Zen Mind, Beginner's Mind and words by and information about a variety artists such as
Ben Shahn and Robert Henri, and the jazz singer Mabel Mercer. The students did
four projects per semester and assignments and exercises between each class.

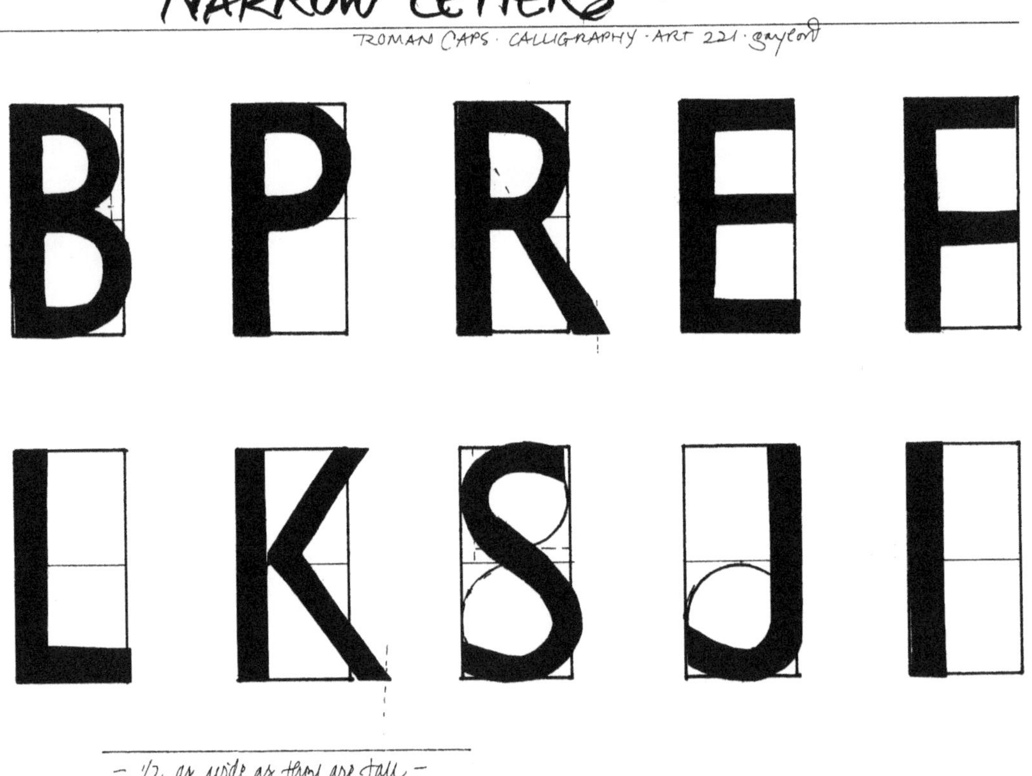

ROMAN CAPS WITH SPEEDBALL B·2

CALLIGRAPHY ART 221 · gaylord

ABCDEFGHIJ
KLMNOPQR
STUVWXYZ

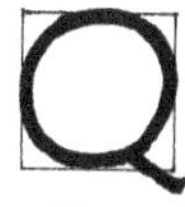
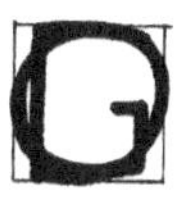
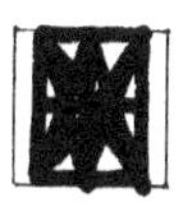
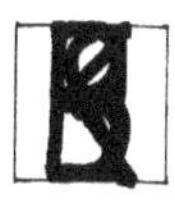
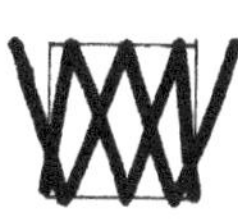

UNCIAL written with Brause 4mm

CALLIGRAPHY · ART 221 · gaylord

ABCDEFGh
IJKLMNOPq
RSCTUVWX
YZ

Pen held at 30° angle.
Letters with ascenders— D, H, K, L
Letters with descenders— F, G, J, P, Q, R, Y
Think ROUND

based on the Uncial alphabet in *Written Letters* by Jacqueline Svaren

The first project used Roman caps written with a Speedball B nib. One project was to do a quote about the alphabet (I gave quotes or they could find their own) and the alphabet itself. Another was to find a black-and-white photograph and recreate the image with lettering, showing the gradations of gray by altering the weight of the letters.

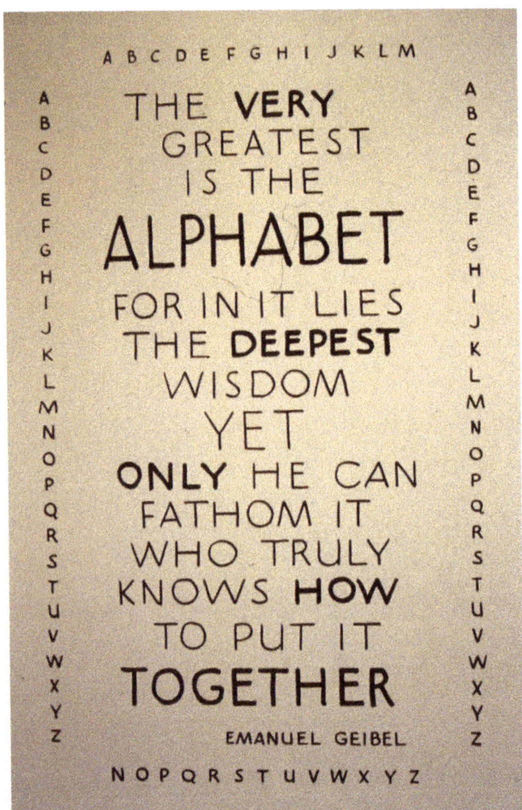

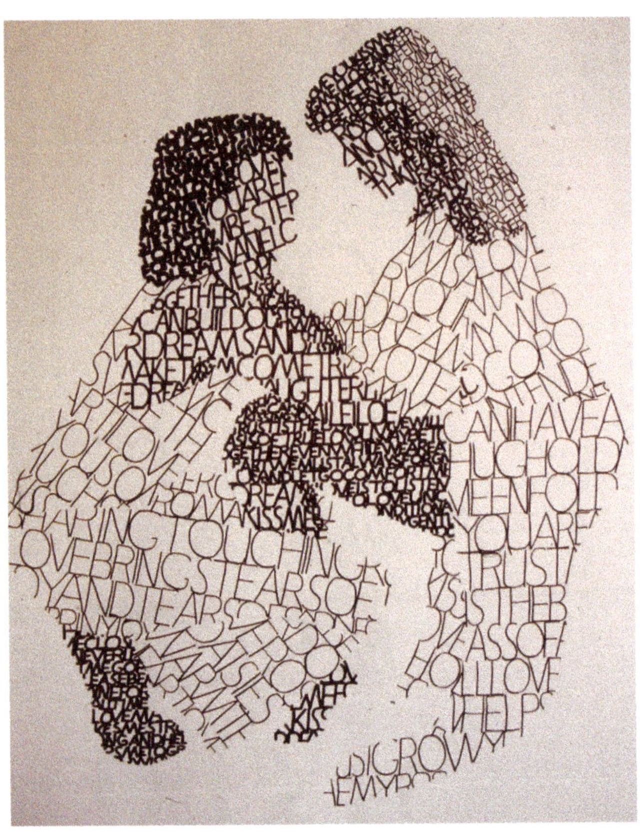

For the Uncial Hand, we made books. I encouraged students to use words that were meaningful to them. Mostly they chose poems and songs. A student interested in fashion worked with the text from a perfume ad.

The assignment for the Foundational Hand was to audiotape something—a TV show, a conversation, something on the radio—and try to convey the changes in voices and volume through letter size, spacing, color, and arrangement. For the final project, students chose the hand, the form, and the content.

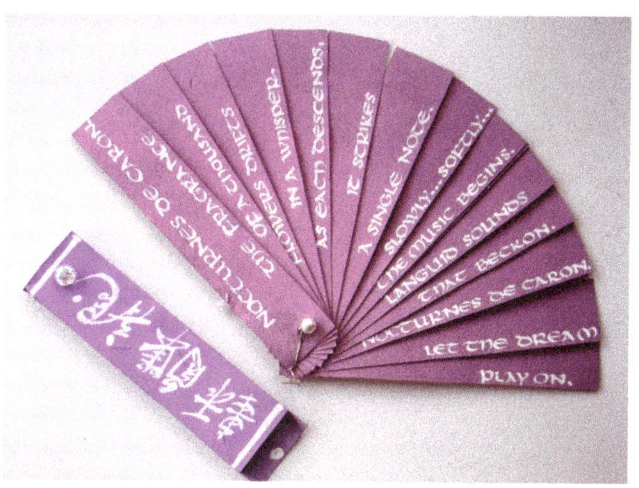

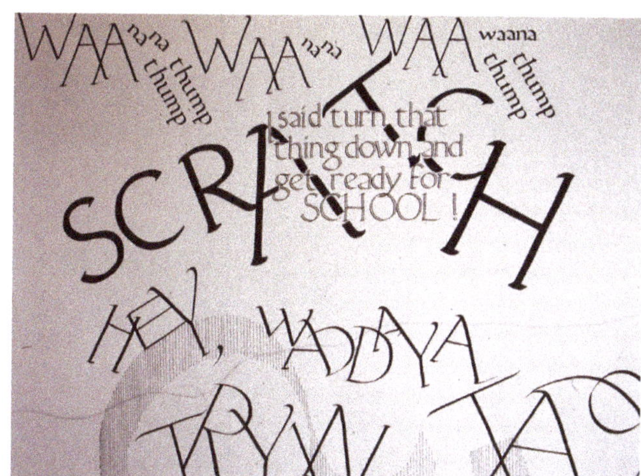

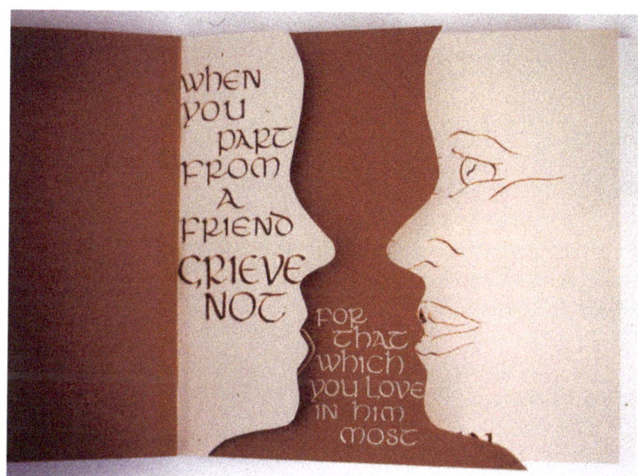

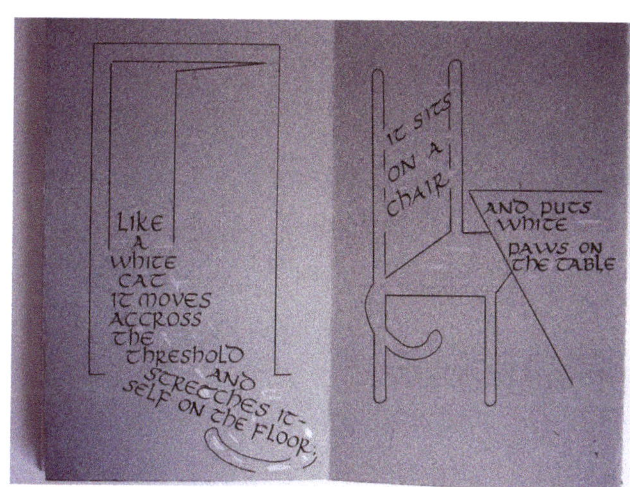

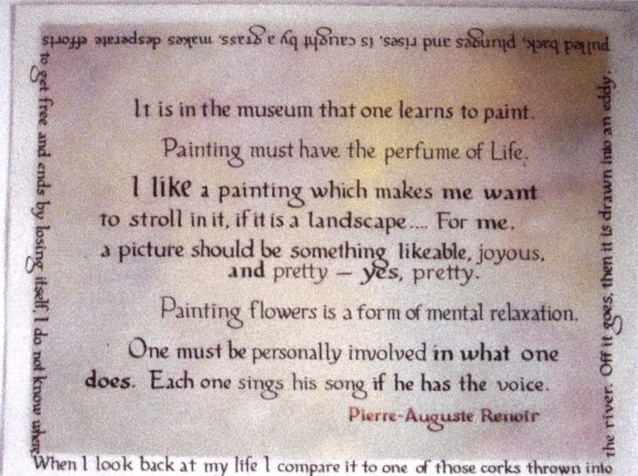

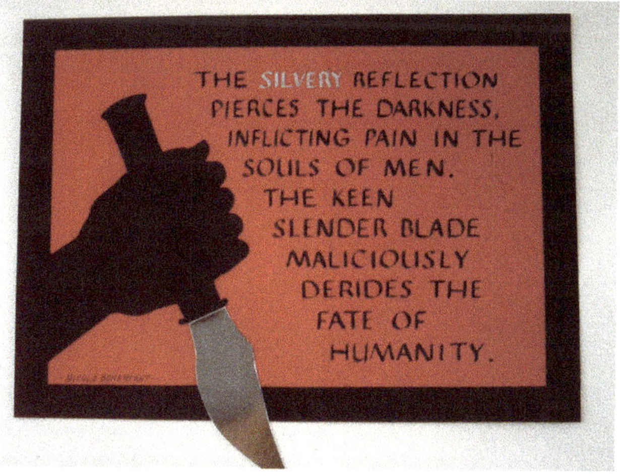

Student Work: Clockwise: Book project with Uncial. Audio project with Foundational. Book project with Uncial. Free choice project with Roman Caps. Free choice project with Foundational. Book project with Uncial. Opposite Page: Projects with Speedball B nibs and Roman Caps.

THE FIRST WORK THAT I CONSIDER to be truly my own was *Childbirth Journey*, a series of fifteen abstract pastel drawings with calligraphy of excerpts from the journal I kept through my pregnancy and the months following the birth of my first child. Here's what I wrote about the work on the back of the exhibit invitation: "As I tried to come to terms with the experiences of pregnancy and childbirth, I felt that while the baby was making a physical journey into the world, I was making an emotional journey to motherhood. The series is an attempt to express the wide range of emotions—up, down, and in-between—that made up the journey."

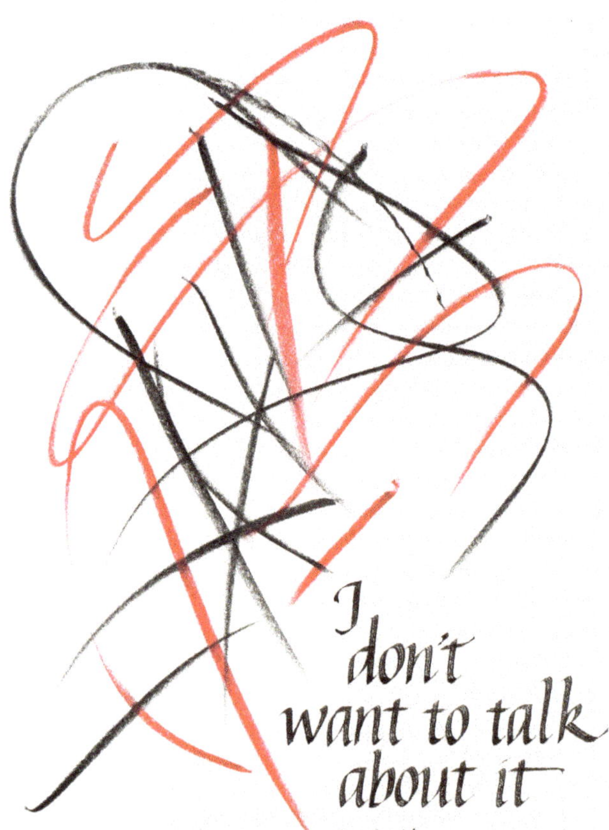

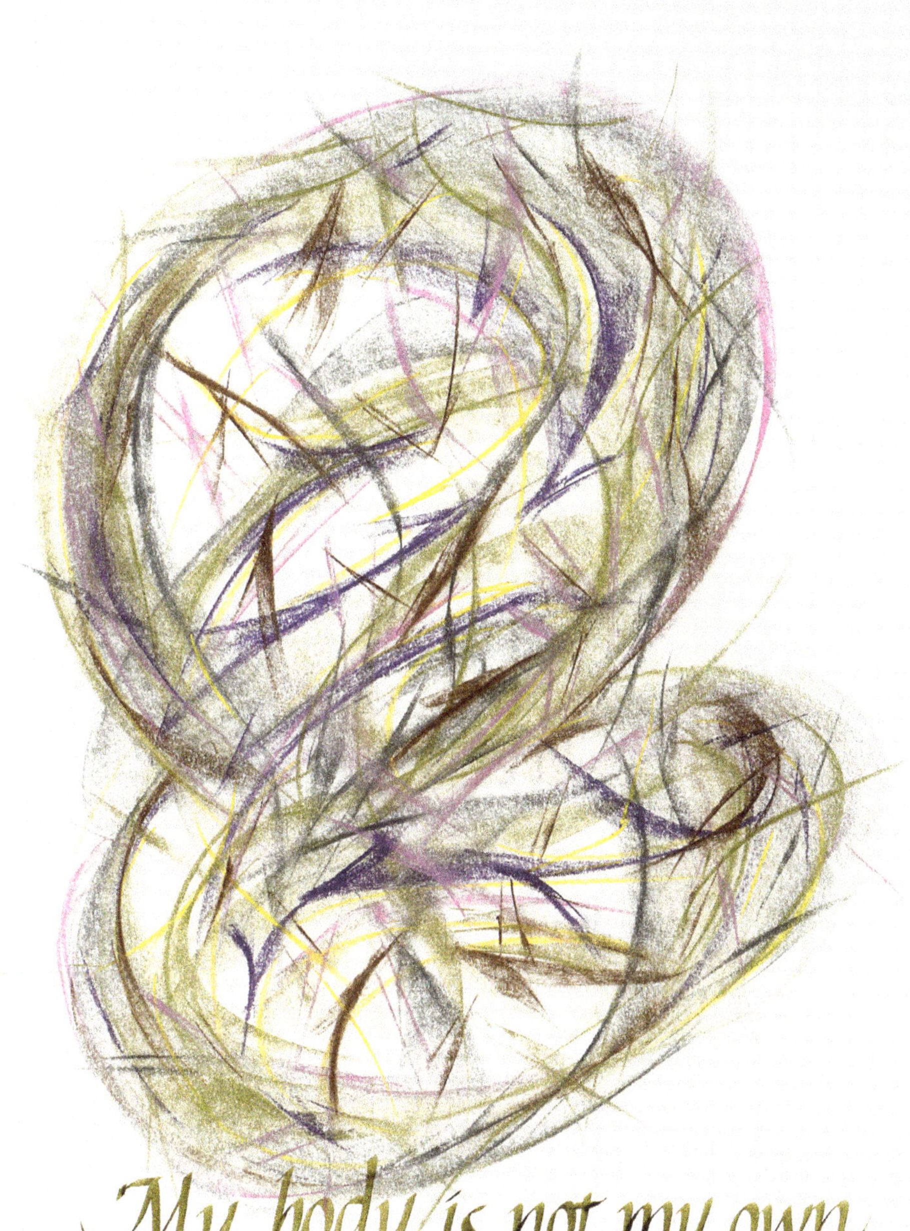

My body is not my own.

I know this being growing inside of me comes from the two of us,
but it feels like a stranger. Its unsettling. Everyone says how happy I must be,
but I'm not. The thought of the responsibility overwhelms me. I'm confused,
I'm ambivalent. I don't know if I want a baby or not.

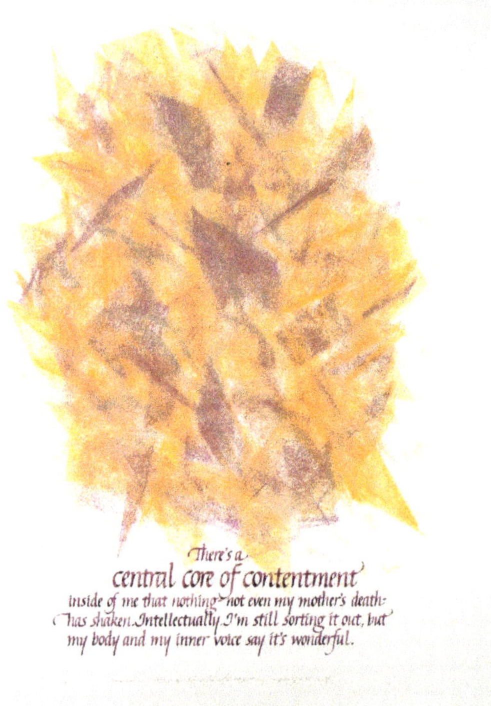
There's a
central core of contentment
inside of me that nothing—not even my mother's death—
has shaken. Intellectually I'm still sorting it out, but
my body and my inner voice say it's wonderful.

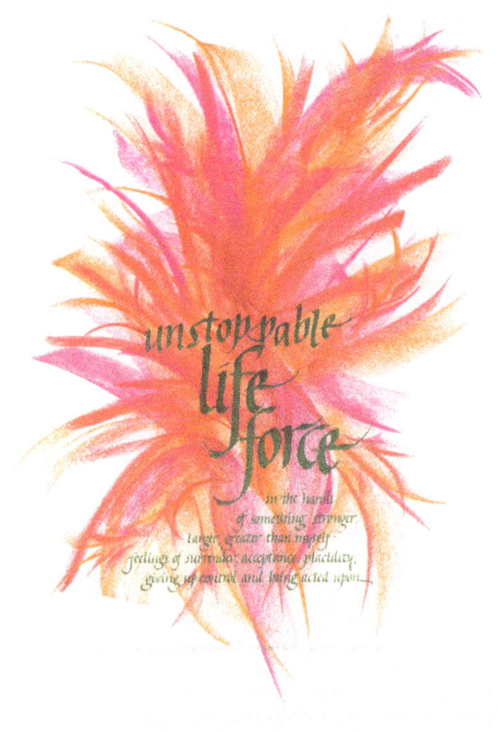
unstoppable
life
force
in the hands
of something stronger,
larger, greater than myself.
feelings of surrender, acceptance, placidity,
giving up control and being acted upon.

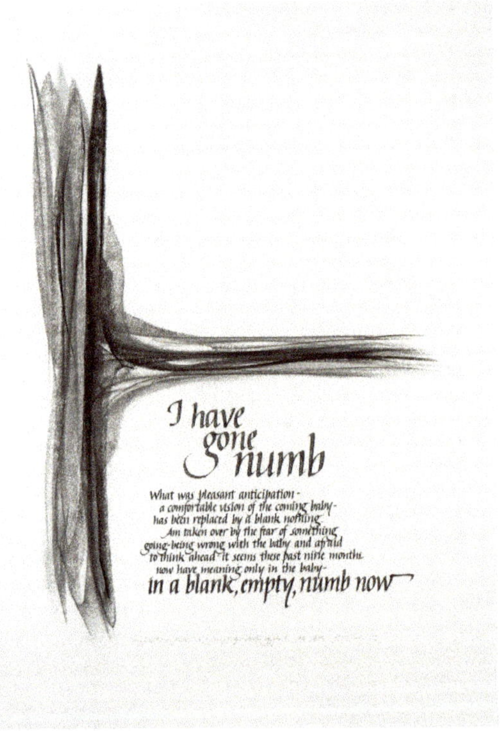
I have
gone
numb
What was pleasant anticipation—
a comfortable vision of the coming baby—
has been replaced by a blank nothing.
Am taken over by the fear of something
going-being wrong with the baby and afraid
to think ahead. It seems these past nine months
now have meaning only in the baby—
in a blank, empty, numb now

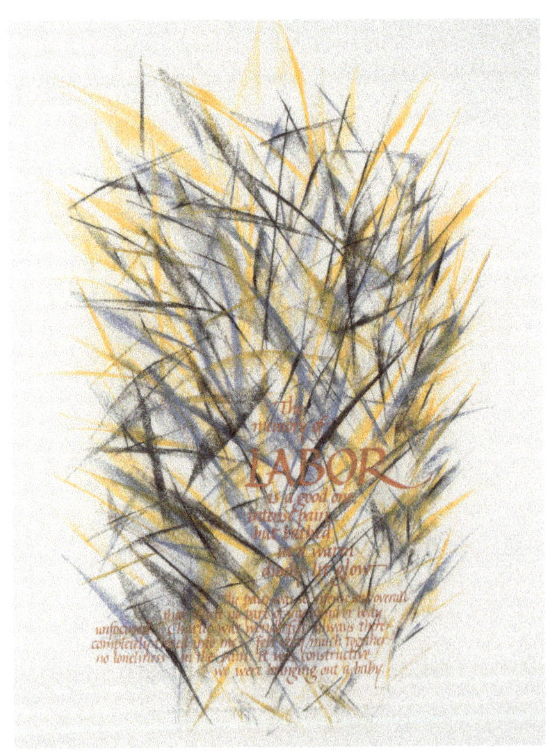
The
memory of
LABOR
is a good one,
intense pain,
but buried
in a warm
dim lit glow—

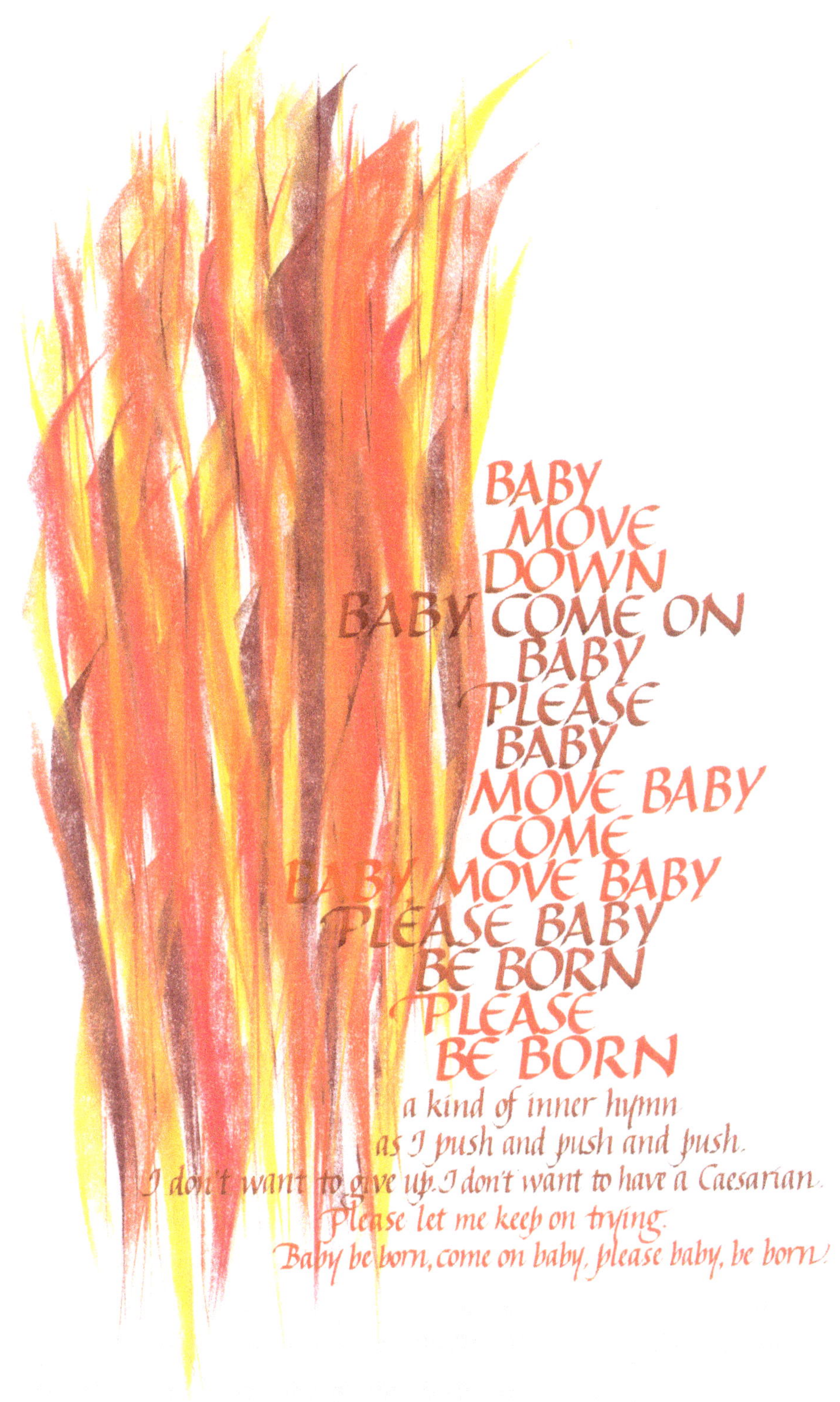
BABY
MOVE
DOWN
BABY COME ON
BABY
PLEASE
BABY
MOVE BABY
COME
BABY MOVE BABY
PLEASE BABY
BE BORN
PLEASE
BE BORN
a kind of inner hymn
as I push and push and push.
I don't want to give up. I don't want to have a Caesarian.
Please let me keep on trying.
Baby be born, come on baby, please baby, be born!

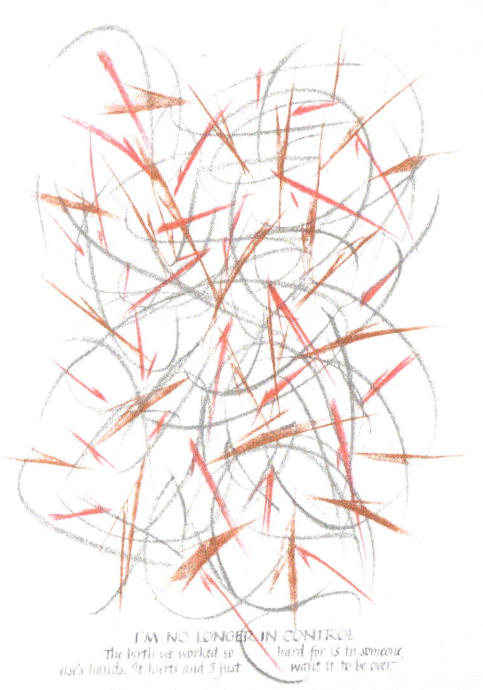
I'M NO LONGER IN CONTROL
the birth we worked so hard for is in someone
else's hands. It hurts and I just want it to be over.

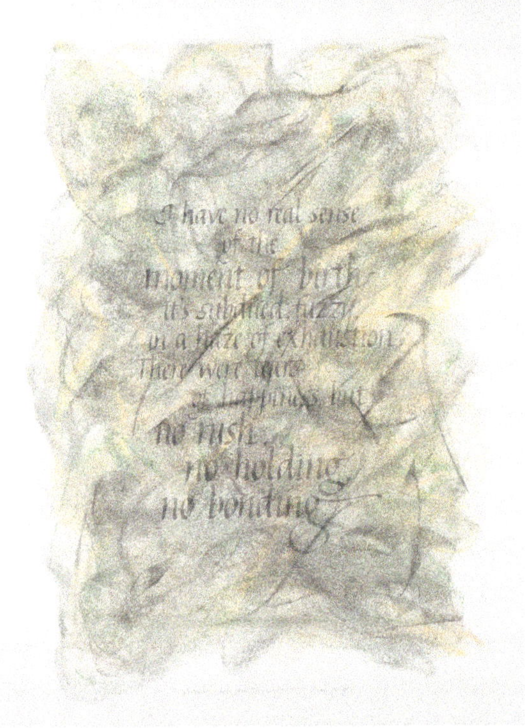
I have no real sense
of the
moment of birth.
It's subdued, fuzzy
in a haze of exhaustion.
There was more
of happiness but
no rush
no holding
no bonding

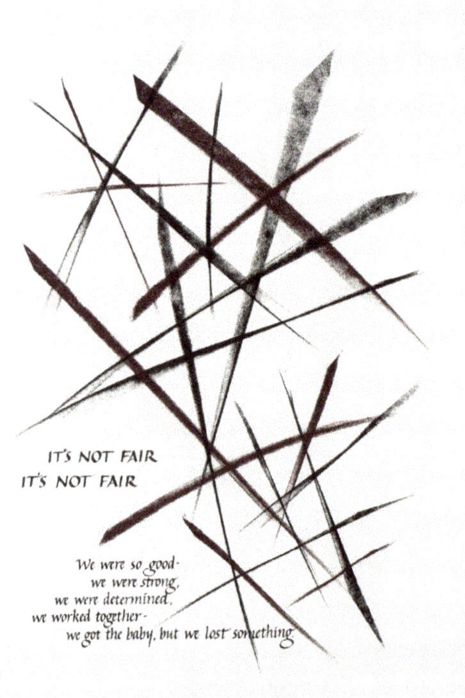
IT'S NOT FAIR
IT'S NOT FAIR

We were so good -
we were strong,
we were determined,
we worked together -
we got the baby, but we lost something.

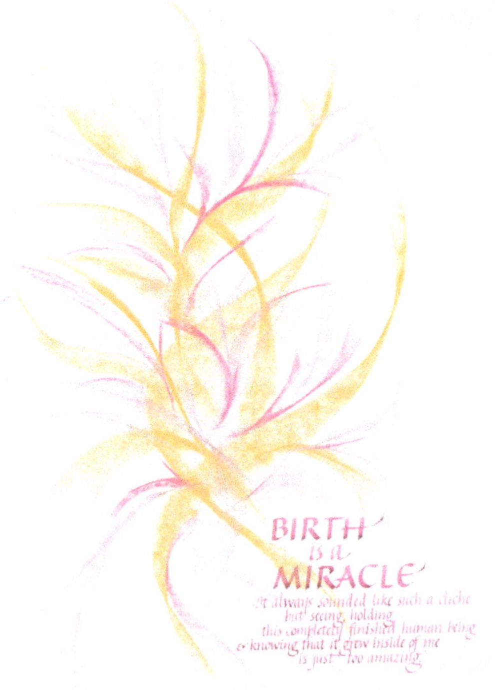
BIRTH
is a
MIRACLE
It always sounded like such a cliche
but seeing, holding
this completely finished human being
& knowing that it grew inside of me
is just too amazing.

All I want to do is sleep,
when the baby nurses.
I can feel him sucking the energy from me.
I'm not ready.
I still want to be taken care of
I miss Mom so much.

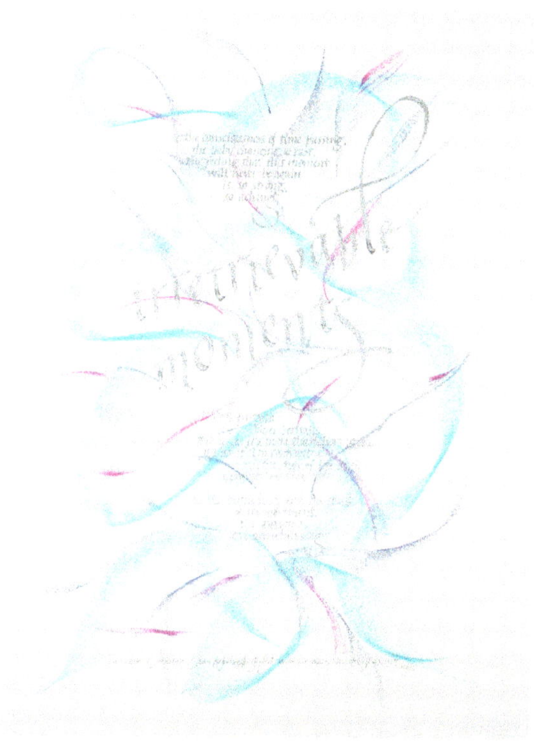

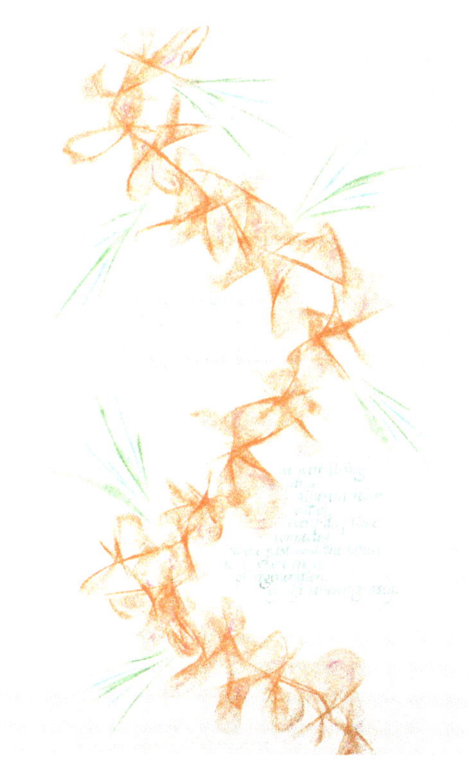

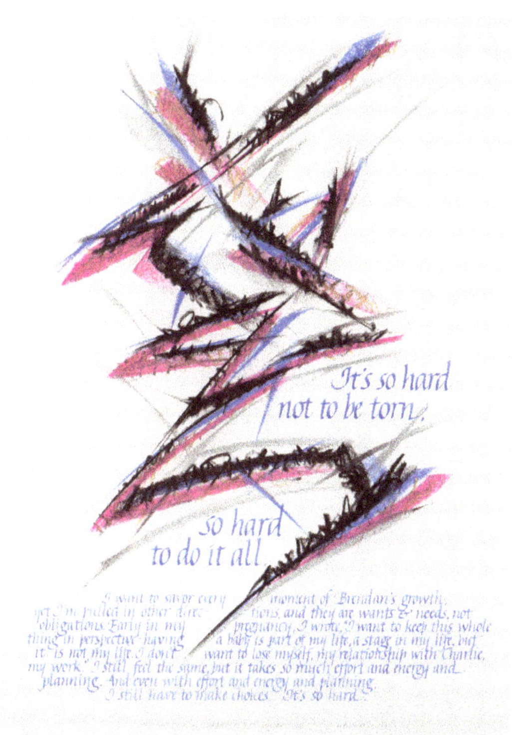
It's so hard
not to be torn,
so hard
to do it all.

I want to savor every moment of Brendan's growth, yet I'm pulled in other directions, and they are wants & needs, not obligations. Early in my pregnancy, I wrote, "I want to keep this whole thing in perspective, having a baby is part of my life, a stage in my life, but it is not my life. I don't want to lose myself, my relationship with Charlie, my work." I still feel the same, but it takes so much effort and energy and planning. And even with effort and energy and planning, I still have to make choices. It's so hard.

In 1986, I exhibited *Childbirth Journey* at the Newburyport Art Association in my new hometown of Newburyport, Massachusetts. After the exhibition, I questioned whether the wall was the right place for the work in the long term. Even though the pieces were powerful on the walls of the gallery, I didn't want to hang them in my home. They were too emotional to look at all the time. I felt they needed to be presented in a more intimate form, which led me to the handmade book.

My first stop on the way to making books was a portfolio of eight-and one-half-inch by eleven-inch offset prints. They combined charcoal drawings, calligraphy, and bits of photocopied natural objects such as milkweed in #3, "Core of Contentment" and asparagus in #4, "Unstoppable Life Force."

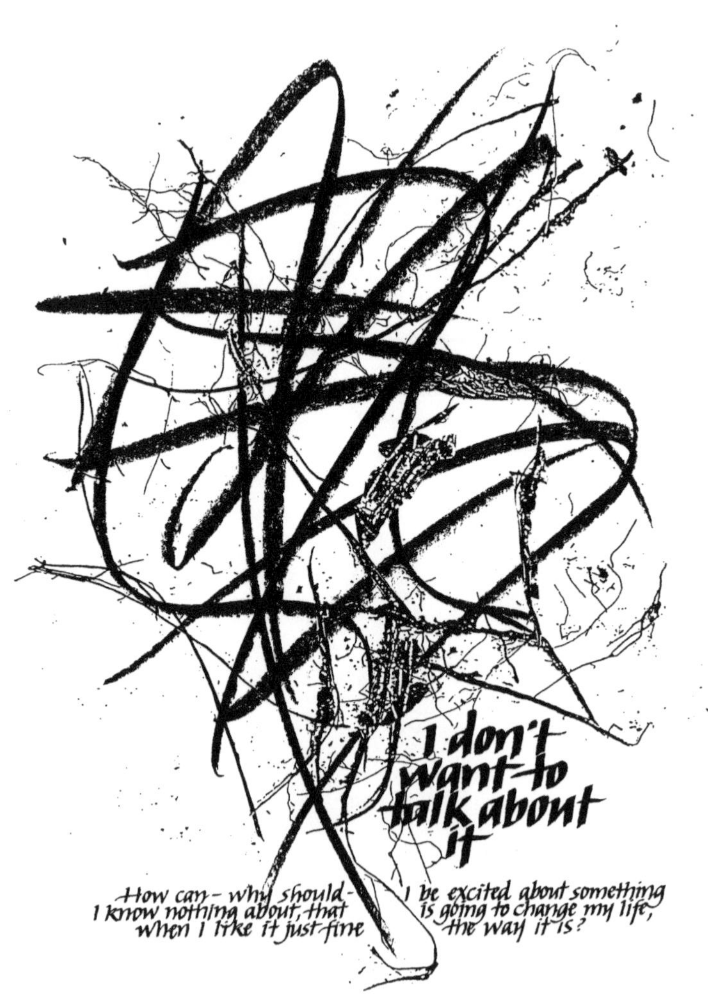

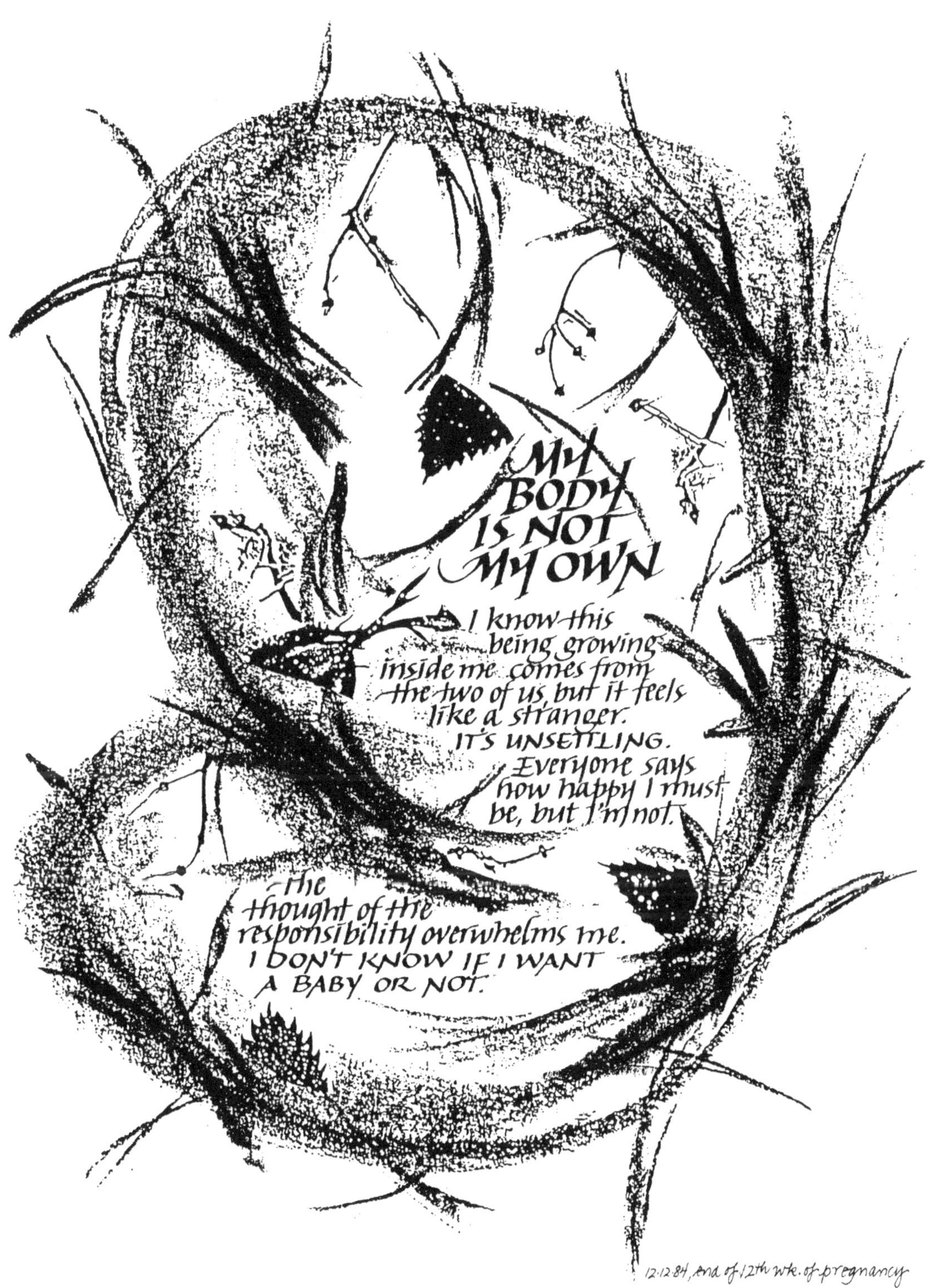
MY
BODY
IS NOT
MY OWN

I know this
being growing
inside me comes from
the two of us, but it feels
like a stranger.
IT'S UNSETTLING.
Everyone says
how happy I must
be, but I'm not.

The
thought of the
responsibility overwhelms me.
I DON'T KNOW IF I WANT
A BABY OR NOT.

12·12·84, end of 12th wk. of pregnancy

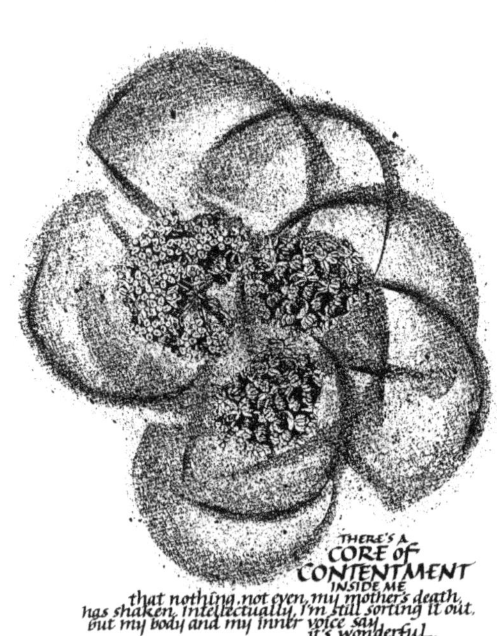

THERE'S A CORE OF CONTENTMENT INSIDE ME
that nothing, not even my mother's death, has shaken. Intellectually, I'm still sorting it out, but my body and my inner voice say it's wonderful.
3-5-85, 24th week of pregnancy

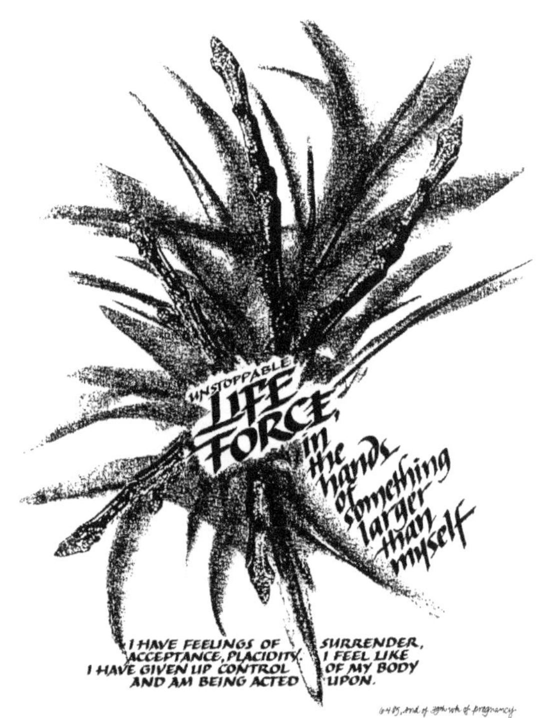

UNSTOPPABLE LIFE FORCE, in the hands of something larger than myself
I HAVE FEELINGS OF ACCEPTANCE, PLACIDITY. I HAVE GIVEN UP CONTROL AND AM BEING ACTED SURRENDER, I FEEL LIKE OF MY BODY UPON.
6-4-85, end of 39th wk of pregnancy

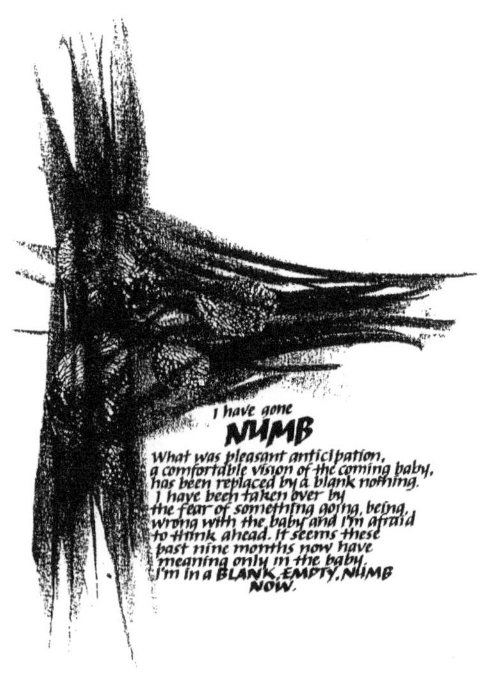

I have gone NUMB
What was pleasant anticipation, a comfortable vision of the coming baby, has been replaced by a blank nothing. I have been taken over by the fear of something going, being, wrong with the baby and I'm afraid to think ahead. It seems these past nine months now have meaning only in the baby. I'm in a BLANK, EMPTY, NUMB NOW.

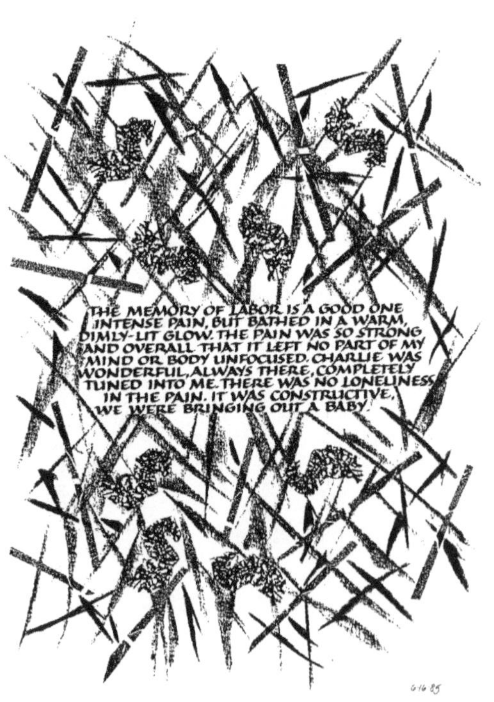

THE MEMORY OF LABOR IS A GOOD ONE INTENSE PAIN, BUT BATHED IN A WARM, DIMLY-LIT GLOW. THE PAIN WAS SO STRONG AND OVERALL THAT IT LEFT NO PART OF MY MIND OR BODY UNFOCUSED. CHARLIE WAS WONDERFUL, ALWAYS THERE, COMPLETELY TUNED INTO ME. THERE WAS NO LONELINESS IN THE PAIN. IT WAS CONSTRUCTIVE, WE WERE BRINGING OUT A BABY.
6-16-85

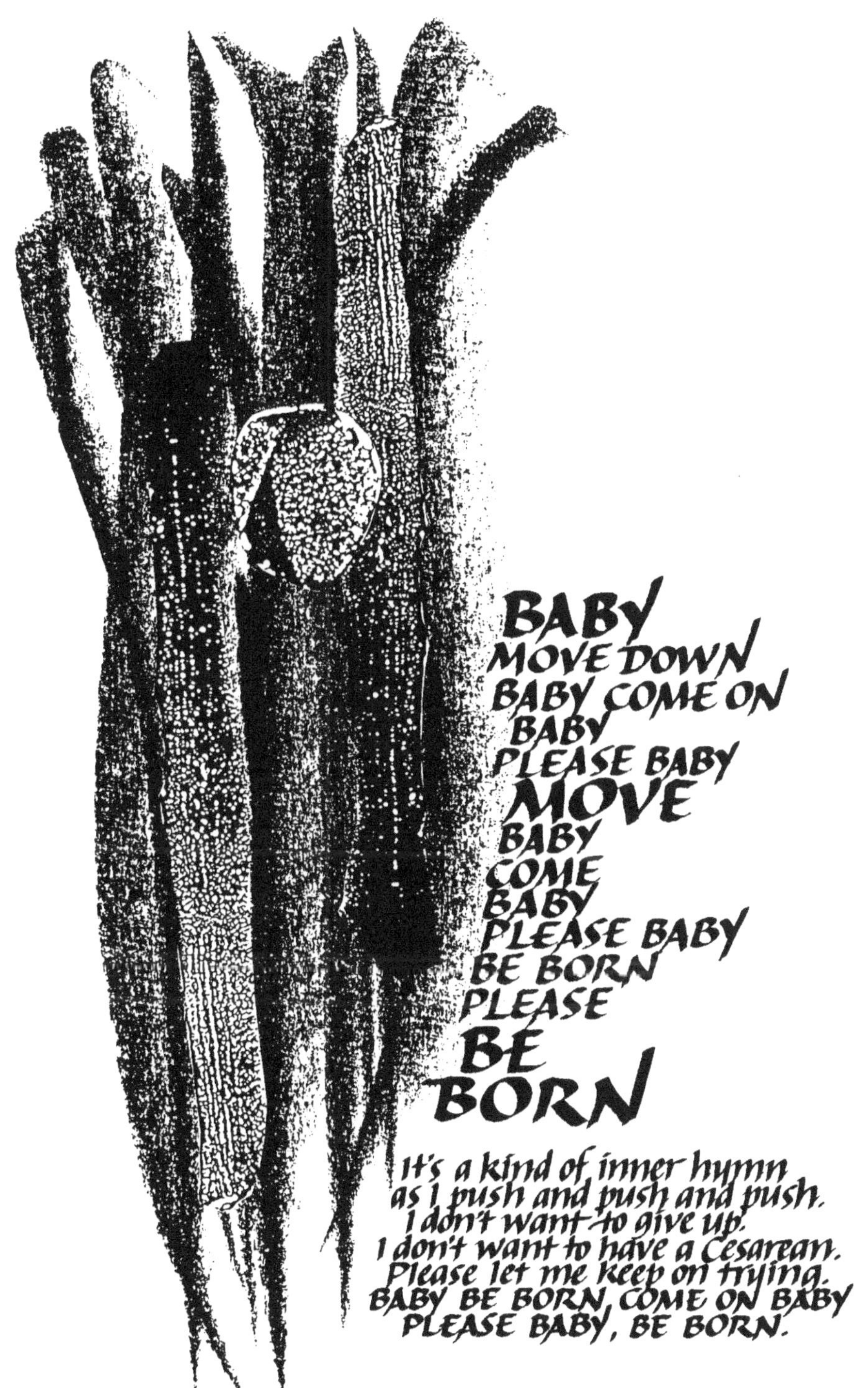
BABY
MOVE DOWN
BABY COME ON
BABY
PLEASE BABY
MOVE
BABY
COME
BABY
PLEASE BABY
BE BORN
PLEASE
BE
BORN

It's a kind of inner hymn
as I push and push and push.
I don't want to give up.
I don't want to have a Cesarean.
Please let me keep on trying.
BABY BE BORN, COME ON BABY
PLEASE BABY, BE BORN.

6·16·85, after 4 hours of pushing

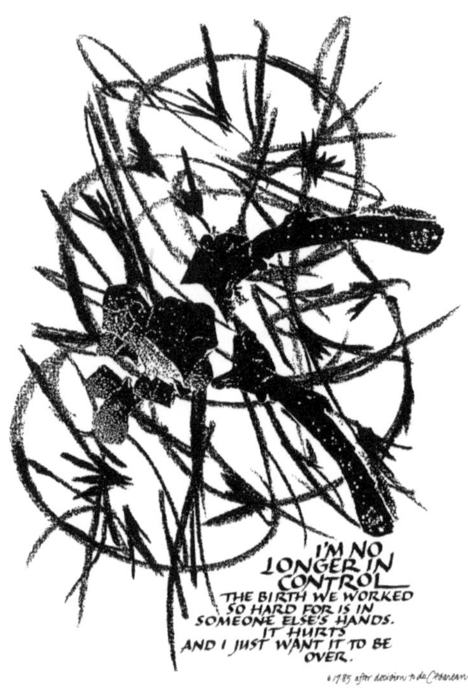
I'M NO
LONGER IN
CONTROL
THE BIRTH WE WORKED
SO HARD FOR IS IN
SOMEONE ELSE'S HANDS.
IT HURTS
AND I JUST WANT IT TO BE
OVER.
6/17/85 after decision to do Cesarean

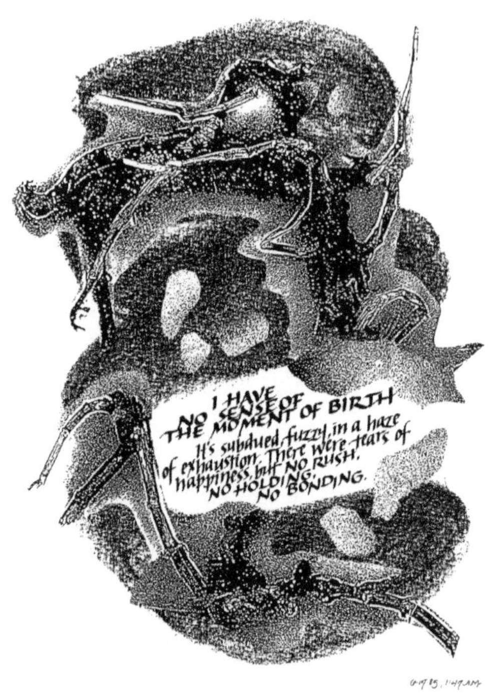
I HAVE
NO SENSE OF
THE MOMENT OF BIRTH
It's subdued, fuzzy, in a haze
of exhaustion. There were tears of
happiness, but NO RUSH,
NO HOLDING,
NO BONDING.

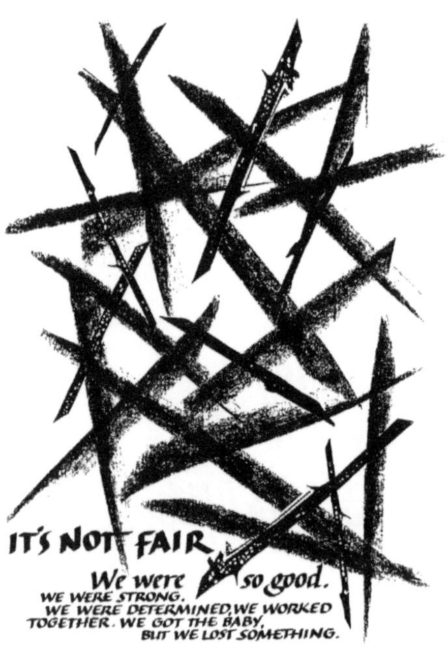
IT'S NOT FAIR.
We were   so good.
WE WERE STRONG.
WE WERE DETERMINED, WE WORKED
TOGETHER. WE GOT THE BABY,
BUT WE LOST SOMETHING.
6/17/85 in recovery after Cesarean

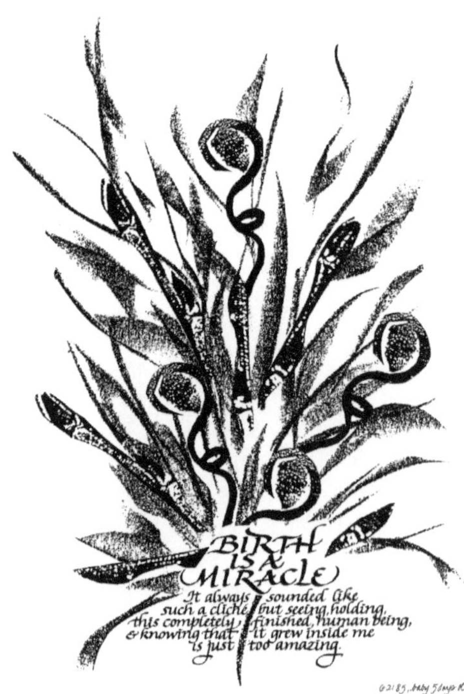
BIRTH
IS A
MIRACLE
It always sounded like
such a cliché, but seeing, holding,
this completely finished, human being,
& knowing that it grew inside me
is just too amazing.

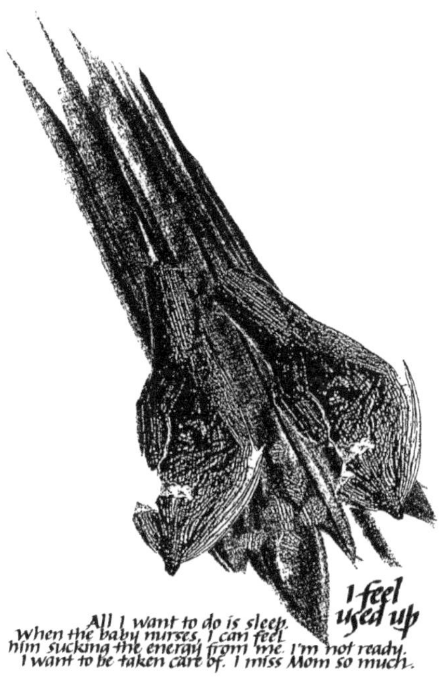

7.12.85, baby 4 weeks old

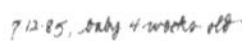

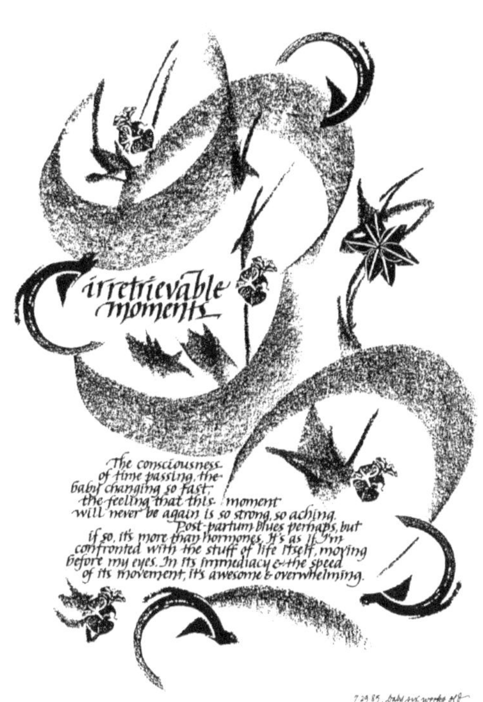

7.29.85, baby 6 weeks old

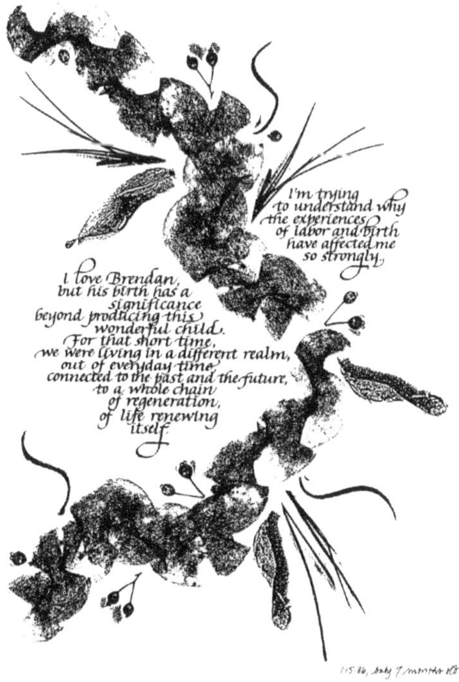

1.15.86, baby 7 months old

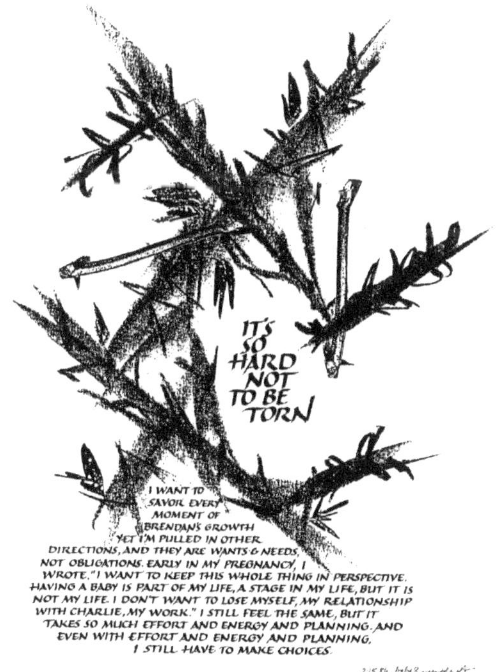

2.15.86, baby 8 months old

THE PHOTOCOPIER BITS IN THE BLACK-AND-WHITE version of *Childbirth Journey* were only part of my exploration of working with the photocopier. I loved the way the images broke down through repeated copying and brought unpredictable results. I used to show up at my local copy shop with a bag of miscellaneous materials and a sheet of acetate to protect the glass. I tried to be respectful and go during slow times. I then leased a photocopier which I purchased at the end of the rental term. I kept it until parts were no longer available. By then, I had a computer and a scanner. A lot of the photocopier work was inspired by being a new mother.

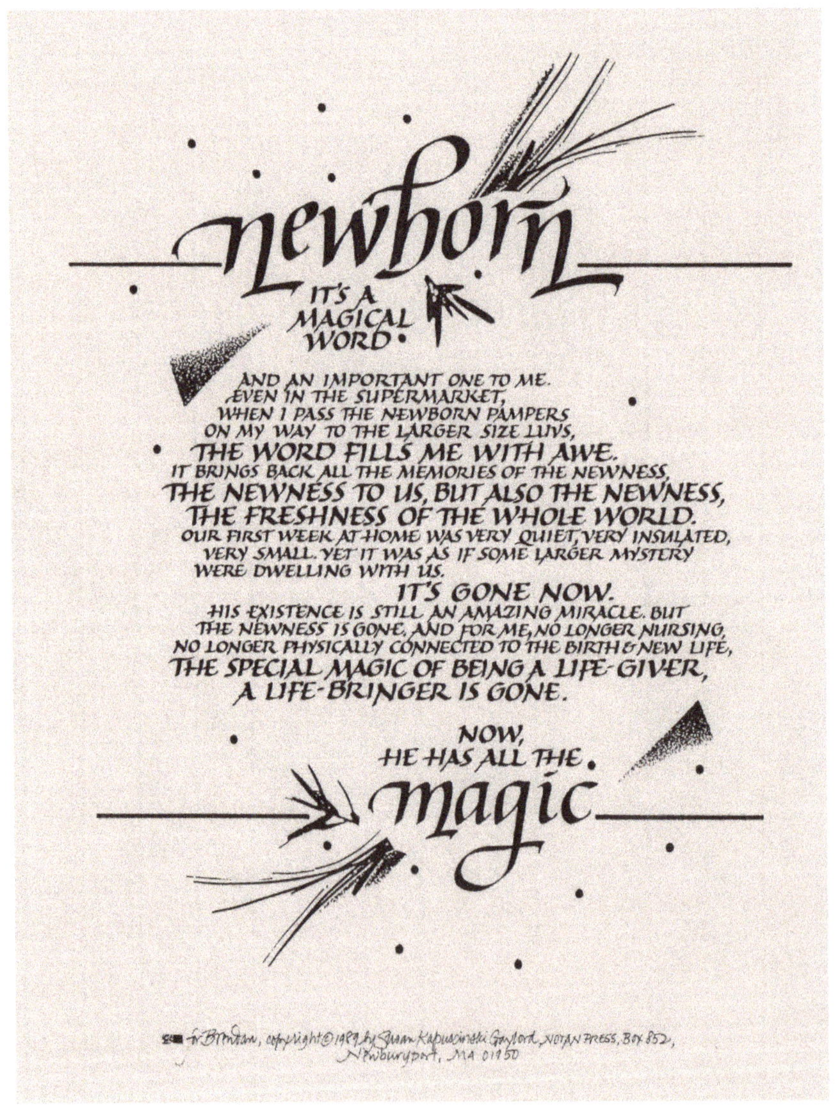

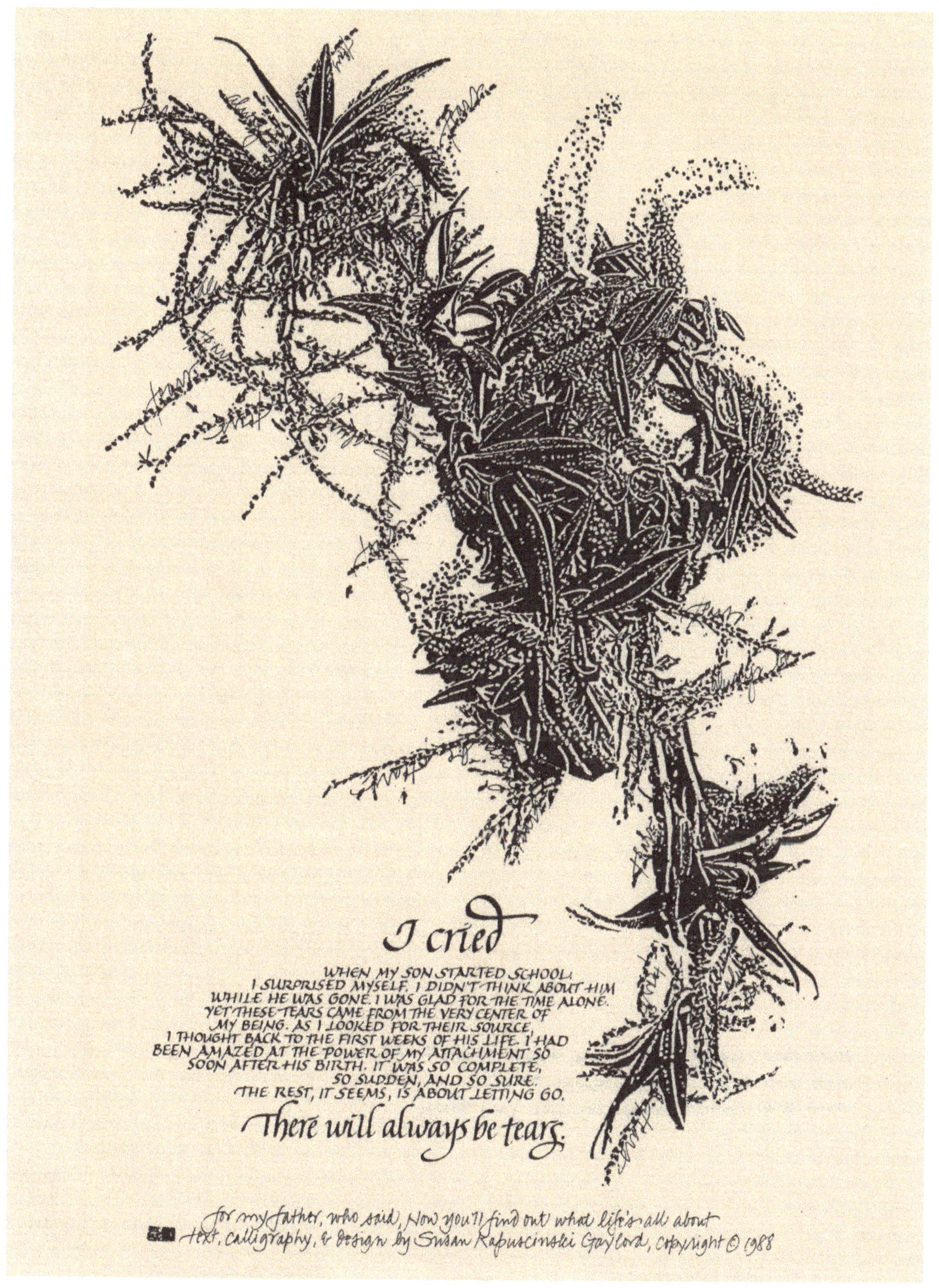
I cried
WHEN MY SON STARTED SCHOOL.
I SURPRISED MYSELF. I DIDN'T THINK ABOUT HIM
WHILE HE WAS GONE. I WAS GLAD FOR THE TIME ALONE.
YET THESE TEARS CAME FROM THE VERY CENTER OF
MY BEING. AS I LOOKED FOR THEIR SOURCE,
I THOUGHT BACK TO THE FIRST WEEKS OF HIS LIFE. I HAD
BEEN AMAZED AT THE POWER OF MY ATTACHMENT SO
SOON AFTER HIS BIRTH. IT WAS SO COMPLETE,
SO SUDDEN, AND SO SURE.
THE REST, IT SEEMS, IS ABOUT LETTING GO.
There will always be tears.
for my father, who said, Now you'll find out what life's all about
text, calligraphy, & design by Susan Kapuscinski Gaylord, copyright © 1988

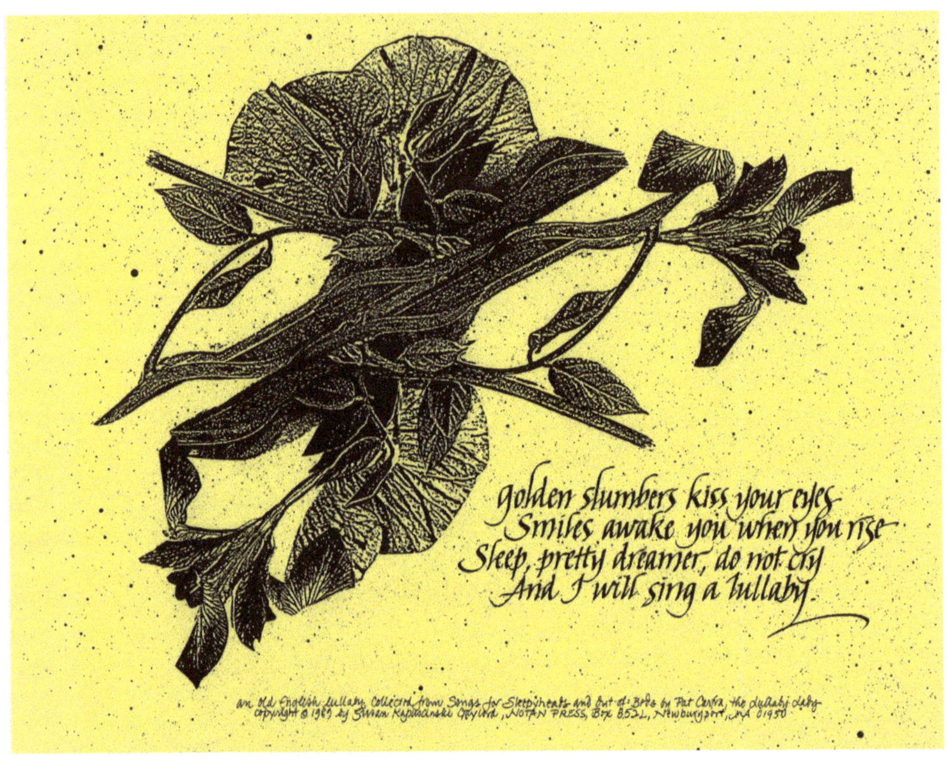
golden slumbers kiss your eyes
Smiles awake you when you rise
Sleep, pretty dreamer, do not cry
And I will sing a lullaby

an old English lullaby, collected from Songs for Sleepyheads and Out-of-Beds by Pat Carfra, the lullaby lady
copyright © 1989 by Susan Kapuscinski Gaylord, NOTAN PRESS, Box 852L, Newburyport, MA 01950

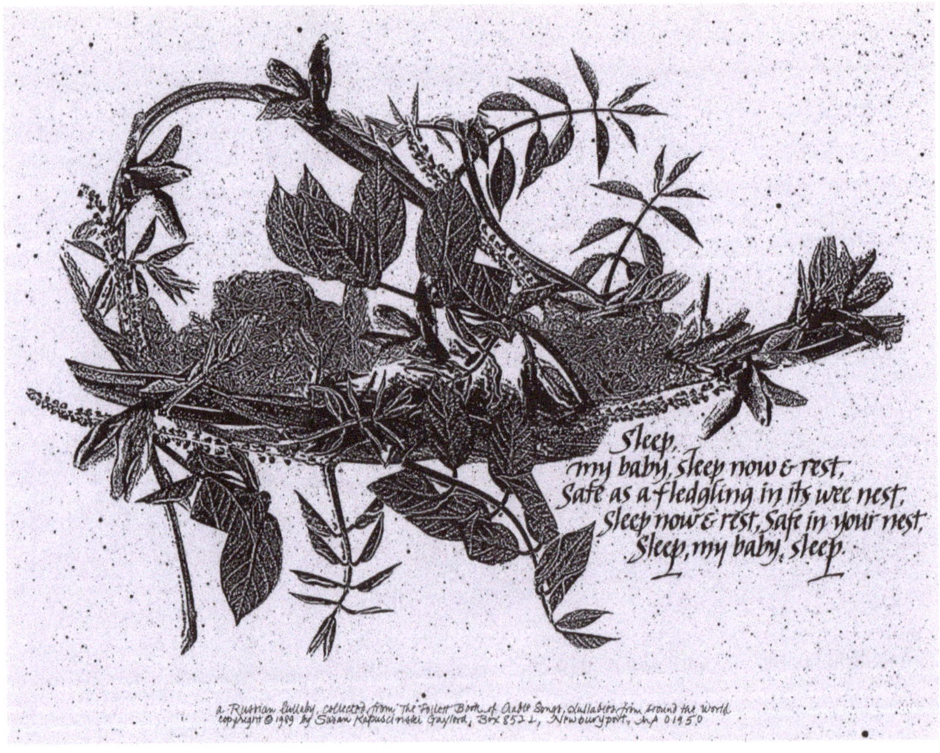
Sleep,
my baby, sleep now & rest,
Safe as a fledgling in its wee nest,
Sleep now & rest, Safe in your nest,
Sleep, my baby, sleep.

a Russian lullaby, collected from The Follett Book of Cradle Songs, Lullabies from around the World
copyright © 1989 by Susan Kapuscinski Gaylord, Box 852L, Newburyport, MA 01950

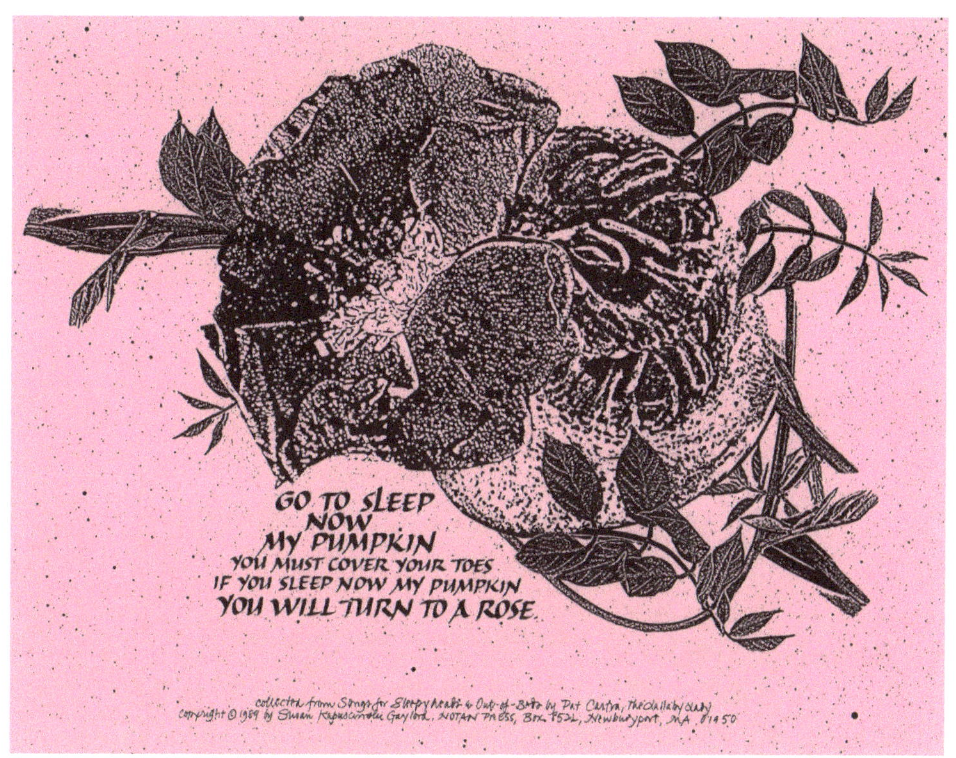
GO TO SLEEP
NOW
MY PUMPKIN
YOU MUST COVER YOUR TOES
IF YOU SLEEP NOW MY PUMPKIN
YOU WILL TURN TO A ROSE

collected from Songs for Sleepy heads & Out-of-Bats by Pat Castra, The Lullaby Club.
copyright © 1989 by Susan Kapuscinski Gaylord, NOTAN PRESS, Box 1522, Newburyport, MA 01950

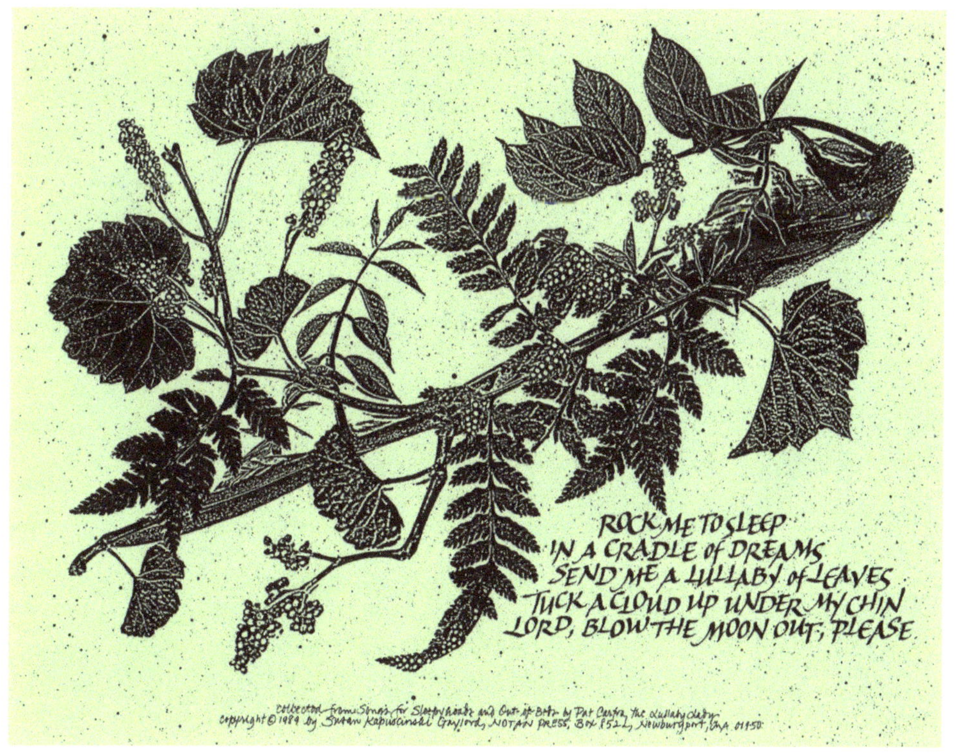
ROCK ME TO SLEEP
IN A CRADLE OF DREAMS
SEND ME A LULLABY OF LEAVES
TUCK A CLOUD UP UNDER MY CHIN
LORD, BLOW THE MOON OUT, PLEASE

collected from Songs for Sleepy heads and Out-of-Bats by Pat Castra, The Lullaby Club.
copyright © 1989 by Susan Kapuscinski Gaylord, NOTAN PRESS, Box 1522, Newburyport, MA 01950

I also did work to celebrate the seasons with the photocopier. The quote below from Henry Glassie's book *All Silver and No Brass: An Irish Christmas Mumming* was published in the *1991 Calligrapher's Engagement Calendar*. I did a series on the Cross Quarter Days of the Celtic calendar, the midpoints between the solstices and equinoxes that mark the beginnings of the seasons. The one on the opposite page is for Samhain, the first day of Celtic winter and the new year.

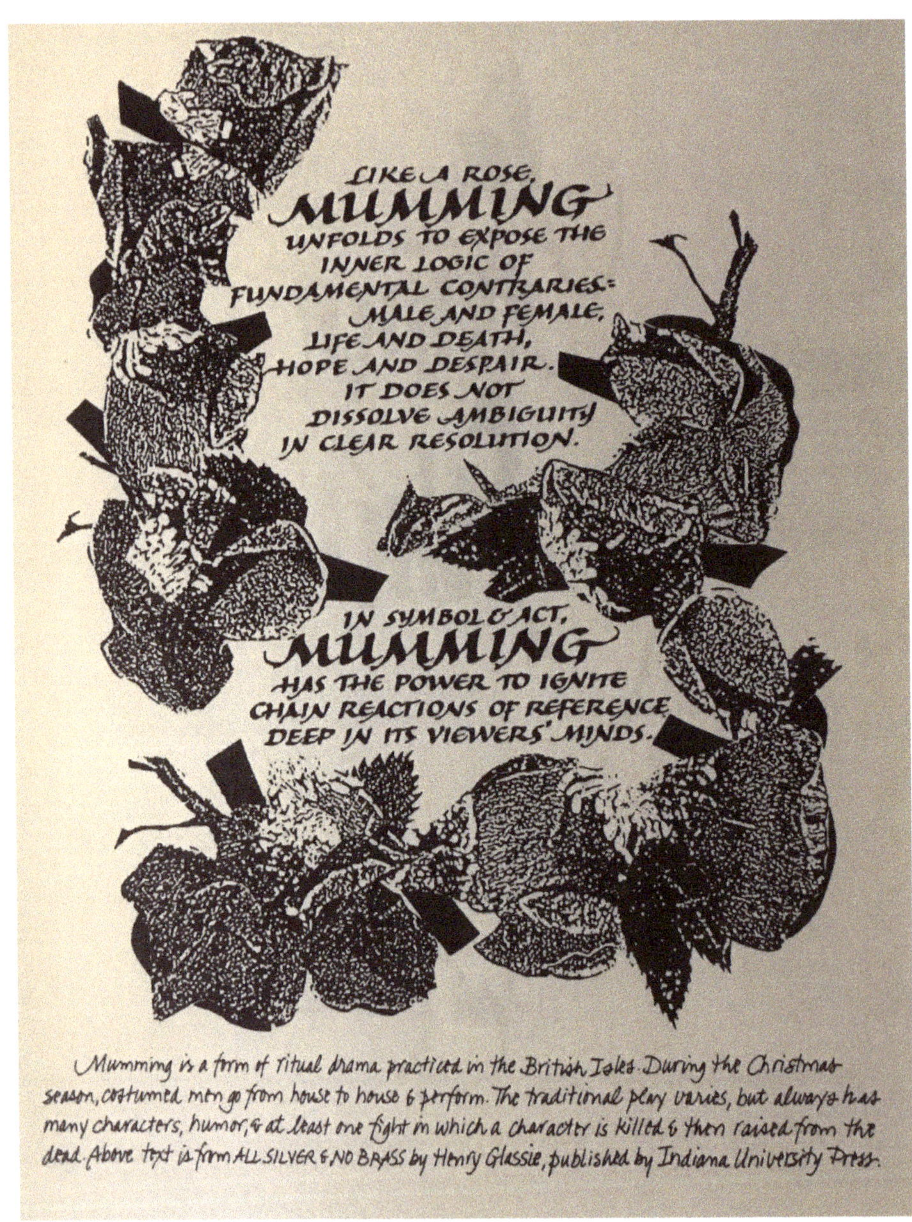

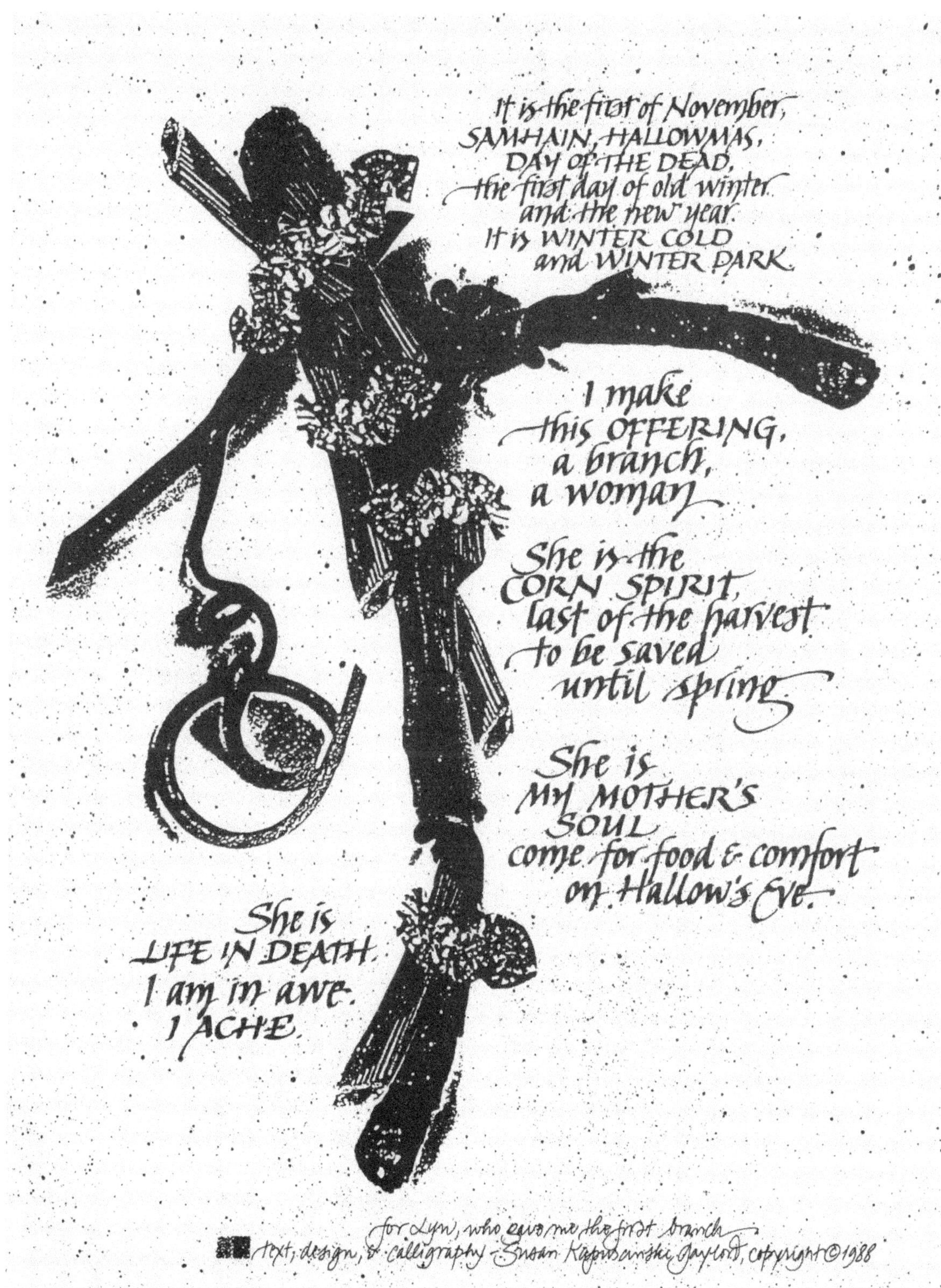
It is the first of November,
SAMHAIN, HALLOWMAS,
DAY OF THE DEAD,
the first day of old winter
and the new year.
It is WINTER COLD
and WINTER DARK.

I make
this OFFERING,
a branch,
a woman.

She is the
CORN SPIRIT,
last of the harvest
to be saved
until spring.

She is
MY MOTHER'S
SOUL
come for food & comfort
on Hallow's Eve.

She is
LIFE IN DEATH.
I am in awe.
I ACHE.

for Lyn, who gave me the first branch
text, design, & calligraphy ~ Susan Kaprubinski Gaylord, copyright © 1988

I gave some talks on the Photocopier and Art. Below is a flyer advertising the talk. On the following page is an illustration of how the image breaks down with repeated copying.

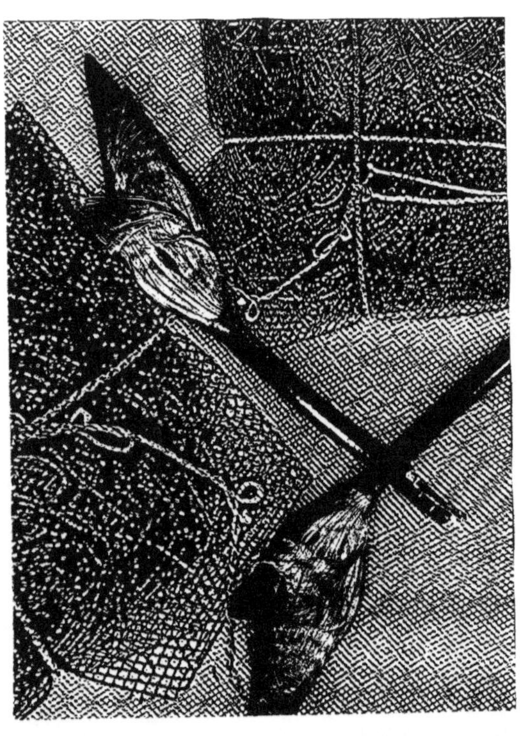

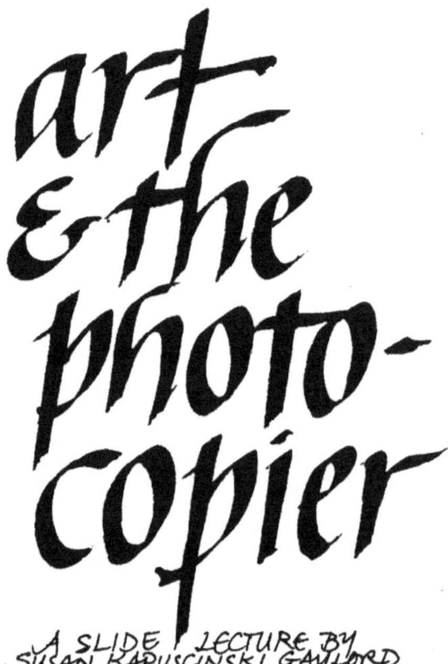

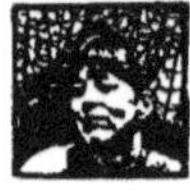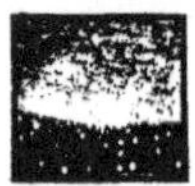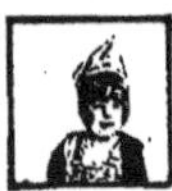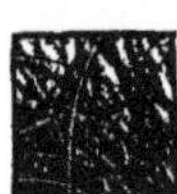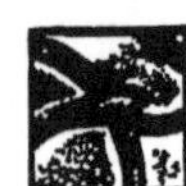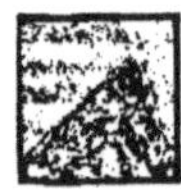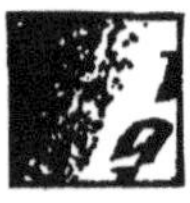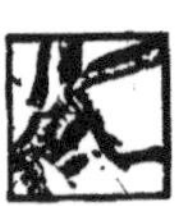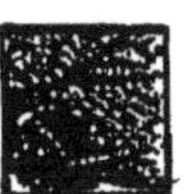

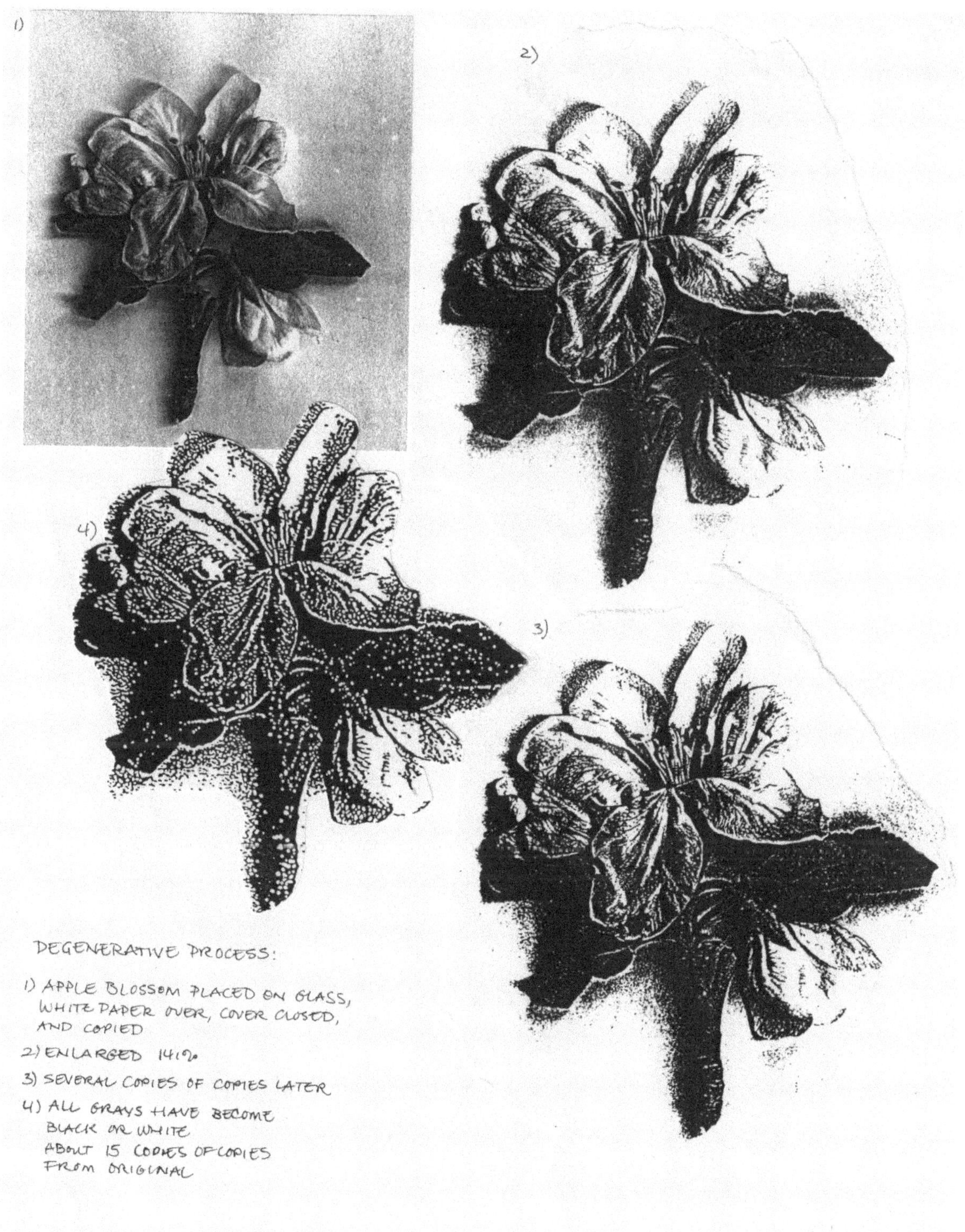
1)
2)
4)
3)
DEGENERATIVE PROCESS:
1) APPLE BLOSSOM PLACED ON GLASS,
WHITE PAPER OVER, COVER CLOSED,
AND COPIED
2) ENLARGED 141%
3) SEVERAL COPIES OF COPIES LATER
4) ALL GRAYS HAVE BECOME
BLACK OR WHITE
ABOUT 15 COPIES OF COPIES
FROM ORIGINAL

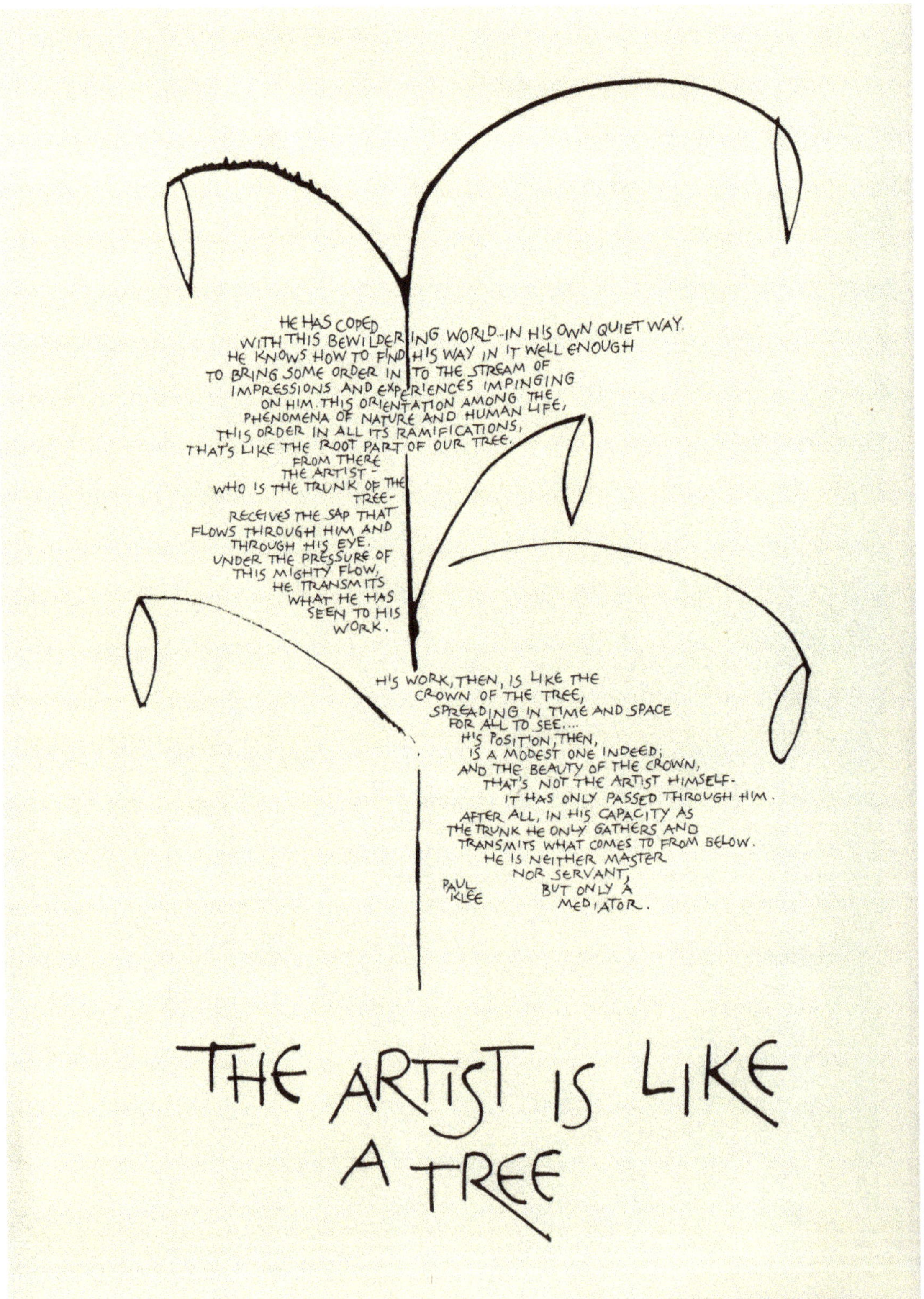

HE HAS COPED
WITH THIS BEWILDERING WORLD. IN HIS OWN QUIET WAY.
HE KNOWS HOW TO FIND HIS WAY IN IT WELL ENOUGH
TO BRING SOME ORDER IN TO THE STREAM OF
IMPRESSIONS AND EXPERIENCES IMPINGING
ON HIM. THIS ORIENTATION AMONG THE
PHENOMENA OF NATURE AND HUMAN LIFE,
THIS ORDER IN ALL ITS RAMIFICATIONS,
THAT'S LIKE THE ROOT PART OF OUR TREE.
FROM THERE
THE ARTIST -
WHO IS THE TRUNK OF THE
TREE -
RECEIVES THE SAP THAT
FLOWS THROUGH HIM AND
THROUGH HIS EYE.
UNDER THE PRESSURE OF
THIS MIGHTY FLOW,
HE TRANSMITS
WHAT HE HAS
SEEN TO HIS
WORK.

HIS WORK, THEN, IS LIKE THE
CROWN OF THE TREE,
SPREADING IN TIME AND SPACE
FOR ALL TO SEE.....
HIS POSITION, THEN,
IS A MODEST ONE INDEED;
AND THE BEAUTY OF THE CROWN,
THAT'S NOT THE ARTIST HIMSELF.
IT HAS ONLY PASSED THROUGH HIM.
AFTER ALL, IN HIS CAPACITY AS
THE TRUNK HE ONLY GATHERS AND
TRANSMITS WHAT COMES TO FROM BELOW.
HE IS NEITHER MASTER
NOR SERVANT,
PAUL
KLEE   BUT ONLY A
MEDIATOR.

THE ARTIST IS LIKE
A TREE

Starting around 1982, I began to look at more art and read more art books. I was particularly interested in Kandinsky and Klee and the abstract expressionists. My attraction to Kandinsky and Klee came from looking at letters as abstract symbols as I studied their negative and positive spaces. The strong black-and-white paintings of the Abstract Expressionist Franz Kline inspired me with their energy. I tried to bring that boldness into my calligraphy and then tried to reach beyond calligraphy to purely abstract work.

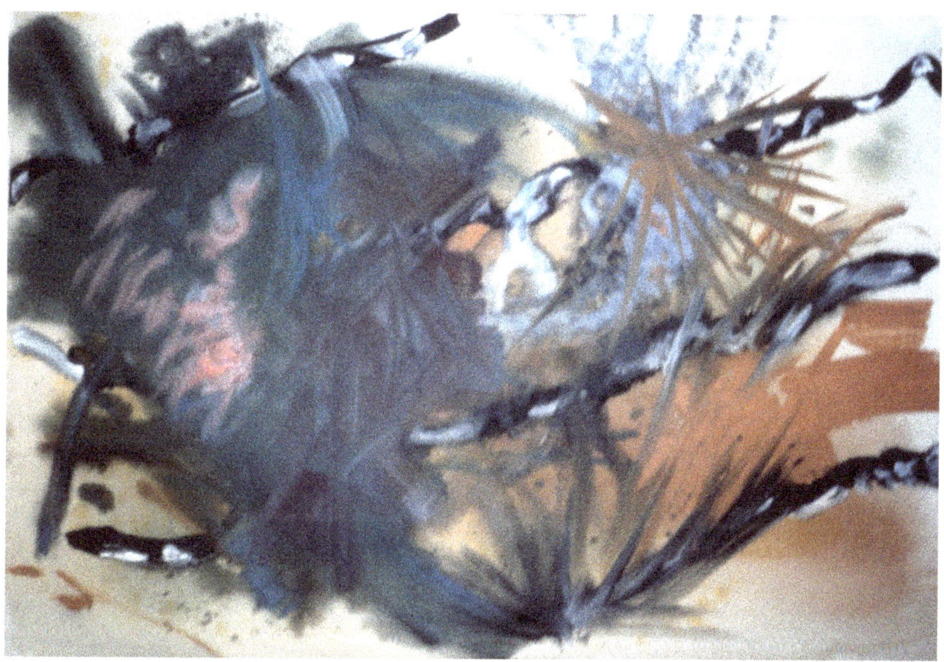

I took a painting class at Cambridge Center for Adult Education (above image) and one in surface design on fabric at the DeCordova Museum School in Lincoln, Massachusetts. At the Innovations '86 Calligraphy Conference in Hoboken, New Jersey, I took a workshop on abstract expressionism and calligraphy with Thomas Ingmire. We moved from working expressively with words to pure mark-making. By the end of the week, I found myself missing words and started putting them back into my work. I didn't know why, but I knew I needed to.

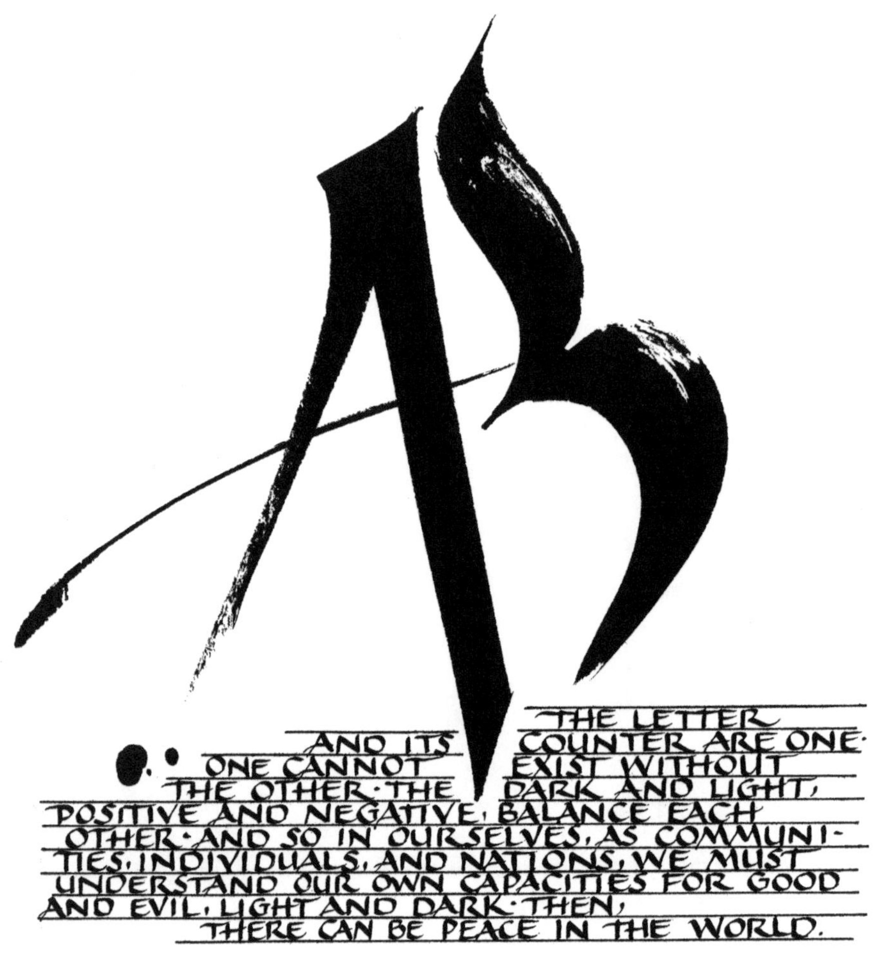

In the fall of 1985, I took a weekend workshop in Boston with Jenny Hunter Groat on Notan, the Japanese design principle based on the interaction of dark (no) and light (tan). I had first encountered the concept in a design class with Brenda Lowen-Siegel at the DeCordova Museum School. I loved Jenny's workshop and I loved Jenny, especially the philosophical depth she brought to the study of calligraphy and design. From her experiences with Zen Buddhism and Jungian analysis, she saw Notan as more than a design principle. It spoke to her of the importance of acknowledging and balancing light and dark, positive and negative, in all aspects of life.

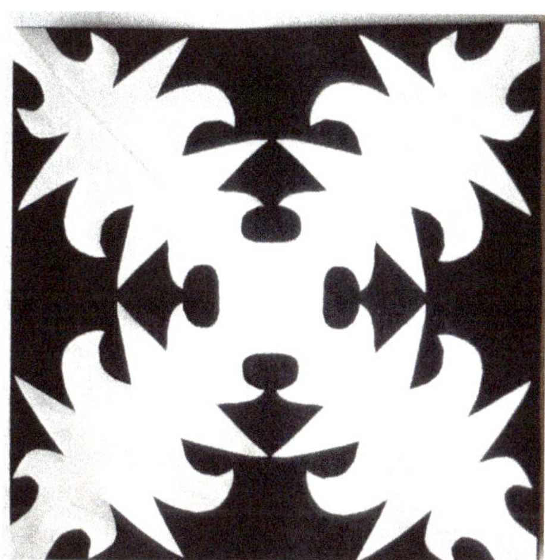 

We did a series of exercises. The goal was to create designs that had an equal balance of light and dark. They trained our eyes to focus on the negative space. I spent many hours after Jenny's workshop playing with pattern design and calligraphy. If you are interested in exploring this Japanese design principle, I recommend *Notan* by Dorr Bothwell, published by Dover Art Instruction.

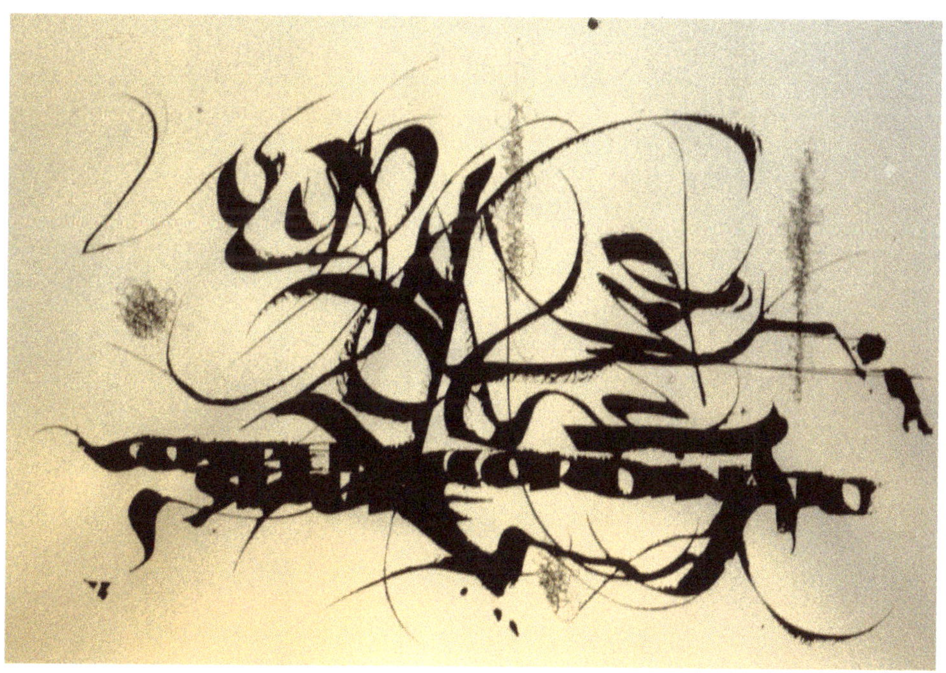

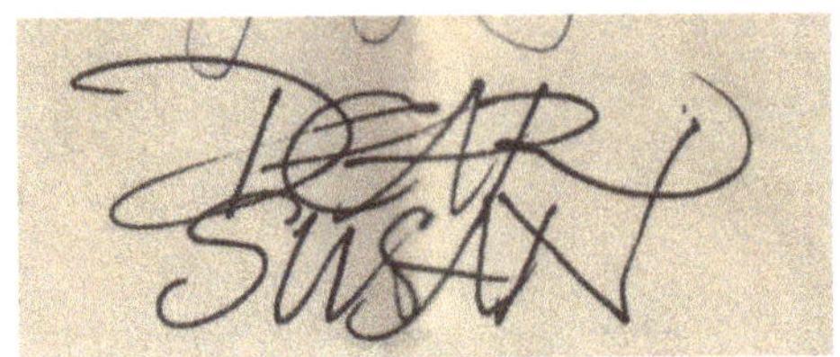

Some time after I took Jenny's Notan workshop, I wrote her a letter. I had never done anything like that before. I described my conflicted feelings about calligraphy, my desire to expand beyond it but not knowing where to go. I'm not sure I ever felt like I truly belonged to whatever I thought the calligraphy community was. As I started to question and try to stretch myself, I didn't feel those efforts were appreciated. I see now that there was a lot I got wrong over the years due to my oversensitivity and insecurity, however, I think there was some truth in my feelings.

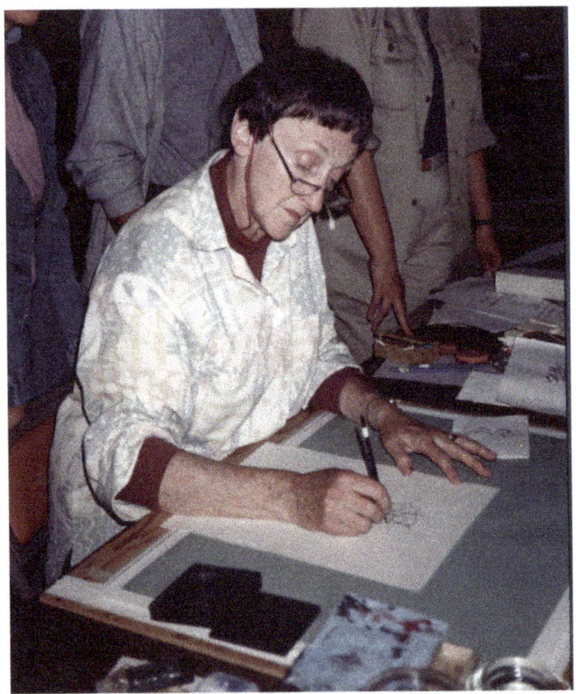

My letter touched a chord in Jenny. She wrote me back a long letter of encouragement, the first of the many times she shared her profound belief: "Follow your heart. Let it and your work lead you."

Jenny's response was the beginning of a correspondence that helped me find my voice and led me to her week-long "Knowing/Not Knowing Retreat/Workshop" at Green Gulch Farm Zen Center north of San Francisco in 1988. During her first evening talk there, she gave me words for my dilemma. She said that there are two kinds of artists—interpretive and originating. Her examples were the ballerina Margot Fonteyn as interpretive and the modern dancer/choreographer Martha Graham as originating. It became clear. I wanted to be an originating artist.

Green Gulch also planted the seeds for my later exploration of nature through gathered objects. After two days of calligraphy in the studio, I went outside and spent the rest of the week creating little environments. I collected things—pine cones, plums, sticks, leaves, owl dung, stones, and grasses. Some I wrapped with paper or wire; most I used as I found them. I would choose a spot on the side of a path and place each object carefully. I would compose, step back, and compose again. They were offerings, devotions, prayers.

Jenny's role in this whole process was magical. First of all, I knew she would understand, even though I wasn't sure I did. She created an atmosphere in which I felt free to follow my inner voice into uncharted territory. She watched me thrill to the new discoveries and struggle to understand their meaning. I silently hungered for her to give me direction, to tell me what it all meant and where I should go from there. I was afraid to ask, and she was too wise to tell. In Jenny's own work, there is depth and power, with an exquisite lightness of touch. In her teaching, it is the same. After the workshop, she wrote to me, "It will ripen and ripen much yet."

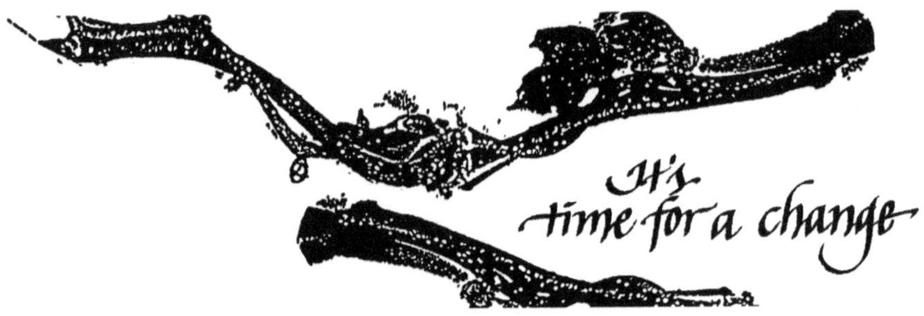

I stopped doing commissioned and commercial calligraphy in 1988. While I made the choice for creative reasons, the business side of things had dwindled after our move to the coastal city of Newburyport despite a lot of effort on my part. Part of the reason may have been that desktop publishing was taking off and people were using their personal computers to create certificates and invitations. I wrote and shared this:

I have begun to do work that pleases me. For the first time, it is truly mine (text, calligraphy, & design). It is very personal, but also seems to speak to and for a lot of people. I feel strongly that I have something to offer & want to use all my time and energy to create & promote my own work. To that end, I am no longer doing any commissioned work.

At this point, my creative work still had calligraphy as its base. Over the next few years, I entered the world of handmade books and taught bookmaking, first to adults in workshops called "Artmaking for Everyone: Simple Handmade Books" and then to children in schools. At first look back, it seems I was particularly harsh in my separation. I began to call myself a book artist and didn't mention the word calligraphy at all. Remembering more deeply, I think I needed to. People would introduce me as a calligrapher. People would talk wistfully about the work I used to do. I had to suppress my natural desire to please. It took a lot of energy not to make exceptions and stick to my plan. In my "Artmaking for Everyone" classes, students would lament that their books didn't look as nice as mine because they couldn't do calligraphy so I stopped using it. The slow drift became decisive. I was on my way to becoming the "originating artist" Jenny had described.

Handmade books opened up a new world to me. I approached them very differently than I had calligraphy. With calligraphy, I was like a sponge. I wanted to learn everything I could. With books, I had a sense of what I wanted to say. Looking for a new vehicle for that content, I was much more selective. I wasn't interested in fine binding. I was drawn to non-Western bindings and simpler forms that allowed me to think about the content in a more three-dimensional way.

In 1987, I made my first artist's book, *Contradictions: Jack Kerouac, Lowell, the River,* using a side-stitched stab binding. After reading about the controversy within Lowell over a proposed monument to its native son, I felt that both the city and the writer contained many contradictions. I made connections between his writing and the city through the image of the Merrimack River. All-hand-lettered, it contained my commentary, quotes from Kerouac, and photocopier manipulations of a photograph of Pawtucket Falls by Betsey Bolton. Three years later, I produced a limited edition version on the photocopier.

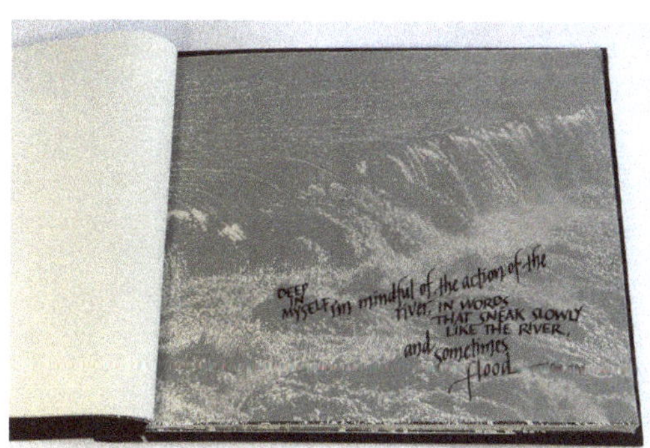
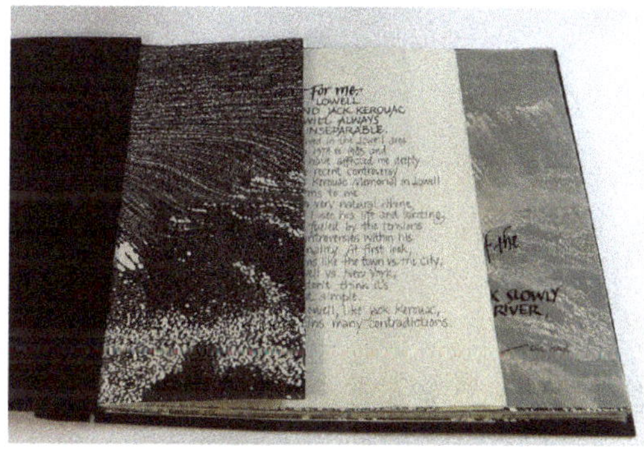
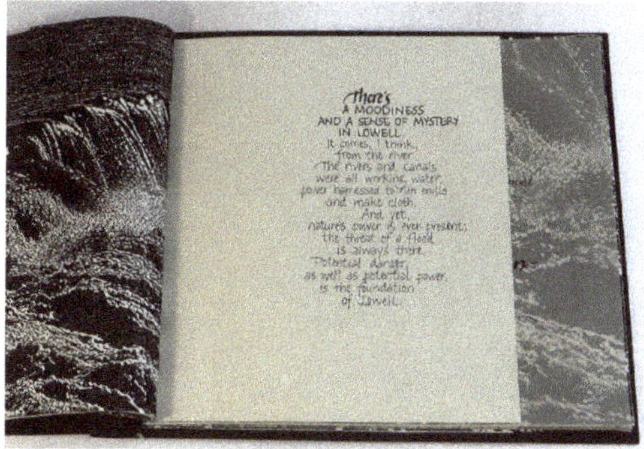
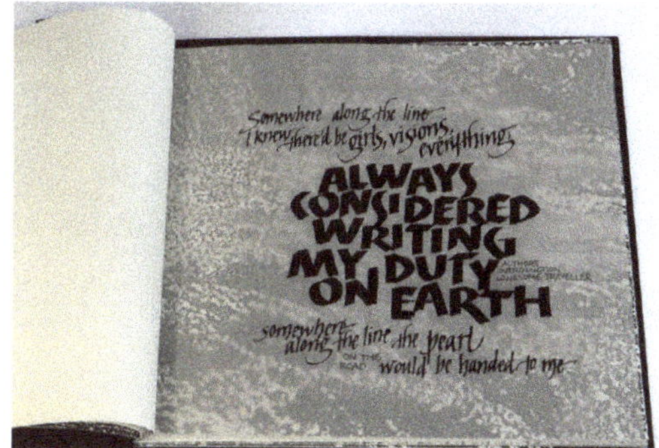

In 1992, I made another limited-edition book, *Lessons from Green Gulch*, about Jenny's workshop. The accordion book has a wrap-around cover and stick closure. Sewn into the accordion are four sections with photocopier imagery created from photographs of Green Gulch, Zen koan and words of wisdom from Jenny in calligraphy, and my text about the experience in type.

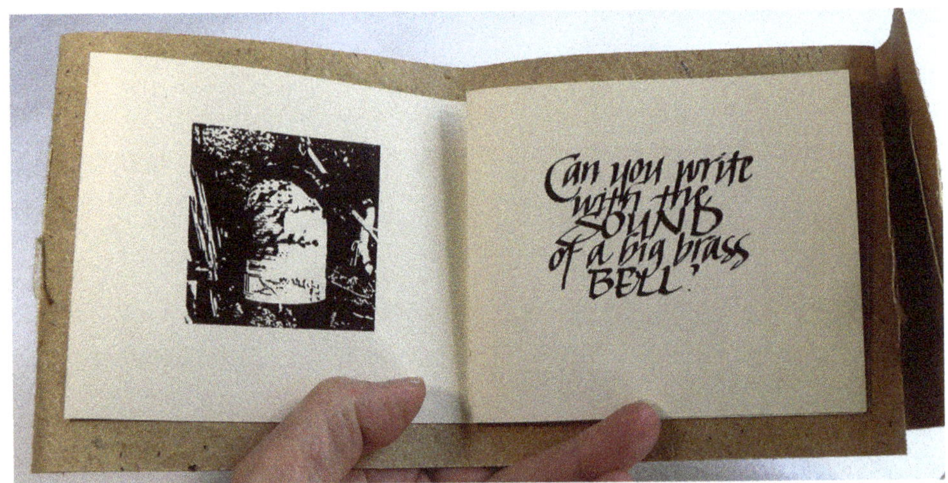

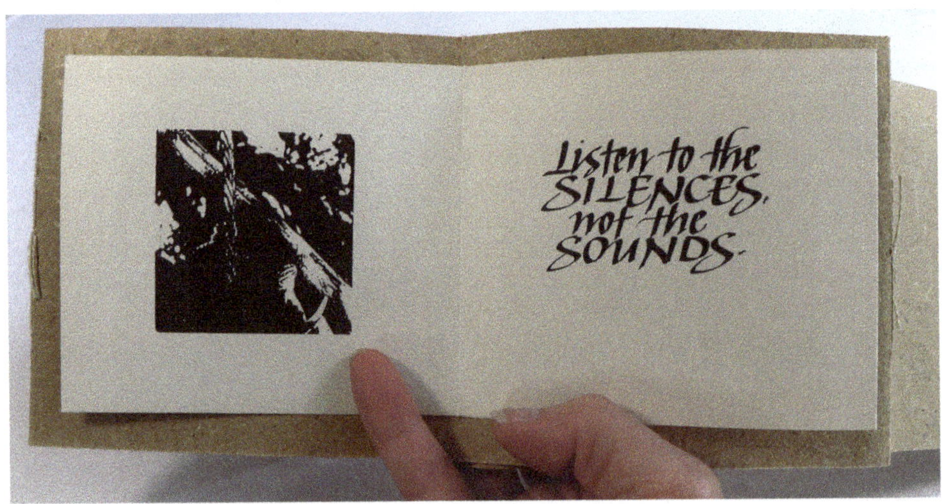

I made the first in a small series of accordion books with pages of covered binder's board in 1990. Up until that point, all my books had soft covers. I thought I needed to try hard covers if I was to be a proper bookmaker. When I covered a piece of binder's board with paper, I loved the way it looked and felt. I didn't want to use it for a cover; I wanted to use it for a page.

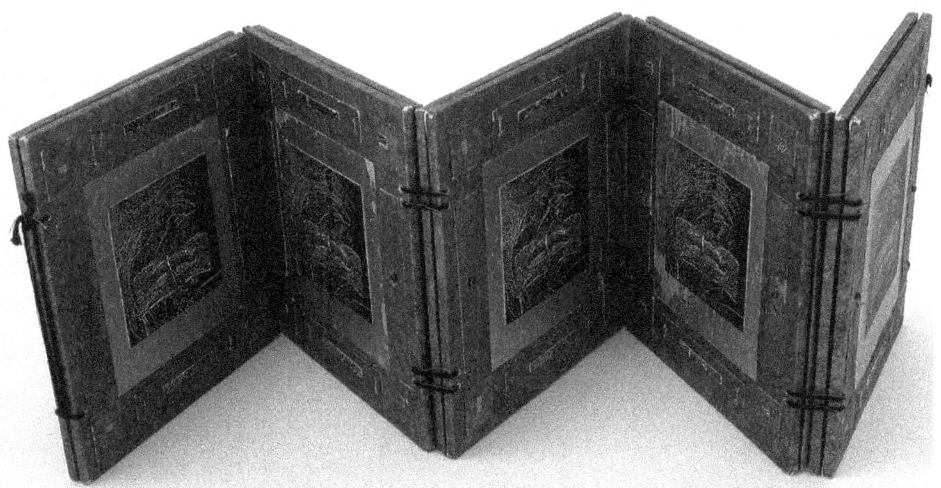

When I made the above book with the not very original title of *Hair and Lips, Aging and Eternal,* I was still holding onto words. The imagery was created from the lips of a photo of a Buddha from Angkor Wat and gray hairs I discovered when I photocopied my ear for an alphabet book I made with my son. I had been reflecting a lot about death after my mother's passing. I felt that the lips represented the eternal and the hair aging, but that each one contained signs of the other. I put images on the front of the pages and written text on the back. When a poet friend looked at the book, she said, "I can see so many things in it. I could look at it again and again." I thought, "Why am I telling her what to see? Why not let the images speak for themselves?" I pasted paper over the text and took my first step away from words.

The book work I am most know for is the Spirit Books, the name I have given to an ongoing series (100 as of this writing) of wordless volumes that rest on cradles of wood and vines. While the Spirit Books were influenced by my experience at Green Gulch, it was a massive pruning in our yard the previous spring that gave me the raw materials. We cut and we cut until our driveway contained a mountain of brush about ten feet high. As I spent days getting the branches into manageable sizes to take to the tree dump, I felt a strong affinity for many of the pieces I held in my hands. They spoke to me of some deeper life force and I brought many of them into my studio.

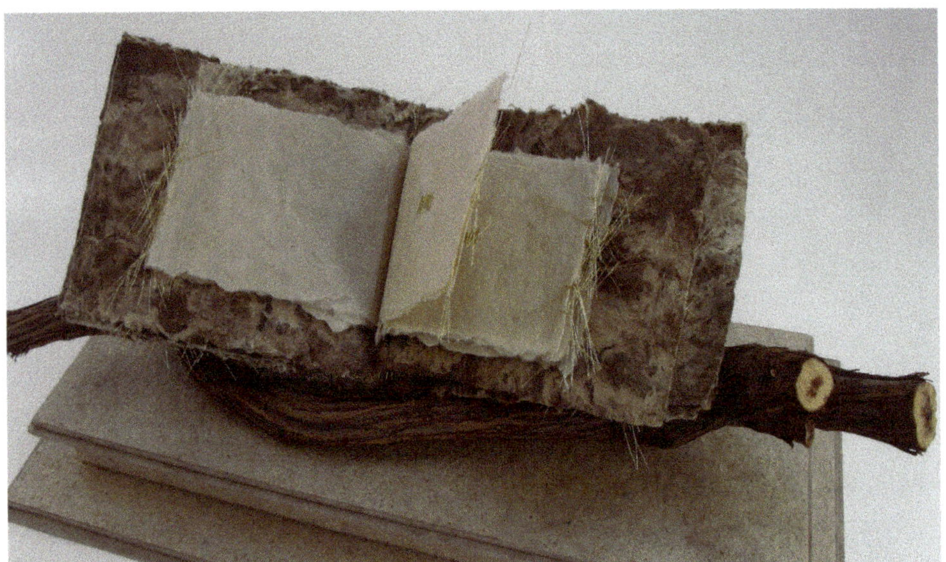

Spirit Book #1: Sewn Prayer

I experimented with the gatherings for several years with mixed results. And then, without any thought, on a fall day in 1992, I made the first Spirit Book in what I can only call an Aha! moment. I put two pieces of thick grape vines together and made a book to rest on top. I didn't have a plan but I knew I wanted the book to have a three-dimensional presence. The pages were made of handmade paper from Bhutan that I had bought during my Green Gulch trip and amate paper made from the inner bark of the fig tree in Mexico. I used round flat beads made from coconut shells, glass seed beads, and pieces of gold Chinese spirit paper which is burned as an offering to the dead.

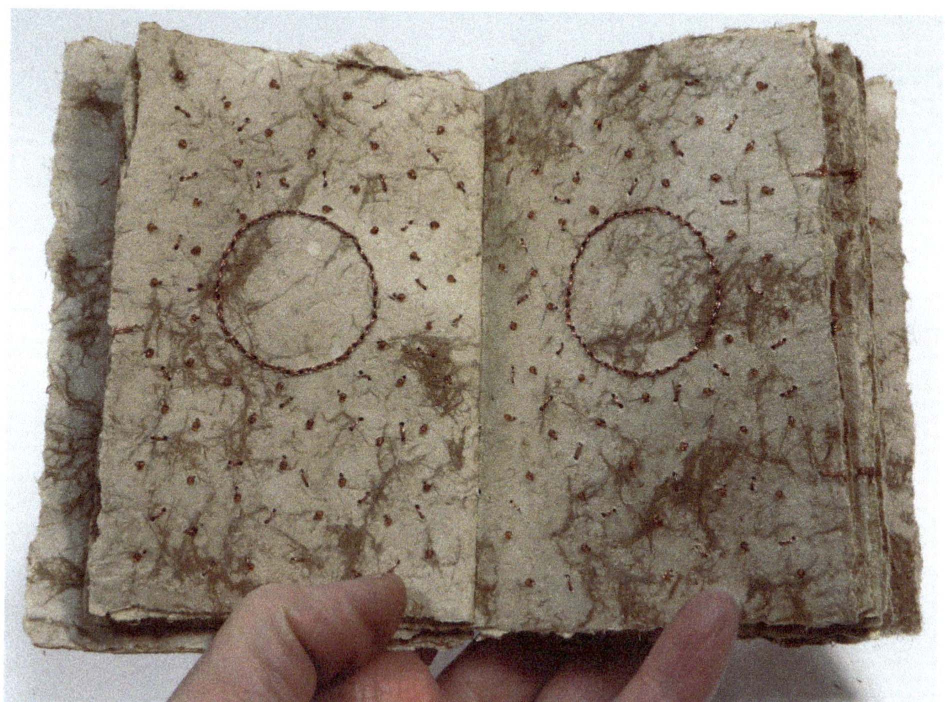

Spirit Book #98: Lunar Meditation

The Spirit Books never start with a sketch or plan. My goal is to make an object that would blend in so well you wouldn't notice it if you walked by it on the forest floor. The papers, all handmade by craftsmen from around the world, are in shades of brown and gray. I always tear them to give an organic look. The pages have pattern in the place of words and images, most often created with stitching and beads. The books rest on cradles which stand on bases of binder's board and paper.

When I start working with the gathered natural materials, I assign a number to the Spirit Book. When it is complete, I give it a name. I write down information about the pages—the kind of papers I used and where they are from, the shapes and patterns made by the stitching—and the cradle—where and when it was gathered, what it is made of. I look through the dictionary and books I have on the meanings of symbols for inspiration. I write down words and try combinations until I arrive at a title.

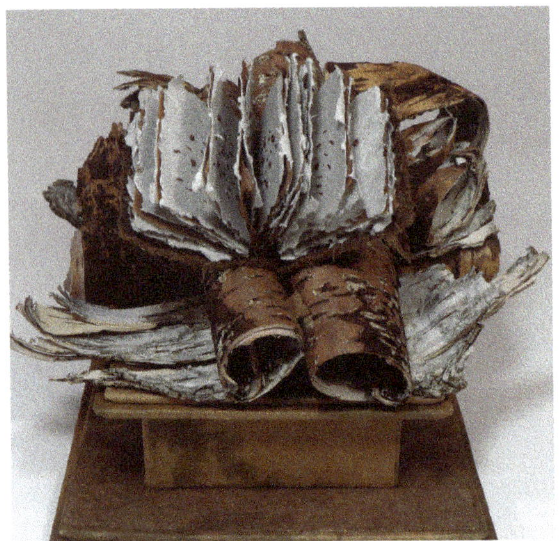

Spirit Book #91: Rising Certainty

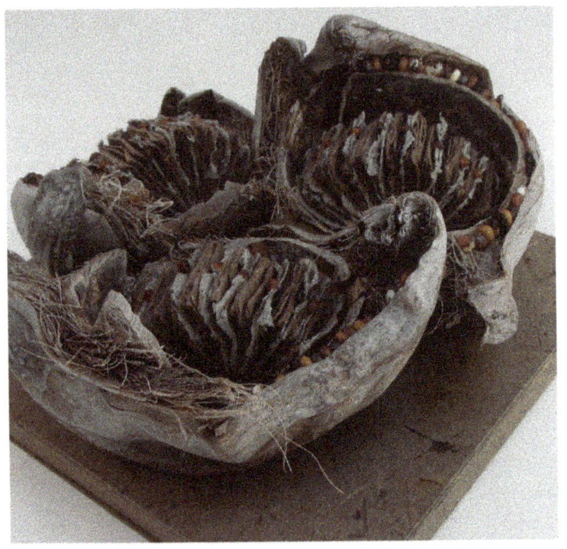

Spirit Book #30: Ixchel's Dream

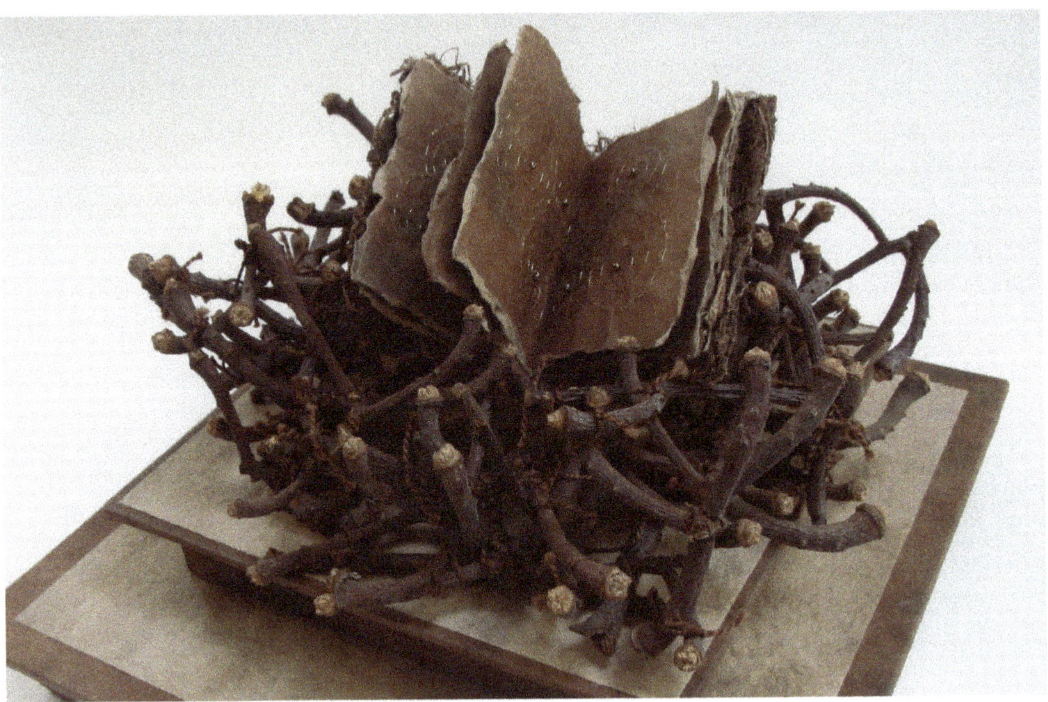

Spirit Book #27: Absorbed Prayer

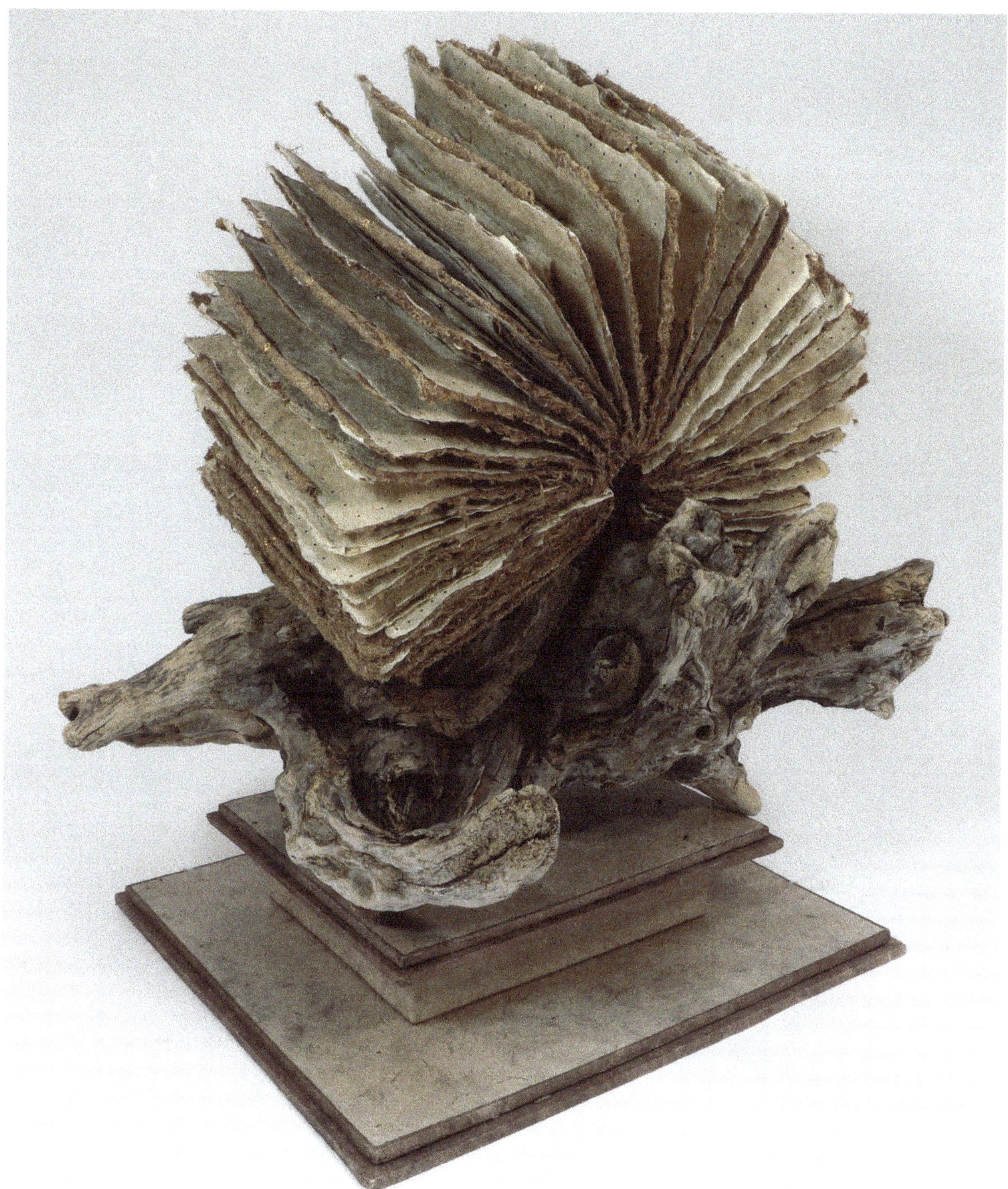

Spirit Book #96: Harmonious Reconciliation

In the height of my calligraphy obsession, I wanted letters everywhere. I was so fortunate to have a willing partner in my friend Sandra Kavanaugh (now a painter but at that time primarily a potter). She did all the hard work so that I had a set of alphabet dishes for six and lettered tiles in our kitchen counter. Each place setting contained a small and large plate, a small and large bowl, a mug, and a goblet. Each place setting had all the letters of the alphabet and all the plates, bowls, mugs, and goblets each also had all the letters of the alphabet. We used pre-made tiles for the kitchen counter. I don't remember if I used a brush or a pen but Sandra has informed me that I used a cobalt blue clay slip to write the letters in the bone alphabet that Jaki Svaren taught in Philadelphia.

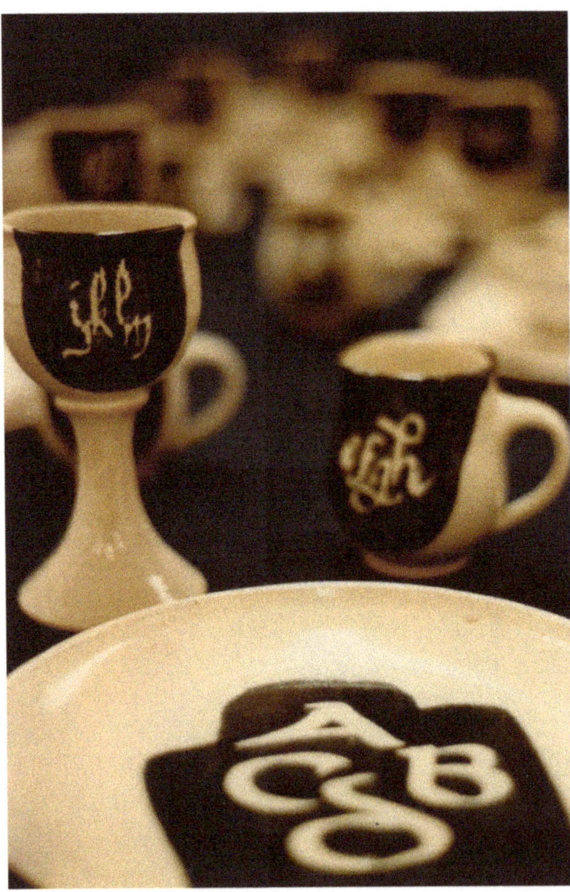
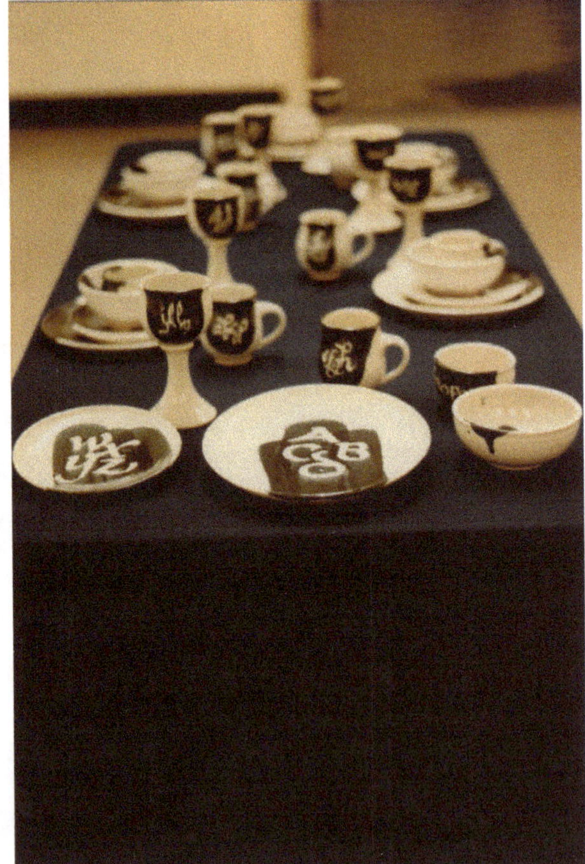

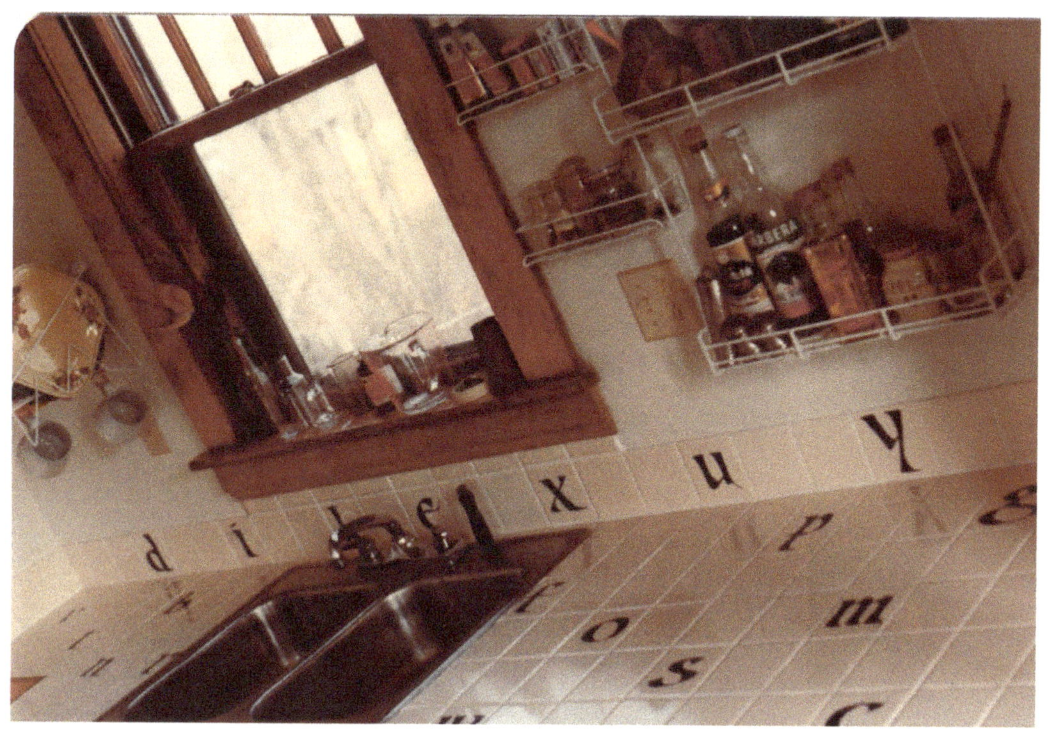

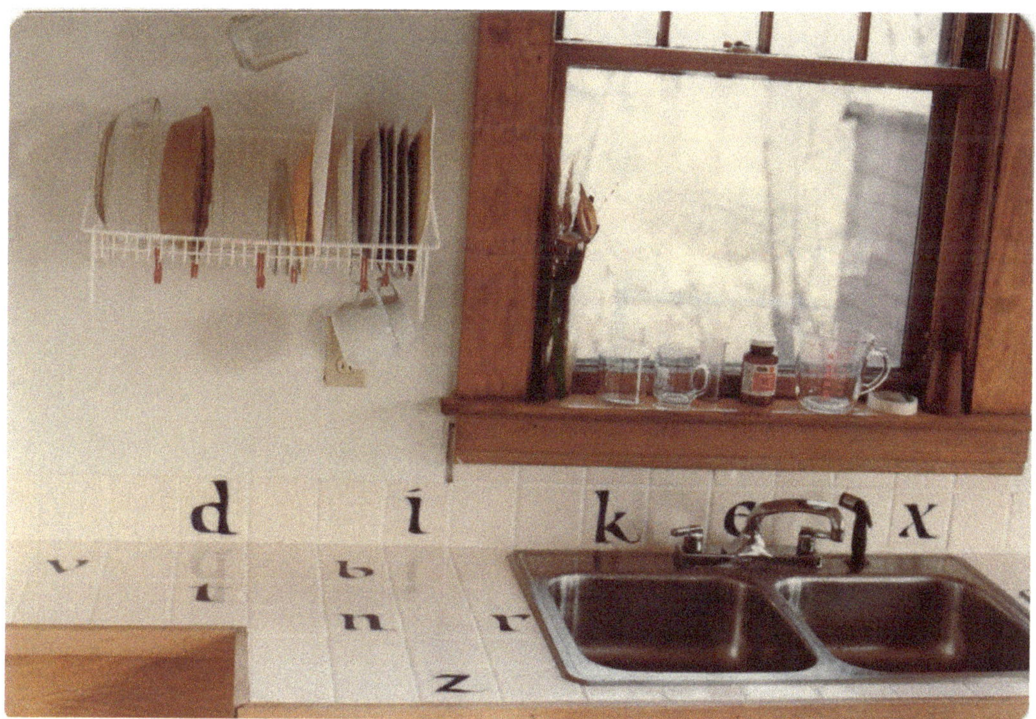

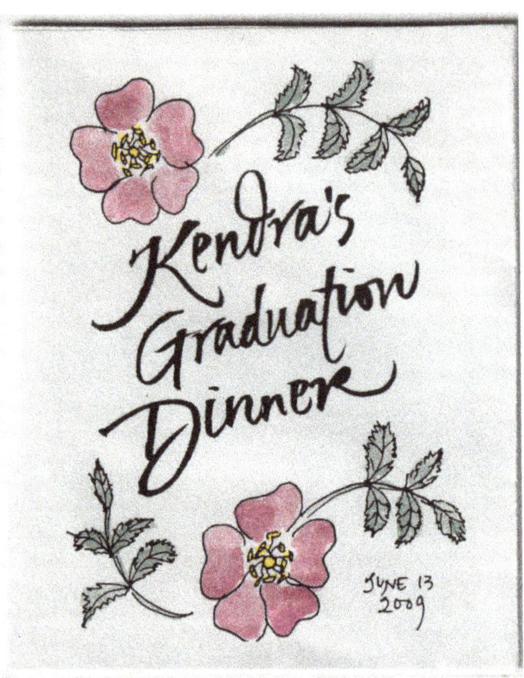

After I moved away from calligraphy in my art, it stayed a part of my life. While I didn't "do calligraphy" for many years, I still used my pens and markers on a regular basis to write recipes, make cards, place cards, and ornaments, send seasonal messages, and create little books to share with friends and family. I continue to do so today.

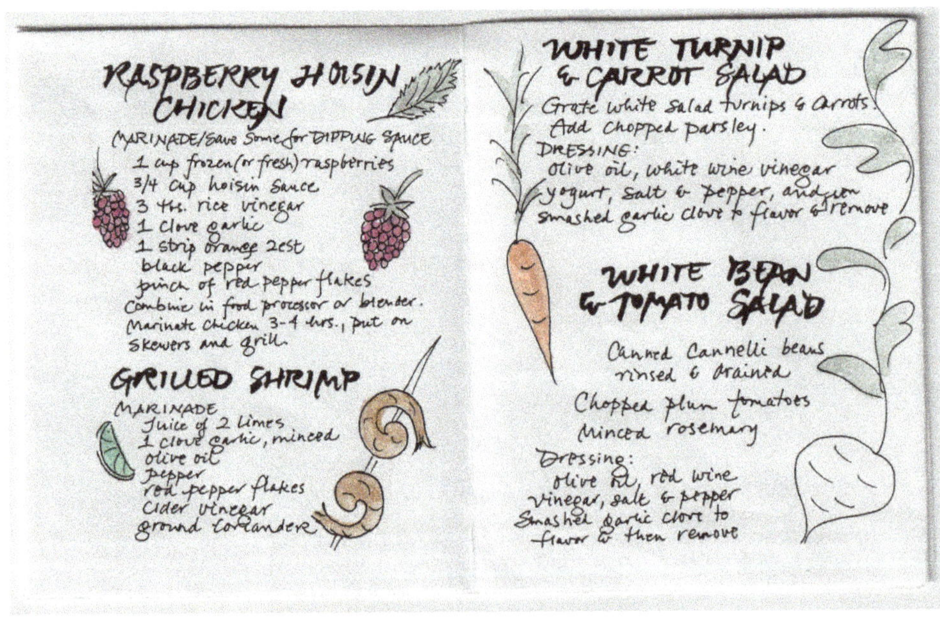

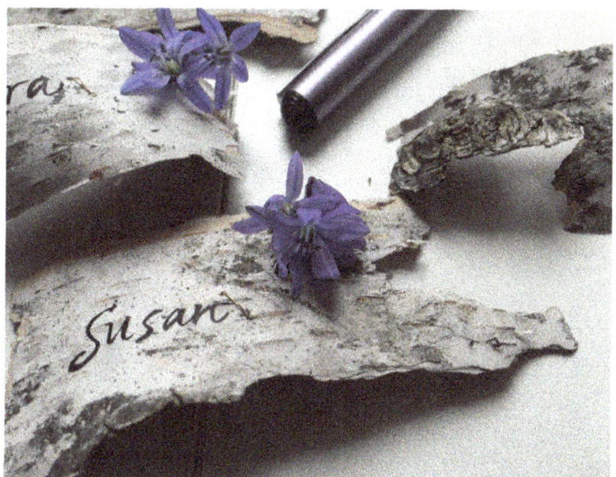
Susan

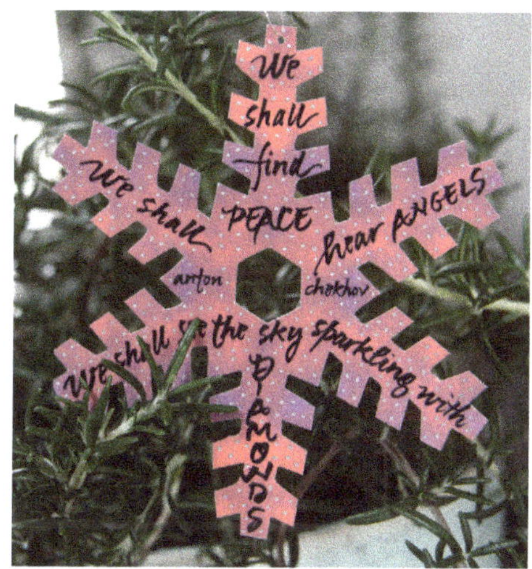
We
shall
find
PEACE
We shall
hear ANGELS
anton   chekhov
We shall see the sky sparkling with
DIAMONDS

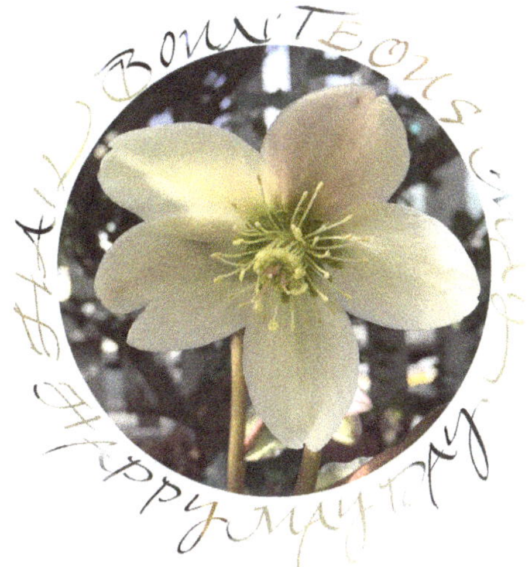

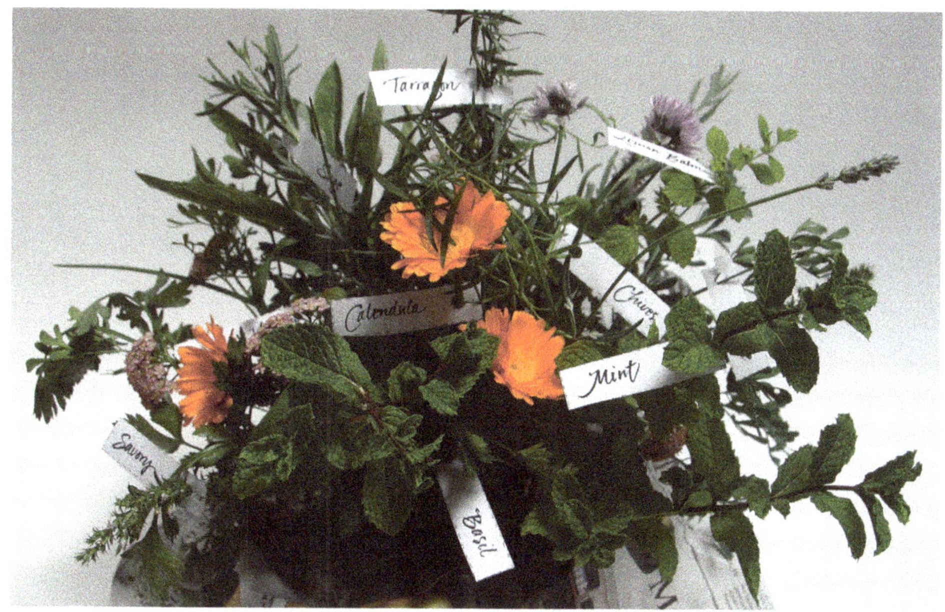
Tarragon
Lemon Balm
Calendula
Chives
Mint
Savory
Basil

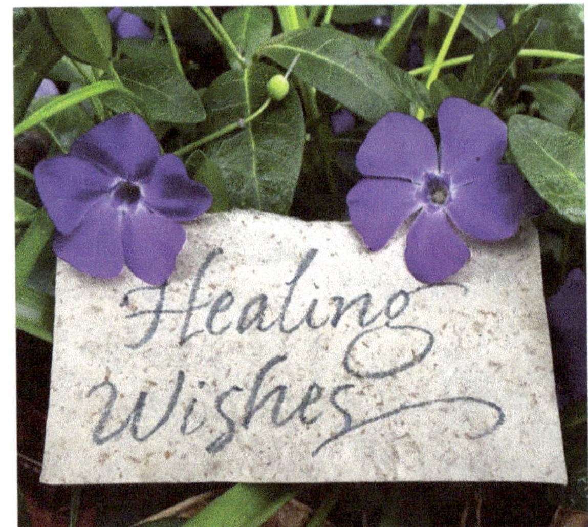
Healing
Wishes

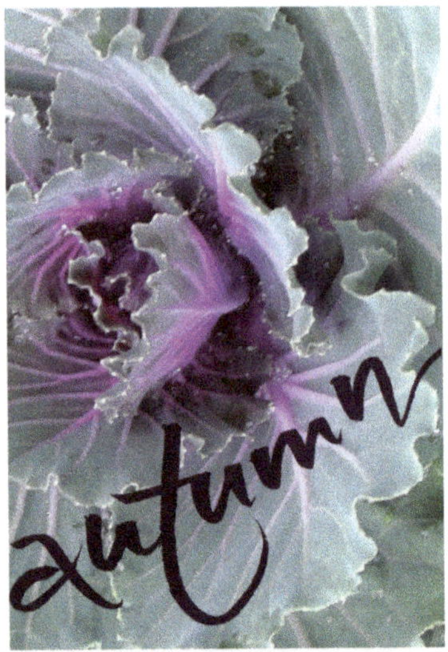
autumn

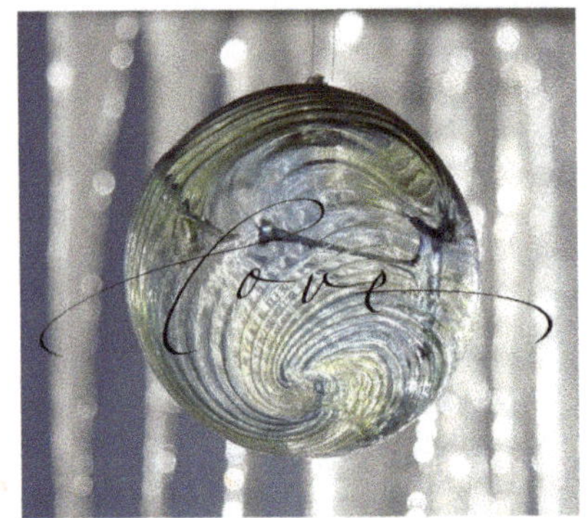
love

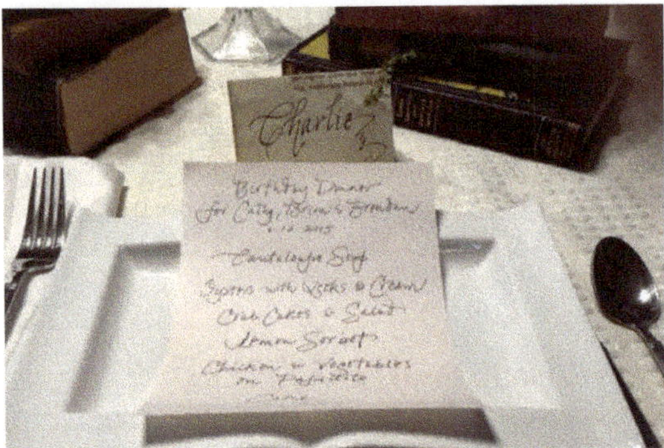

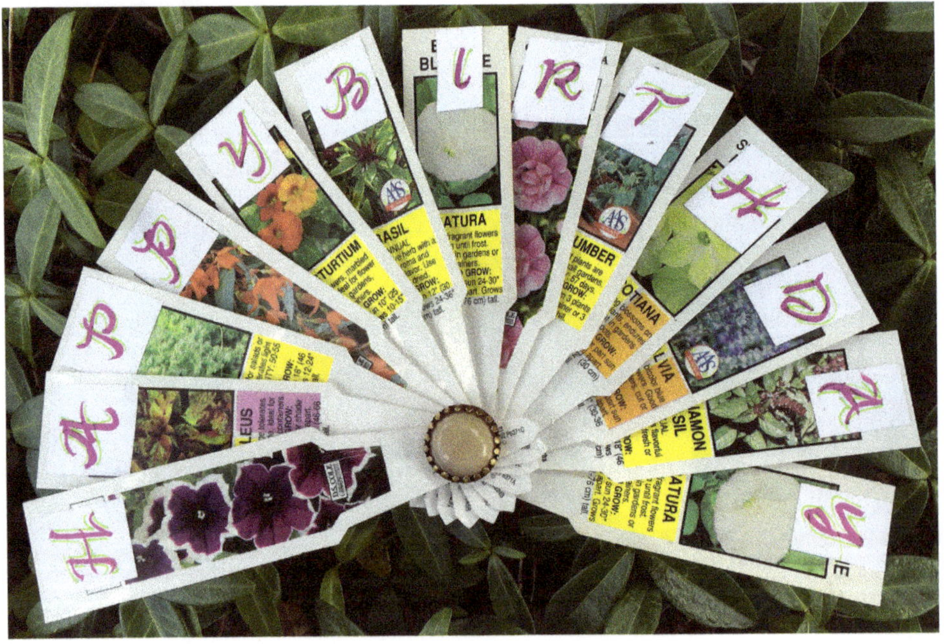

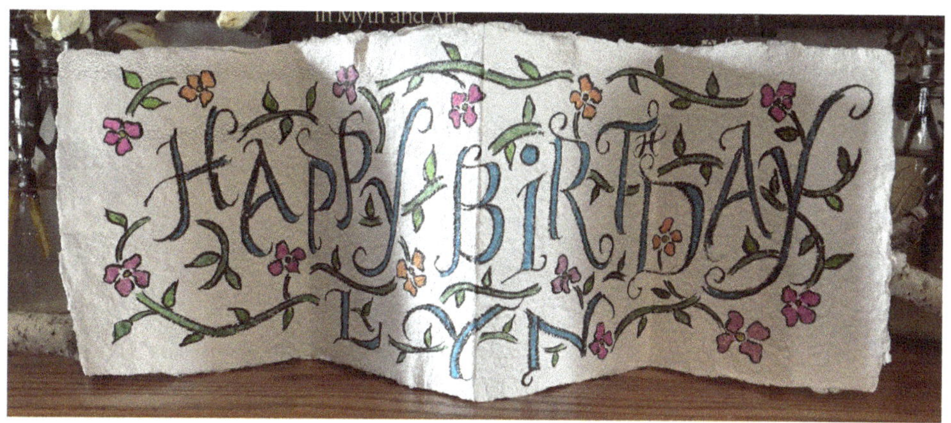

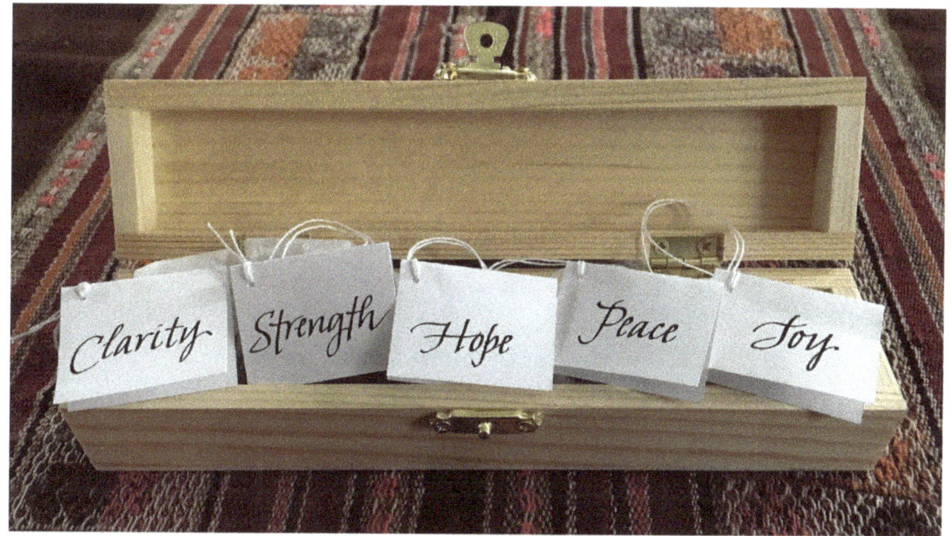
Clarity
Strength
Hope
Peace
Joy.

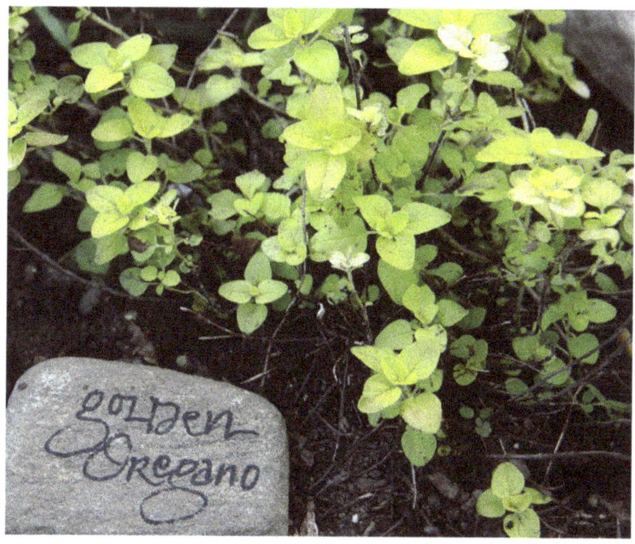
golden
oregano

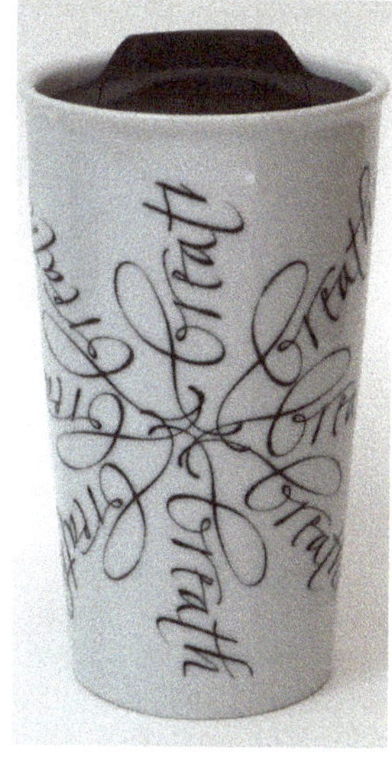

I've lettered many of my holiday cards over the years. Although I've created cards completely by hand, I have more often printed them—at local copy shops, with silkscreen (once), and with my inkjet printer. The card below was the first one I did using calligraphy. I was so excited I spent the extra money for offset printing. My current list is large, and I have switched to digitally printed postcards by my friends at Scarlet Letter Press in Salem, Massachusetts.

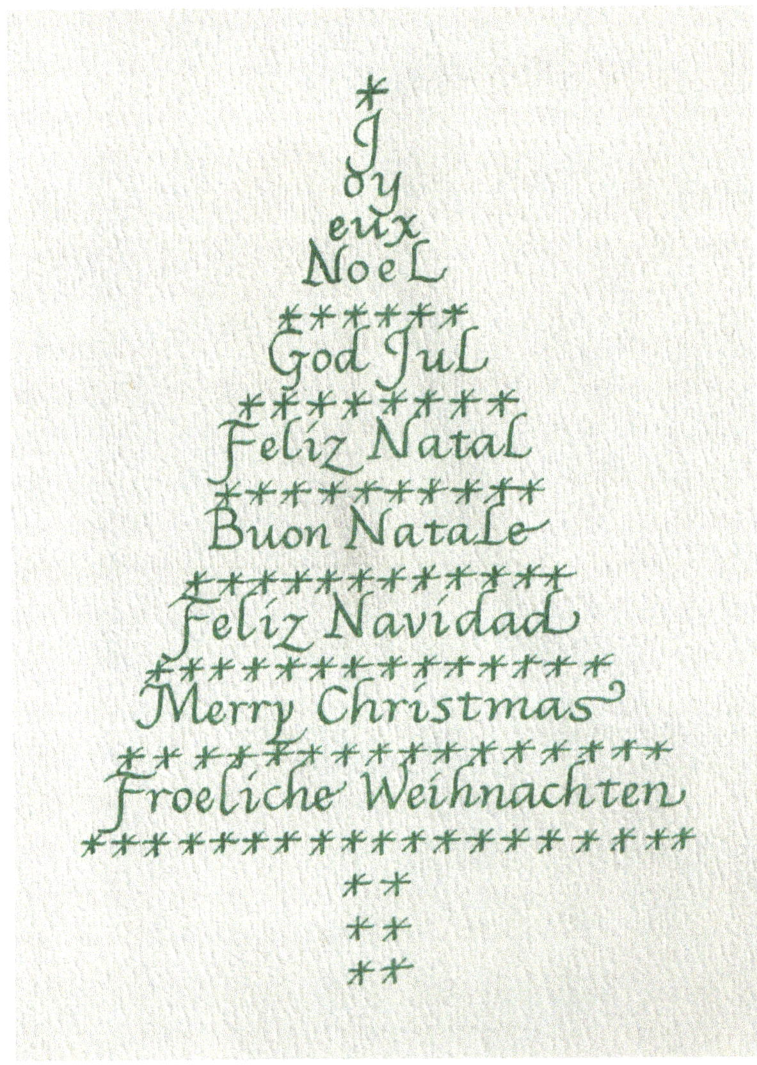

Opposite Page: Clockwise: Dashing through the snow: Written with white ink on black paper, printed on red paper. Fra Giovanni quote: Written with a scroll pen, printed on light-green stationery. Wassail: Silkscreen. Solstice: Written in gold marker. Winter solstice: Flower design from photograph of a peony and lettering with brush pen. Lord of the Dance: Brush drawing by my one-and-a-half-year-old son.

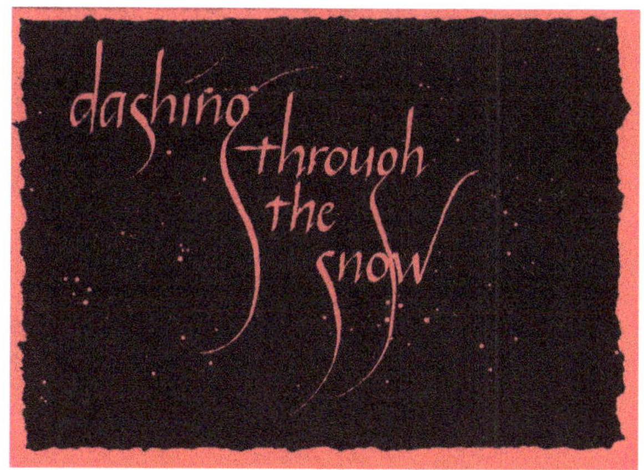

dashing
through
the
snow

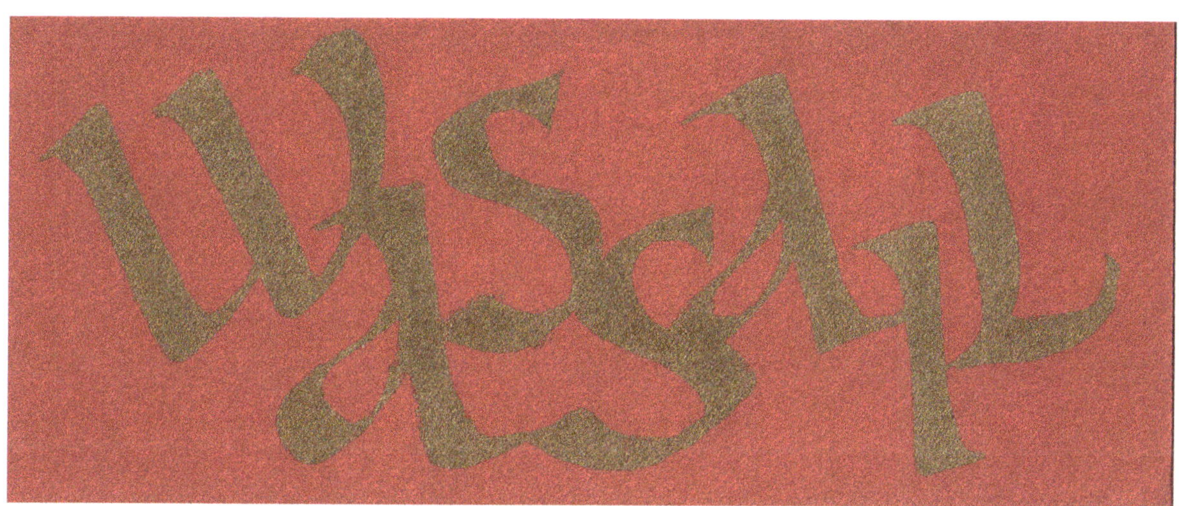

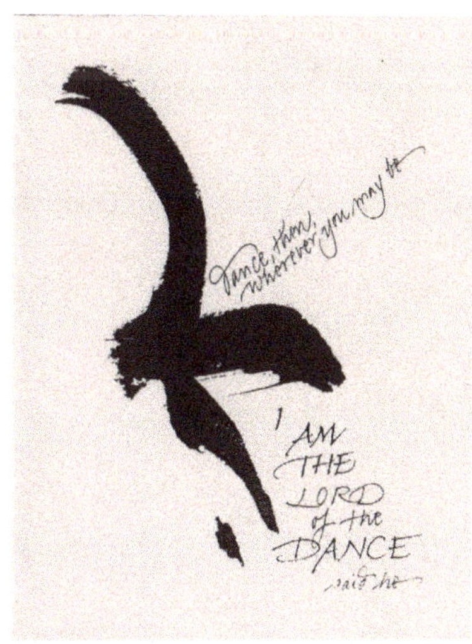

Dance then, wherever you may be
I AM THE LORD of the DANCE
said he

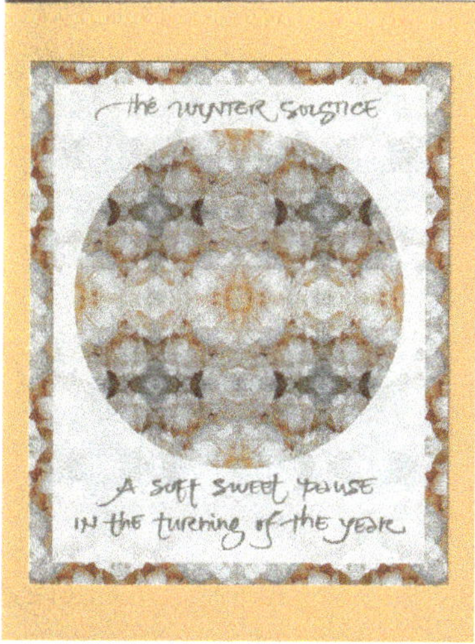

the WYNTER SOLSTICE
A soft sweet pause
in the turning of the year

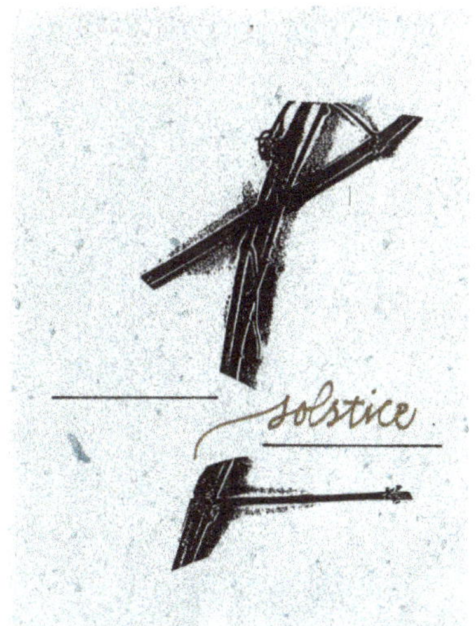

solstice

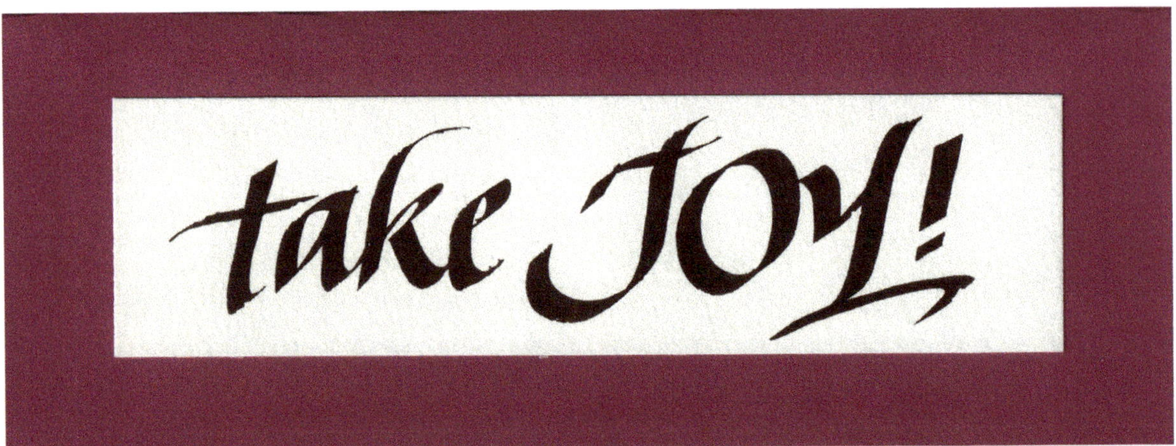

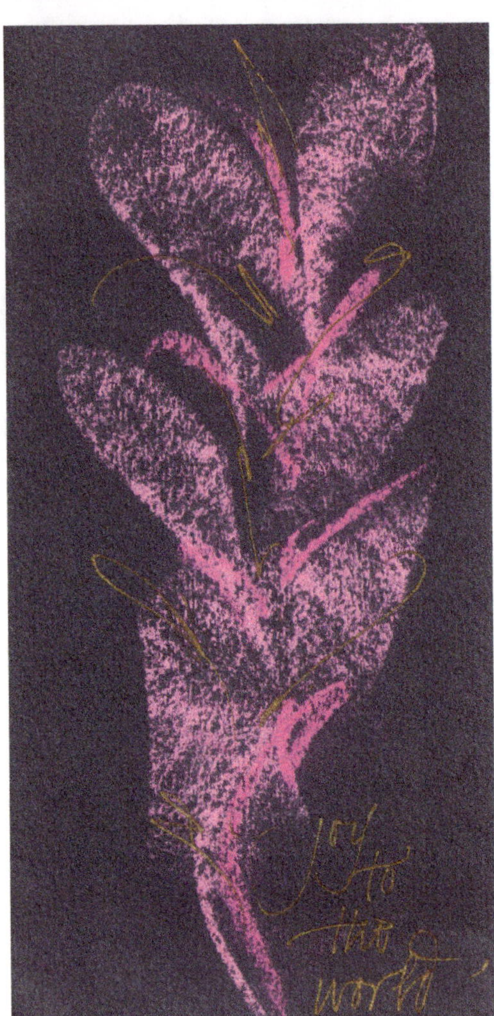

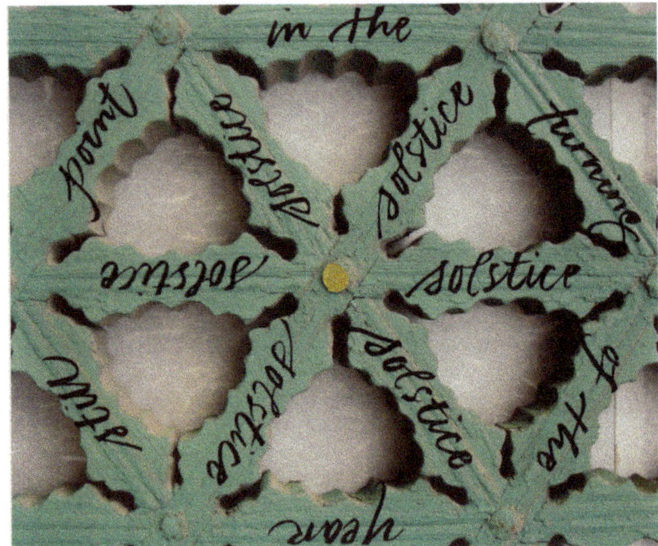

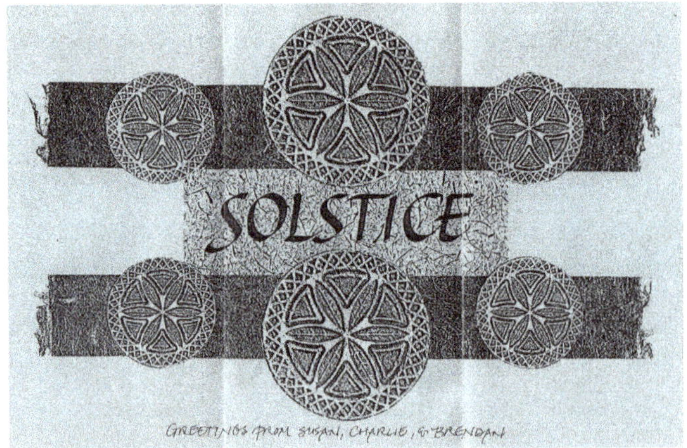

Clockwise: Take joy: Hand-lettered on each card. Solstice: Photo of temple screen in Korea with lettering added in Photoshop. Solstice: Photocopied pizelle cookie and textured papers. Joy to the World: Pastel design and gold marker on card done the first Christmas after the birth of my first child.

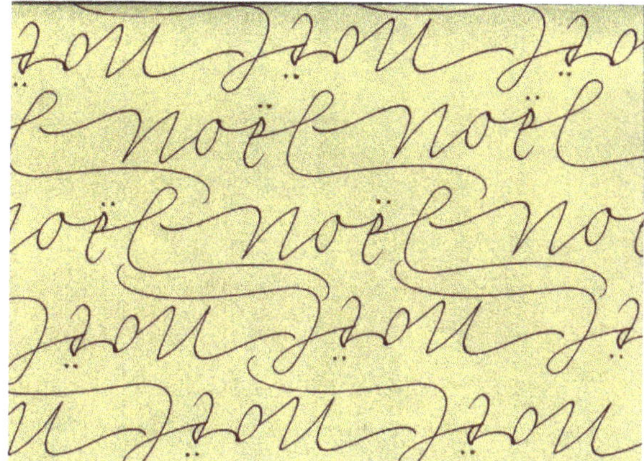

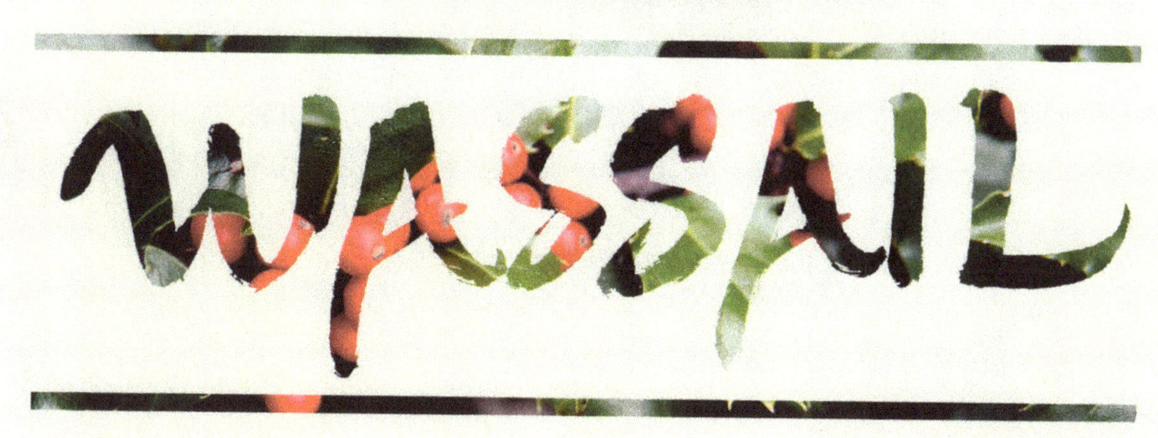

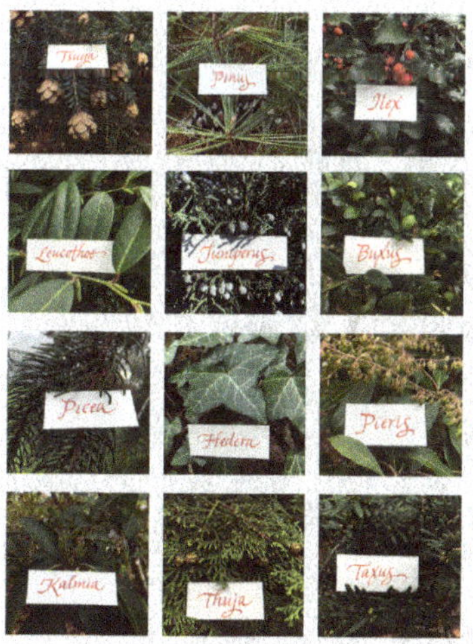

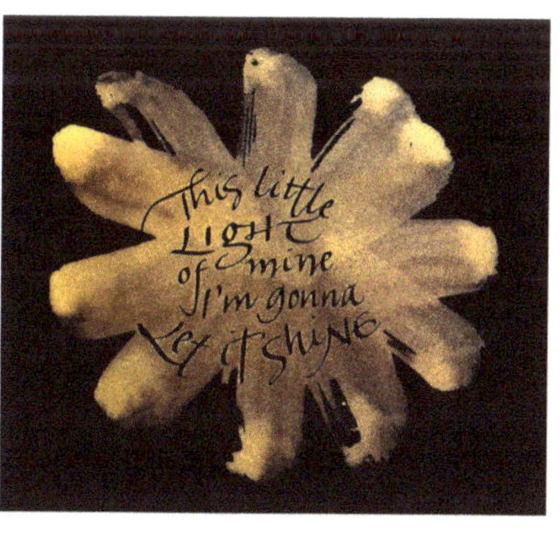

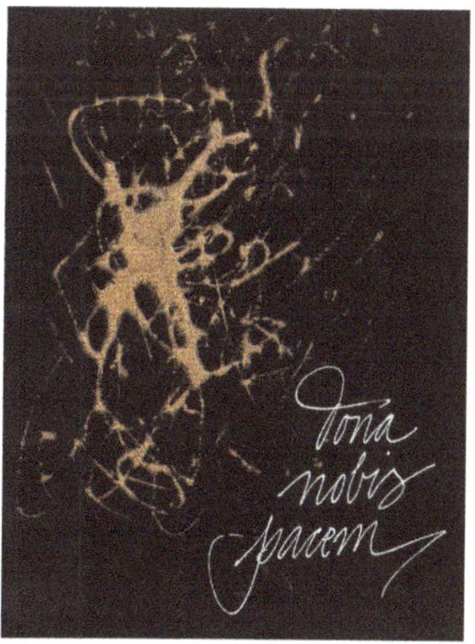

Clockwise: Hope: Lettering screened over image in Photoshop. Noel: Written with automatic pen, pattern designed in Photoshop. Wassail: Lettering combined with holly photo in Photoshop. Dona nobis pacem: Gold gouache design, lettering with silver marker. This little light: Lettering laser-printed on black paper, sun design made with brush and bleach. Technique learned in Carol DuBosch's folded pen workshop. Evergreens with Latin names: lettered tags photographed with plants.

In 2005, I had an exhibition of the Spirit Books at the Carney Gallery at Regis College in Weston, Massachusetts to celebrate what I thought would be the conclusion of the series. After having made fifty, I thought I was finished. Five years later, I found myself looking longingly at branches and bark and missing the quiet hours of stitching pages and began again. In the intervening years, I took advantage of the time to broaden my creative horizons. At the Newburyport Art Association, I took a workshop with Bruce Iverson on Chinese brush painting which reignited my love of working with ink.

I decided to participate in the annual Outdoor Sculpture at Maudslay exhibition at Maudslay State Park in Newburyport in 2007. I made gestural drawings with hemlock branches and waterproof liquid sumi ink on narrow banners of long-fibered handmade paper from Nepal and attached them to hemlock trees. Although the banners had survived rain and wind in a test situation, they were unable to withstand the solid week of rain that came right after they were installed. While I was able to repair them enough to be presentable for the three-week run of the exhibit, they never returned to their initial glory. I didn't let that stop me from trying similar projects in a couple of other locations. After more unexpected weather challenges, I abandoned them as a project partly because of the technical difficulties and partly because they had become repetitive.

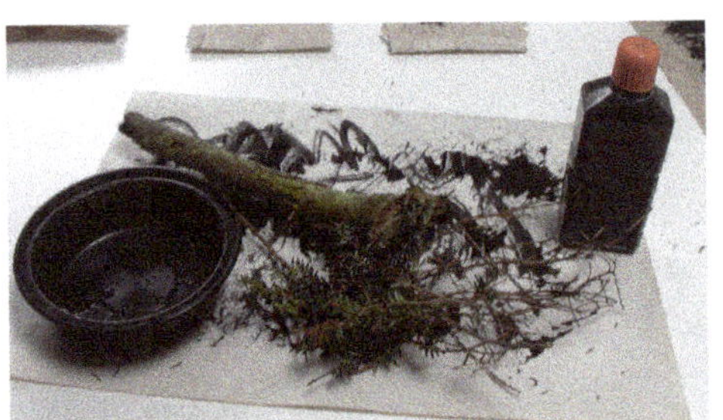

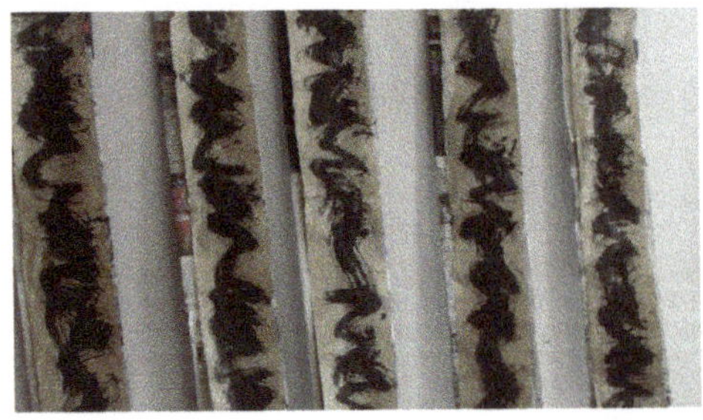

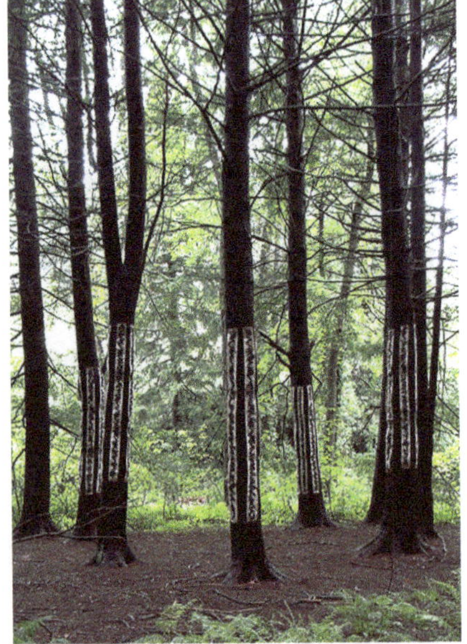

The next year I was having trouble figuring out what to do. I turned to what had been my source of inspiration for so many years before—words. The theme was Trace (creating work that adheres to the theme is optional), and I chose to work with the words of nineteenth-century poet John Greenleaf Whittier who had often visited Maudslay when it was a private estate. For *Whispered Fragments: John Greenleaf Whittier*, I hung Tyvek strips with lines from his poems written with Sharpie marker from two old apple trees.

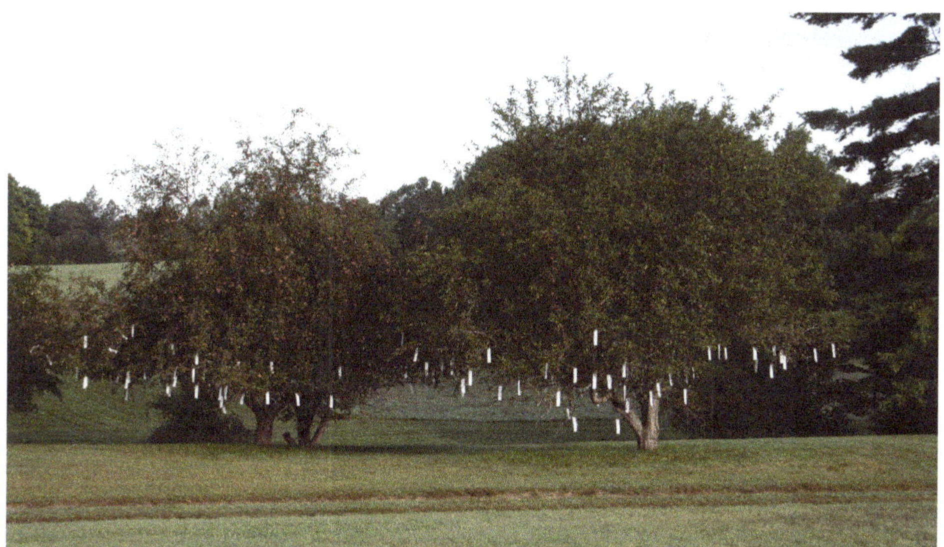

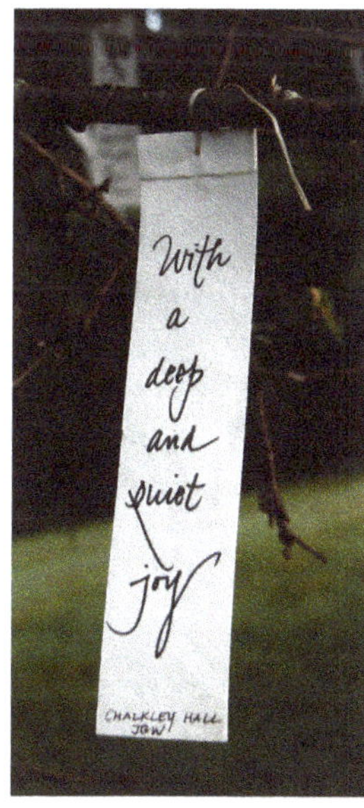

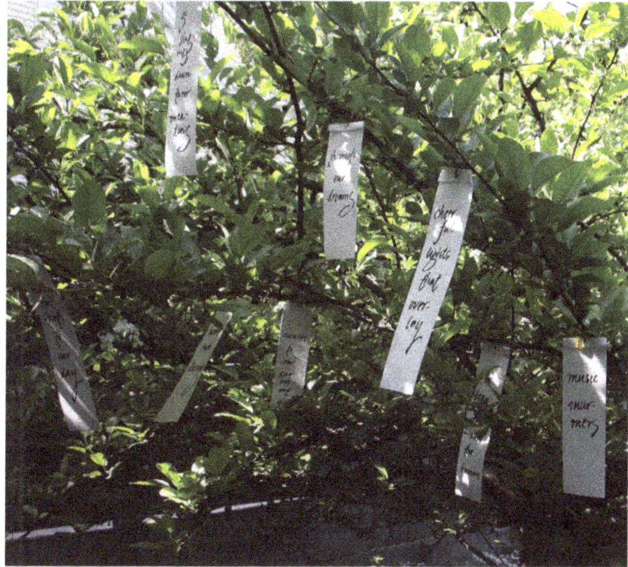

Martha Brookes Hutcheson was the designer of Maudslay's formal garden. In her book *The Spirit of the Garden* she wrote: "The garden is . . . the resting-place of the spirit—the place of inspiration and promise, of tranquility and intense personal claim." In 2010, I lettered the quote on bricks that were placed on top of the brick wall that surrounds the garden. After painting the quote on the bricks with a thick black paint, I shook sand over it to give it texture. I then painted over the letters with gray to look like the cement between the bricks.

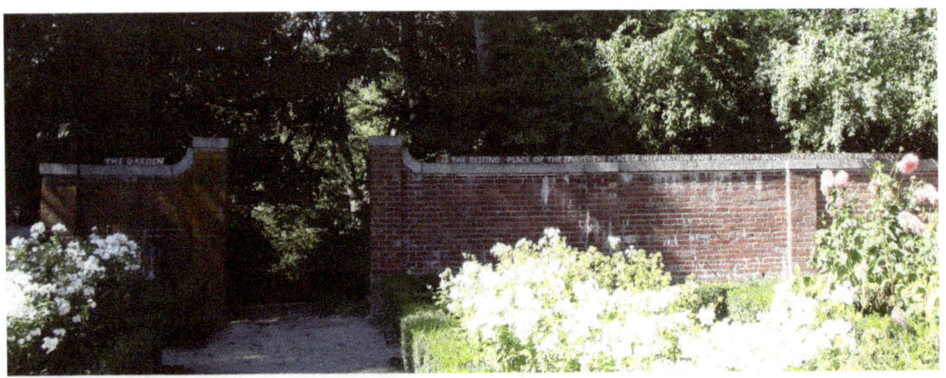

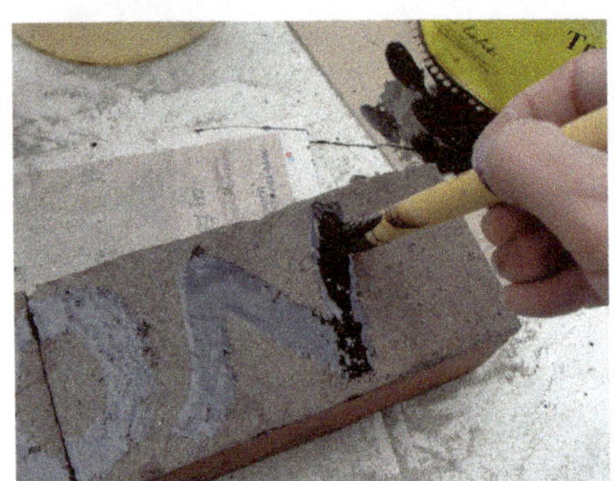

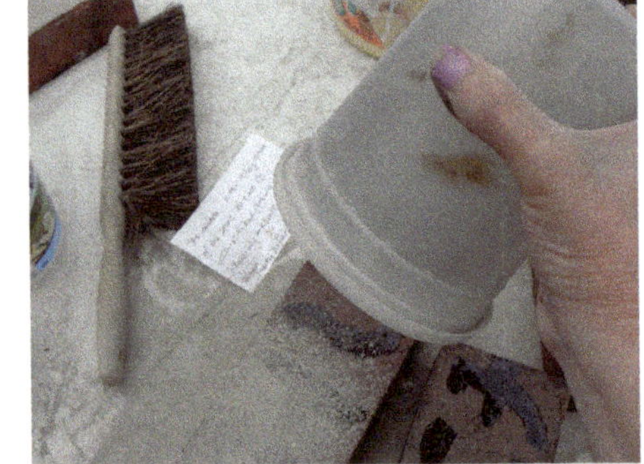

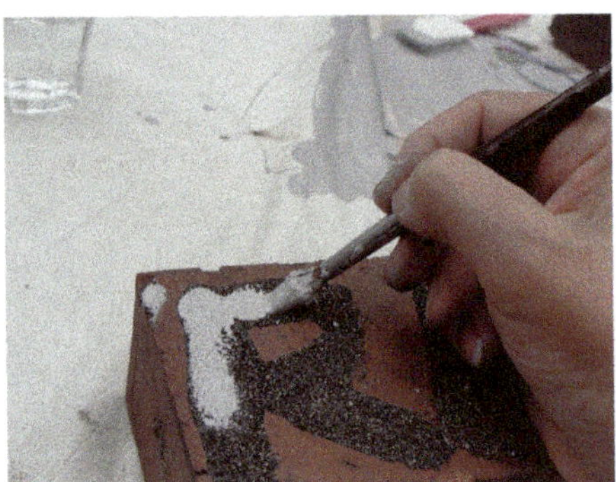

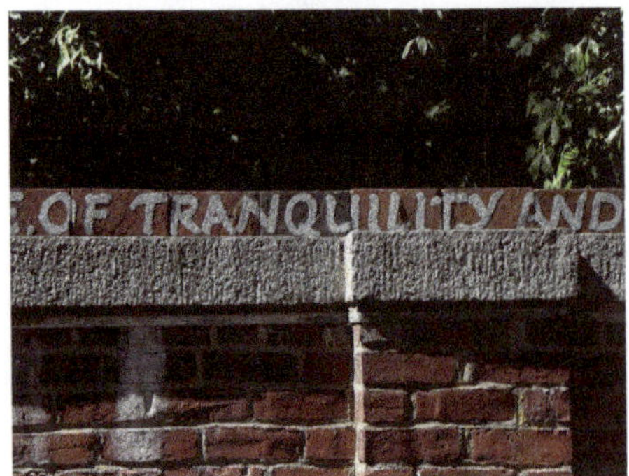

In 2012, the theme was "Inside Out." Thinking of how our breath brings the outside in and lets the inside out, I chose to work with the word "Breathe." I was taking a jewelry class in working with sea glass, stone, and wire with artist Lisa Scala of Georgetown, Massachusetts and wanted to use some of the techniques I was learning. I wrote letters with a brush on strips of Tyvek weighted on the bottom with stones and hung them from the branch of a tree.

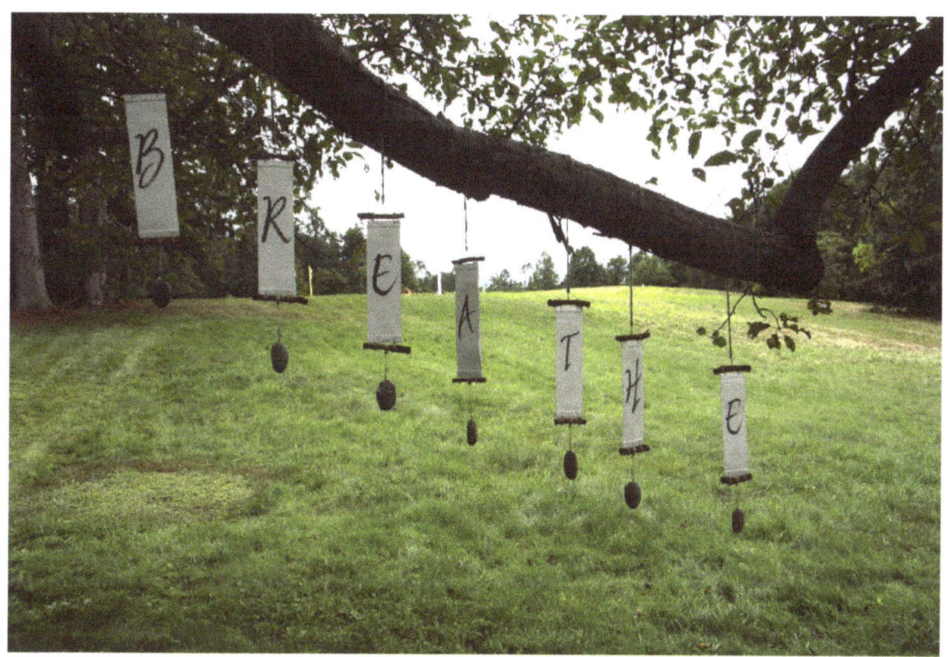

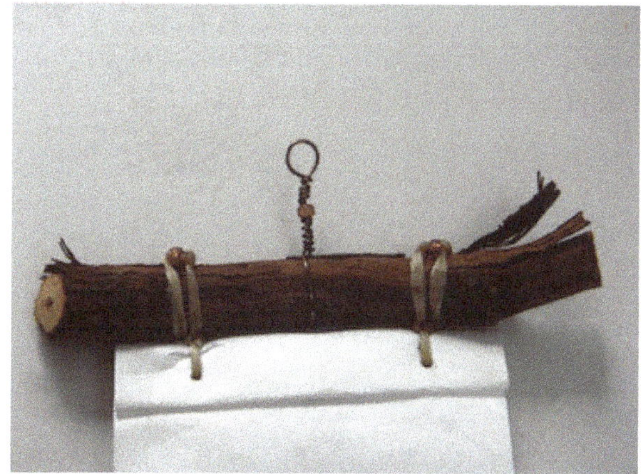

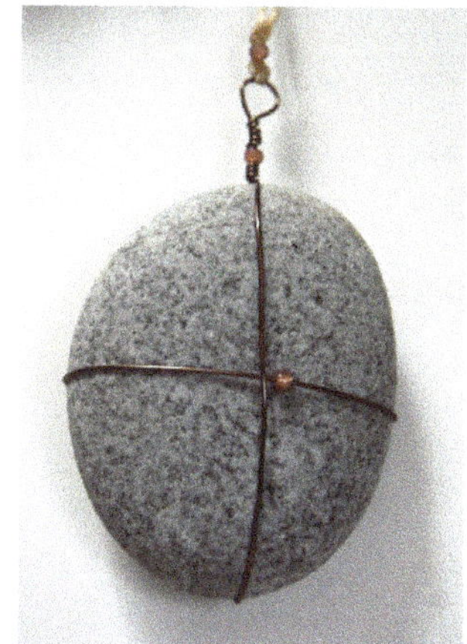

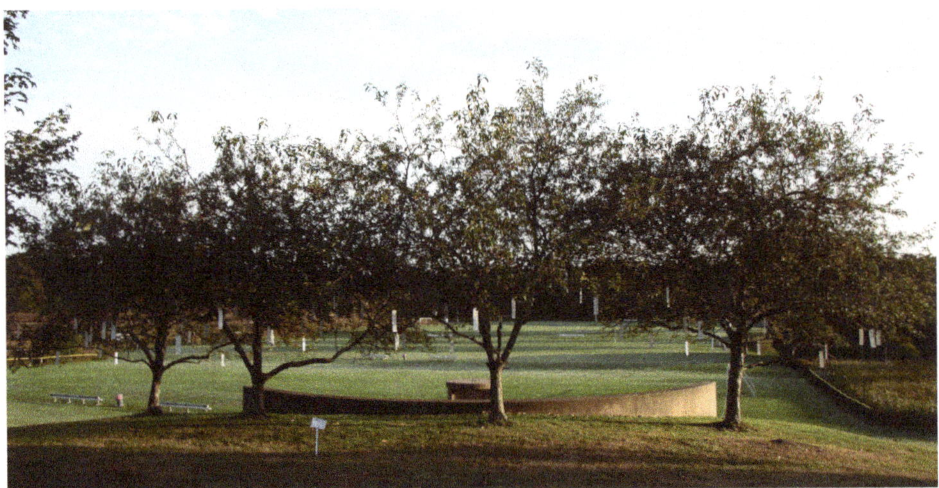

My final piece of outdoor work was installed in 2015 at Flying Horse Sculpture at the Pingree School in South Hamilton, Massachusetts. I continued *Whispered Fragments* with the words of Emily Dickinson. It turned out that the four crab apple trees that looked so peaceful when I first viewed them were in a wildly windy location. I had many difficulties with the installation and spent untold hours trying to find a secure way of hanging the strips on the trees. I started with square knots, then redid every one with a knot I learned from an experienced fisherman. When that didn't work, I went to a bait and tackle shop and got spinners that were supposed to bring in forty-pound fish without a problem.

I started with eighty-eight strips. Only twenty remained on the trees when the time came to dismantle the installation a couple of months later. I have now removed outdoor installations from my repertoire.

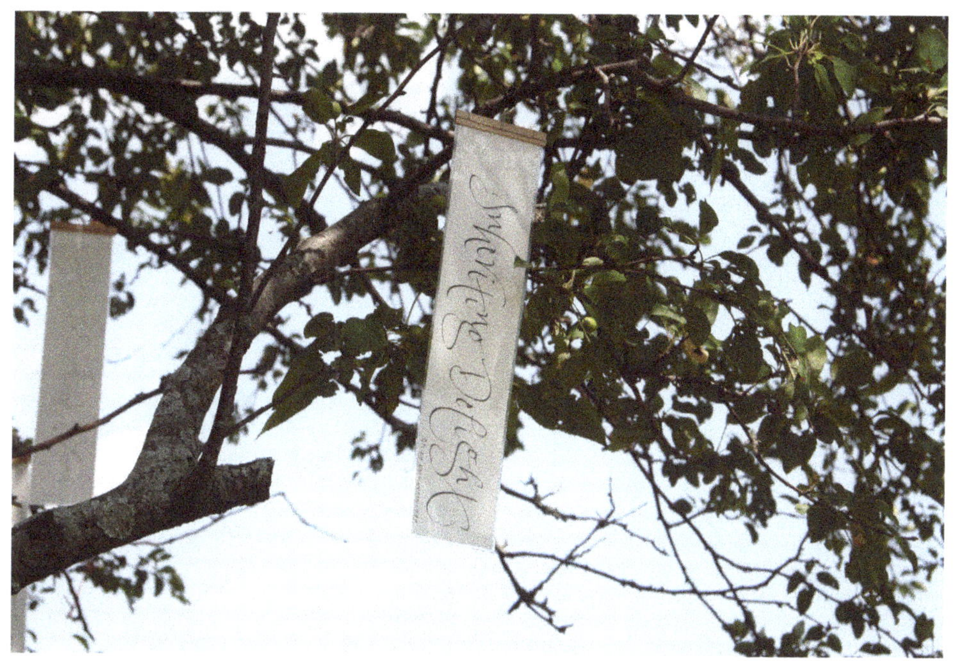

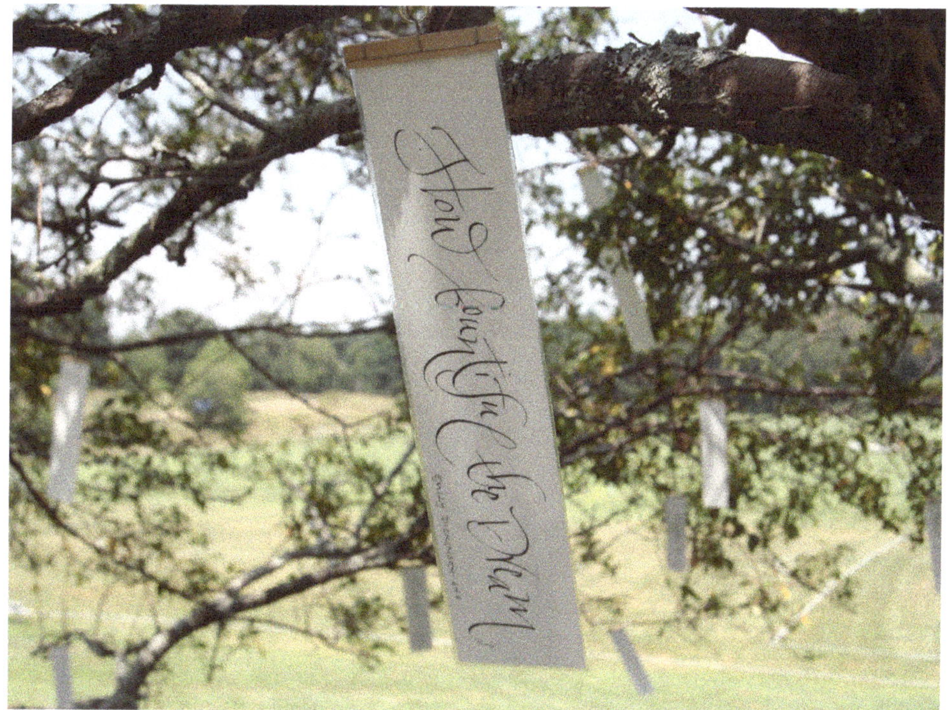

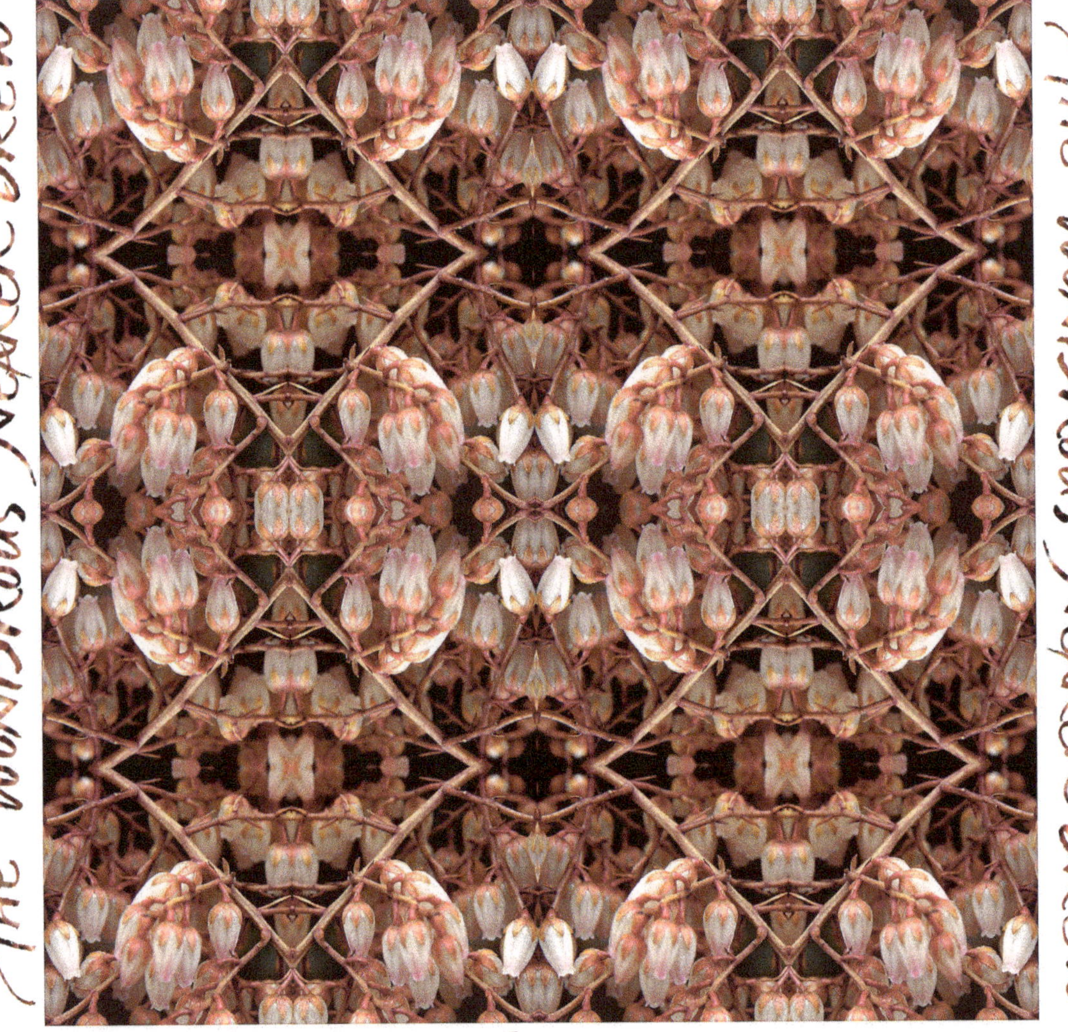
THE WONDROUS NEARER DREW
THE WONDROUS NEARER DREW
THE WONDROUS NEARER DREW
THE WONDROUS NEARER DREW

In addition to exploring my connection to nature through the Spirit Books and outdoor installations, I experimented with photography and computer manipulation. As with the Spirit Books, I wanted to express my sense of life beyond what is seen with the eye. The Emily Dickinson series, which consists of thirty images, began on a crisp mid-April day in 2008 when I took a photograph of our pink Pieris shrub. When I brought the image into the computer, I played around with cropping and then duplicating and rotating. I found myself with a kaleidoscopic square.

I have been a longtime lover of the poetry of Emily Dickinson. Lines from her poems echo in my mind long after reading them. One is "The wondrous nearer drew" from poem 93. The words and image seemed to be a perfect pairing. I lettered the line with my Pentel Brush cartridge pen, scanned it into the computer, and integrated it into the image.

I took more photographs of flowers and read through all the poems in *The Complete Poems of Emily Dickinson* edited by Thomas H. Johnson. I concentrated on the individual lines rather than the meaning of the poems. I avoided all lines that had a sense of color, season, or object. It was important to me that the flower image not compete with or be an illustration of the words. I chose lines that I felt captured the beauty, freshness, and mystery of her language. The flowers were found in gardens (mine, friends', and on garden tours) and along roadsides. All are from Emily Dickinson's home state of Massachusetts.

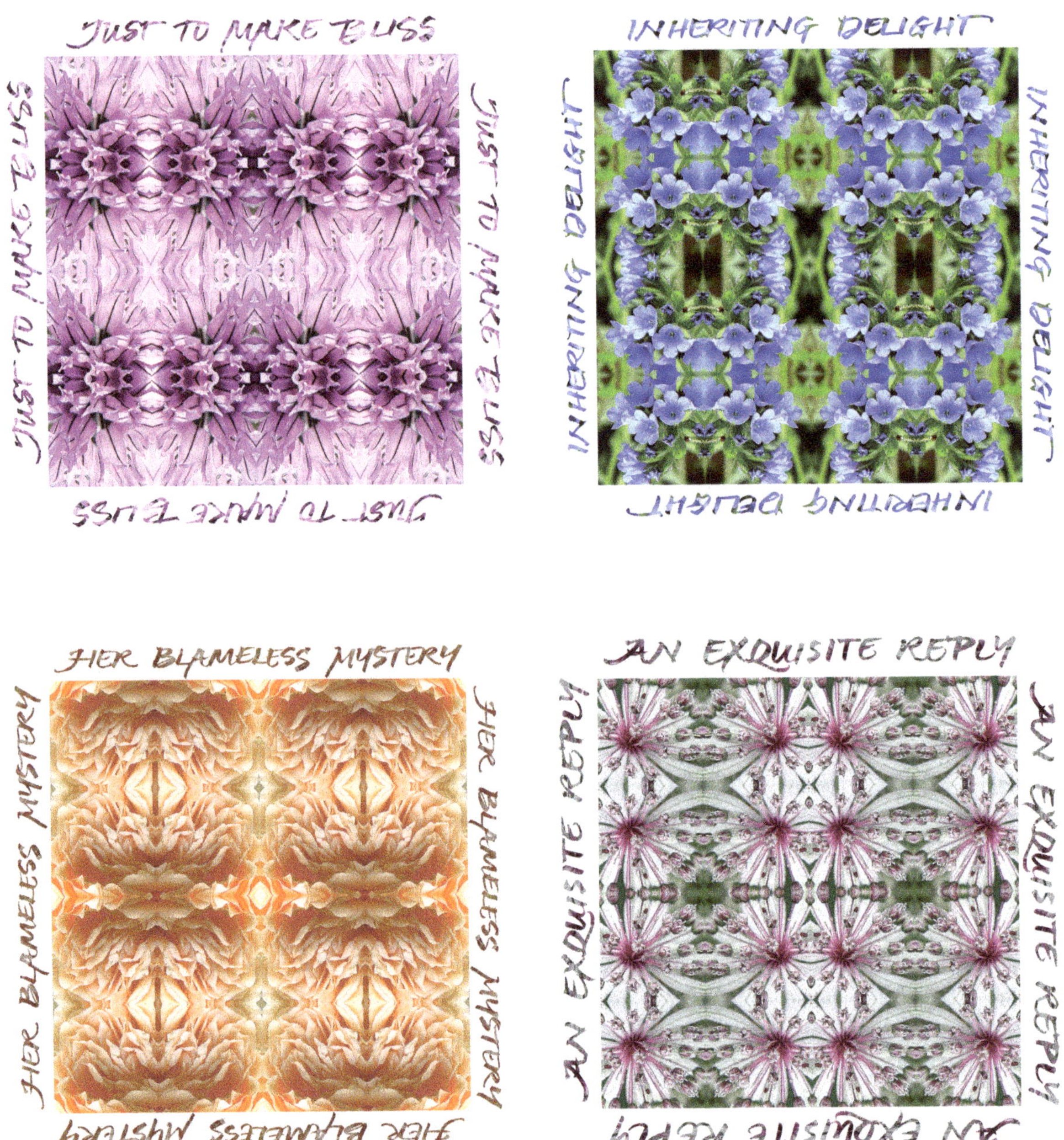

Clockwise: Bliss: Poem 333, Chives. Delight: Poem 499, Virginia Bluebells. Reply: Poem 500, Astrantia. Mystery: Poem 271, Rose.

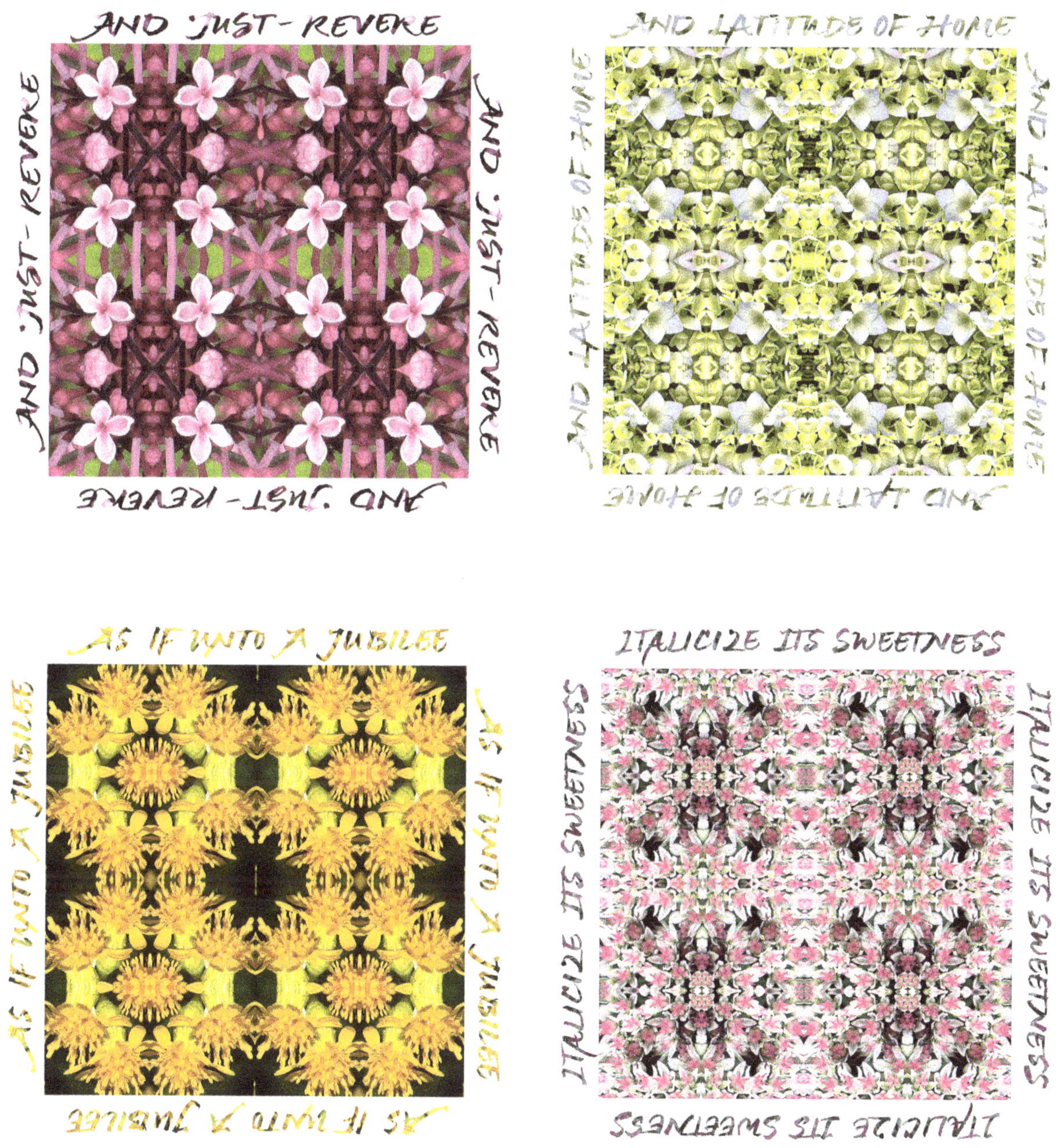

Clockwise: Revere: Poem 283, Lilac. Latitude: Poem 624, Hydrangea. Sweetness: Poem 1717, Sedum. Jubilee: Poem 593, Goldenrod.

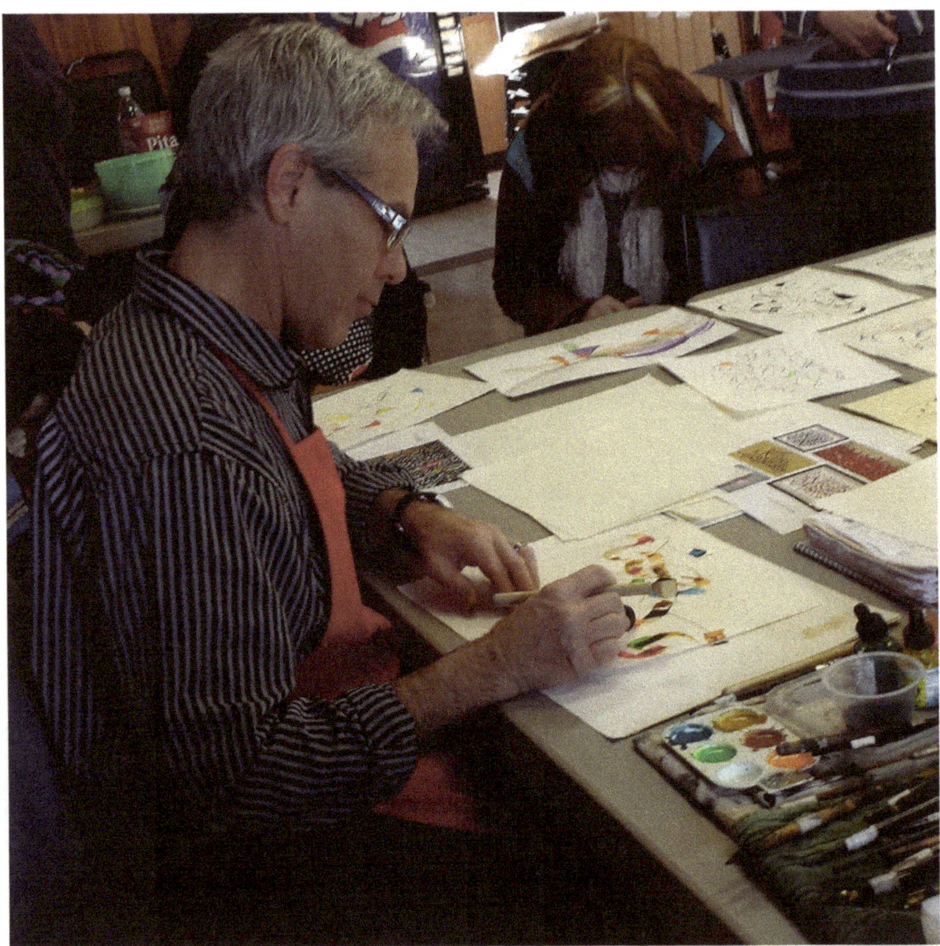

In 2014, I took my first workshop since the week with Jenny at Green Gulch in 1988. Sponsored by Masscribes and called "Contemporary Scripts," it was taught by Mike Gold. The title and description sounded right up my alley. I was nervous about taking a workshop after so many years, but was encouraged by the fact that Mike had studied privately with Jenny. We had corresponded when he wrote an appreciation of Jenny after her passing for *Letter Arts Review*.

The workshop was perfect. Mike taught attitude and approach more than technique. He said, "Don't just make letters. Make art." He was generous, thoughtful, and kind. He took Edward Johnston's analysis of manuscripts—slope, scale, pen angle, spacing (between letters, between words, between lines), shape, baseline, speed, texture—and gave exercises for playing with changes.

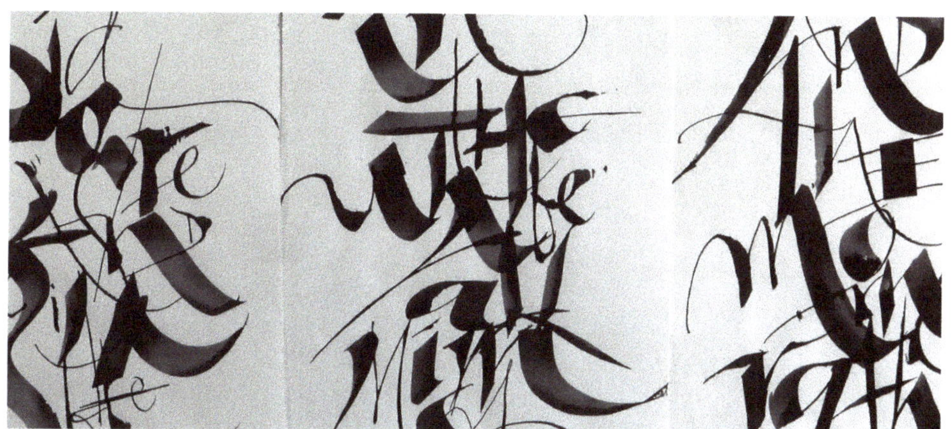

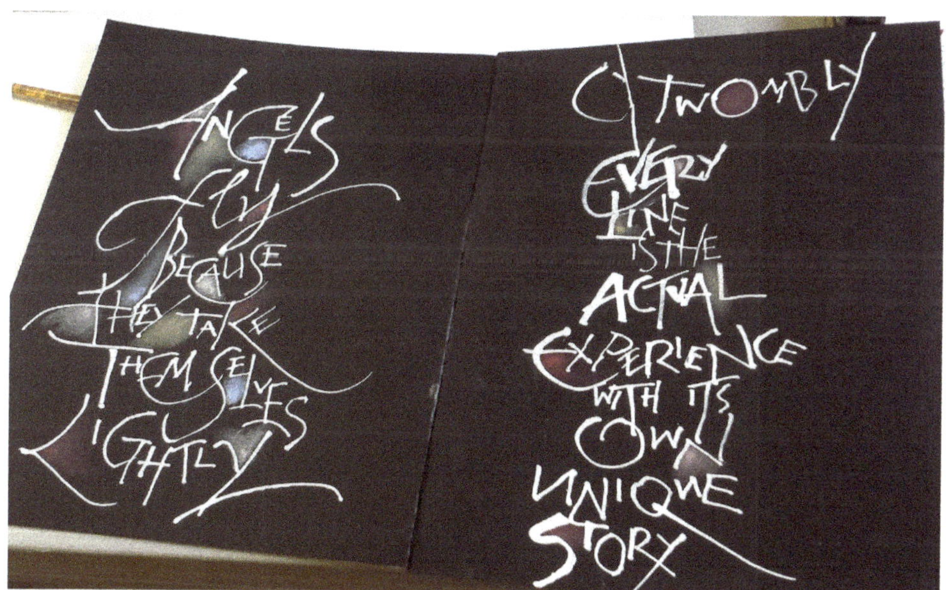

Above: Higgins Eternal Ink with automatic pen. Below: White gouache with ruling pen and pan pastels.

The workshop gave me confidence in the work I was already doing and led me to new explorations. Shortly after Mike's workshop, I made a solstice card using lines from St. Julian of Norwich, "All shall be well and all shall be well and all manner of thing shall be well." I first wrote it in standard upper-and-lower case. When I realized that the many double 'l' combinations were keeping the eye from moving around the page, I combined upper and lower cases throughout the body of the text. I liked the way the mixture looked and continue to use it frequently. The Einstein quote on the opposite page was used for a solstice card. The John Berger quote was shared at fellow artist and friend Deirdre McCullough Grunwald's Celebration of Life at Brush Art Gallery in Lowell.

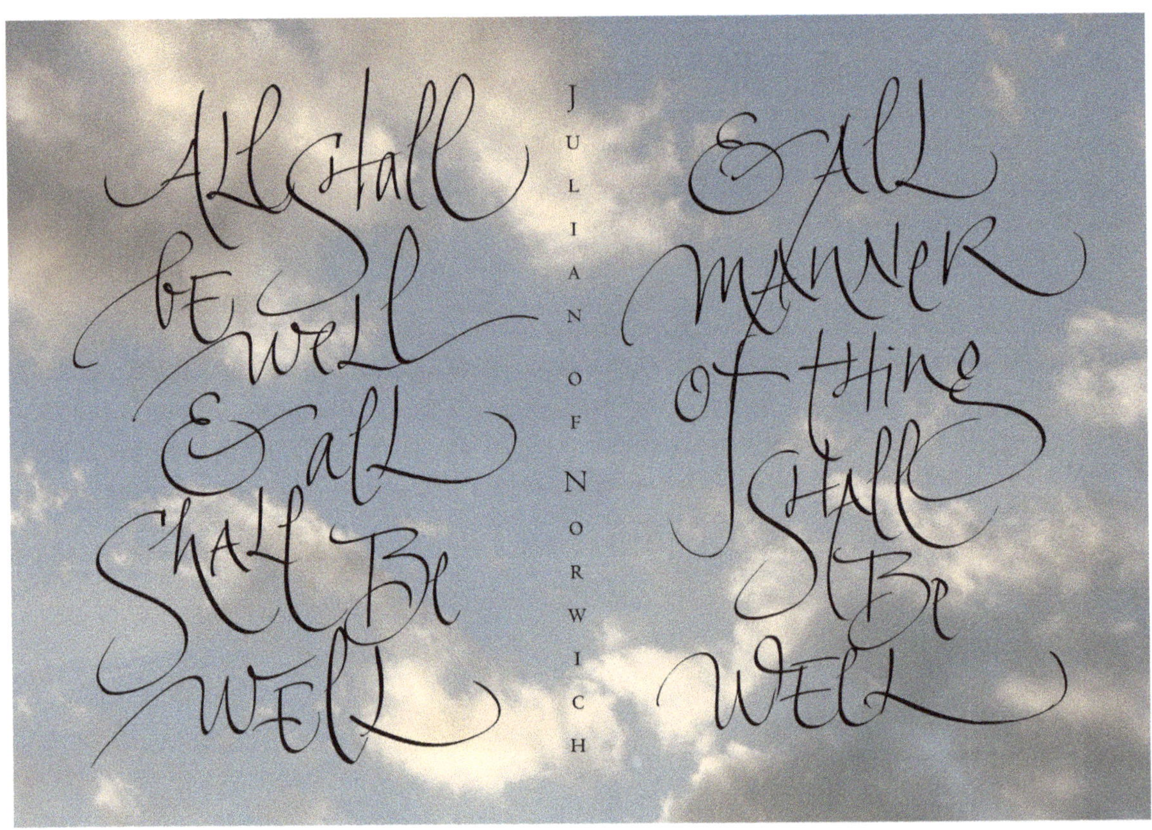

Our task must be
to free ourselves by
widening our
circle of compassion
to embrace all living
things and the
whole of Nature and
its Beauty

ALBERT EINSTEIN

That we find a crystal
or a poppy beautiful means
that we are less alone,
that we are more deeply
inserted into existence
than the course of a
single life would lead
us to believe.

JOHN BERGER · THE SENSE OF SIGHT

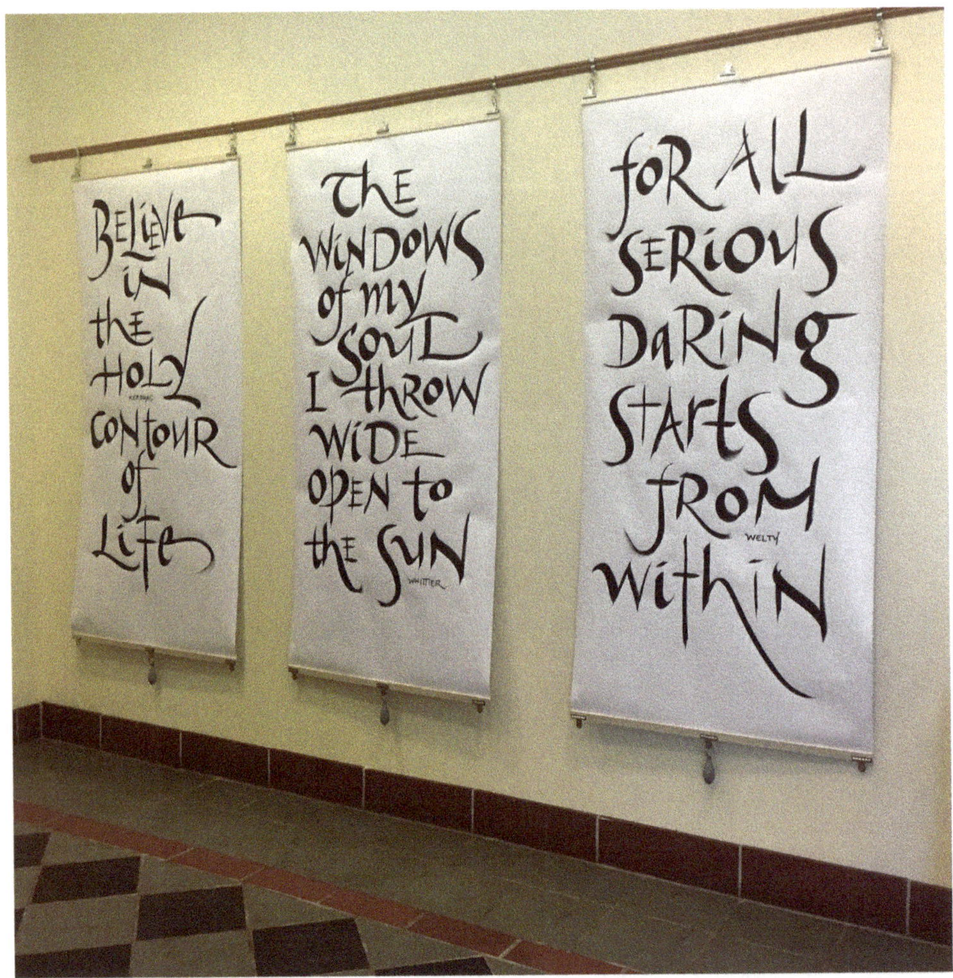

THE NEXT YEAR, I CONTACTED THE CLARE Gallery at the Franciscan Center for
Urban Ministry in Hartford, Connecticut about an exhibition of the Spirit Books.
Although the director was interested, the gallery could only accommodate two-
dimensional work. Through a series of email conversations, we arrived at the decision
to exhibit my calligraphy. I wanted to work large to change the viewer's relationship
with the words and I didn't want the expense or the formality of framed work. The
final plan was to letter large-scale banners live in the gallery.

I called the exhibit "The Power of Words." I chose short quotes, from an equal number of men and women, that I felt would give comfort and courage. I wanted the design of the lettering to be both bold and airy. I used Golden Liquid Acrylic with flow medium added and a 1¼-inch Silver Black Velvet brush. I liked that the softness of the brush's edge made letters that were not too crisp. I used rolls of paper that I cut to make four-foot wide by six-and-a-half-foot long banners.

Knowing that the gallery presentation in January 2017 would be a performance of sorts, I prepared by repeatedly writing the quotes full size on newsprint. In the studio, everything was set up to duplicate the experience in the gallery except the quality of the paper. I wrote each of the ten quotes about eight times. The lettering in the gallery went well. I only left out one letter (in the first banner on the left on the opposite page) and I noticed it right away. The free-form layout allowed me tuck it in before I went on to the next line.

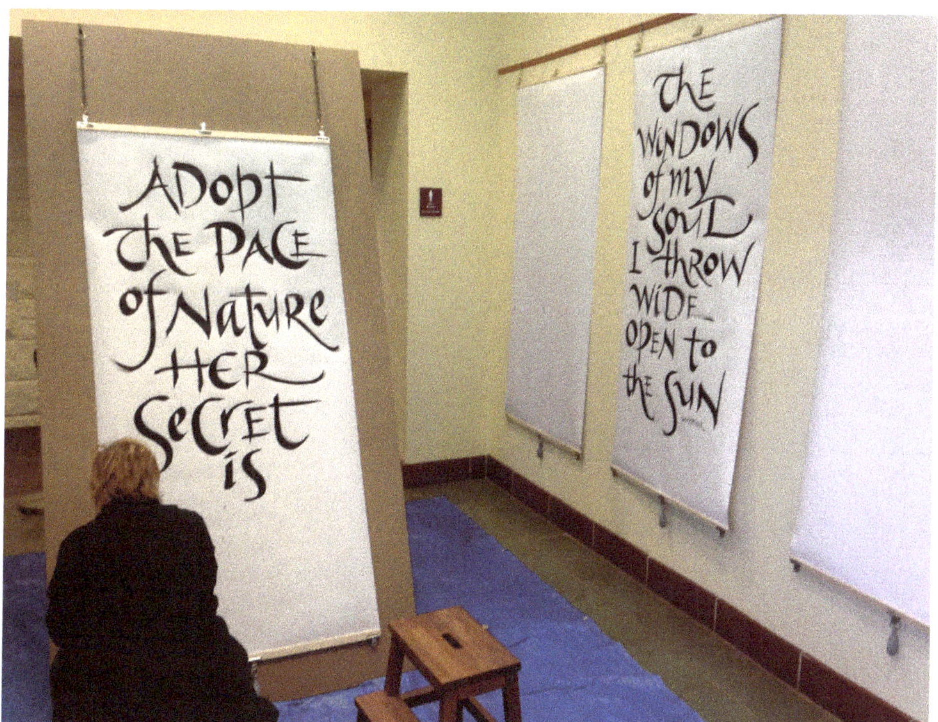

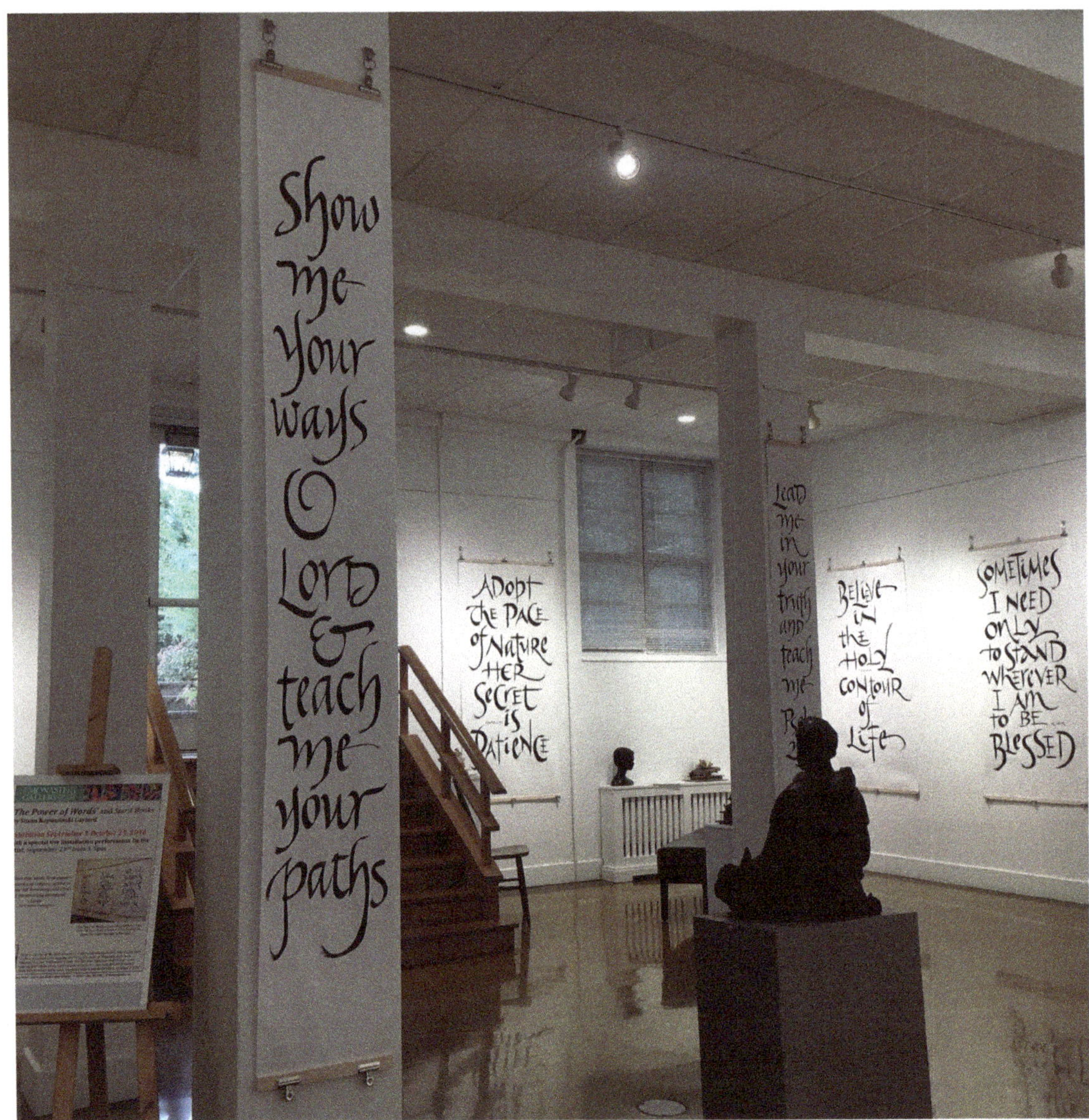

The banners were exhibited again in the fall of 2018 at the Monastery Gallery in
West Hartford along with nine Spirit Books. I lettered two new, much narrower
banners, again before an audience. I enjoy the immediate experience and feel great
relief when it is over.

In 2017, I did a word-based installation at the Cape Ann Museum's White-Ellery House in Gloucester, Massachusetts. This time it was temporary, on view for four hours and then recycled. I used words from the 1847–50 journals of Hannah S. Babson who began writing them just before her twelfth birthday. Her words evoked everyday life in another era.

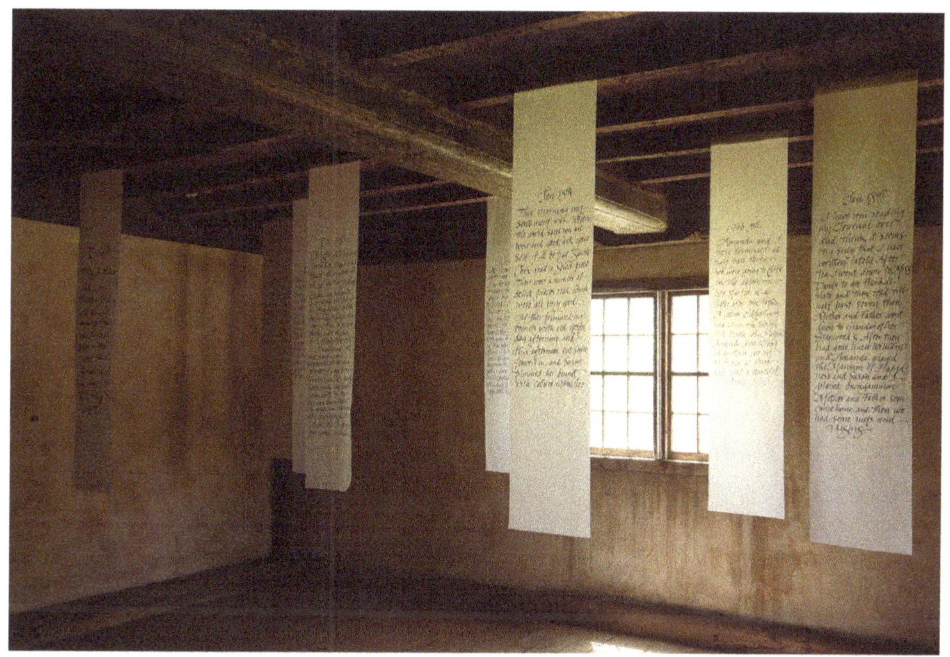

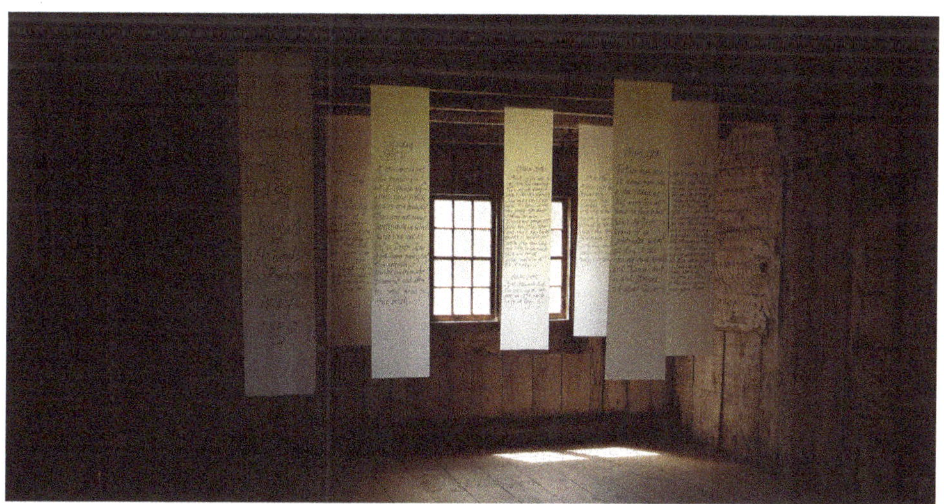

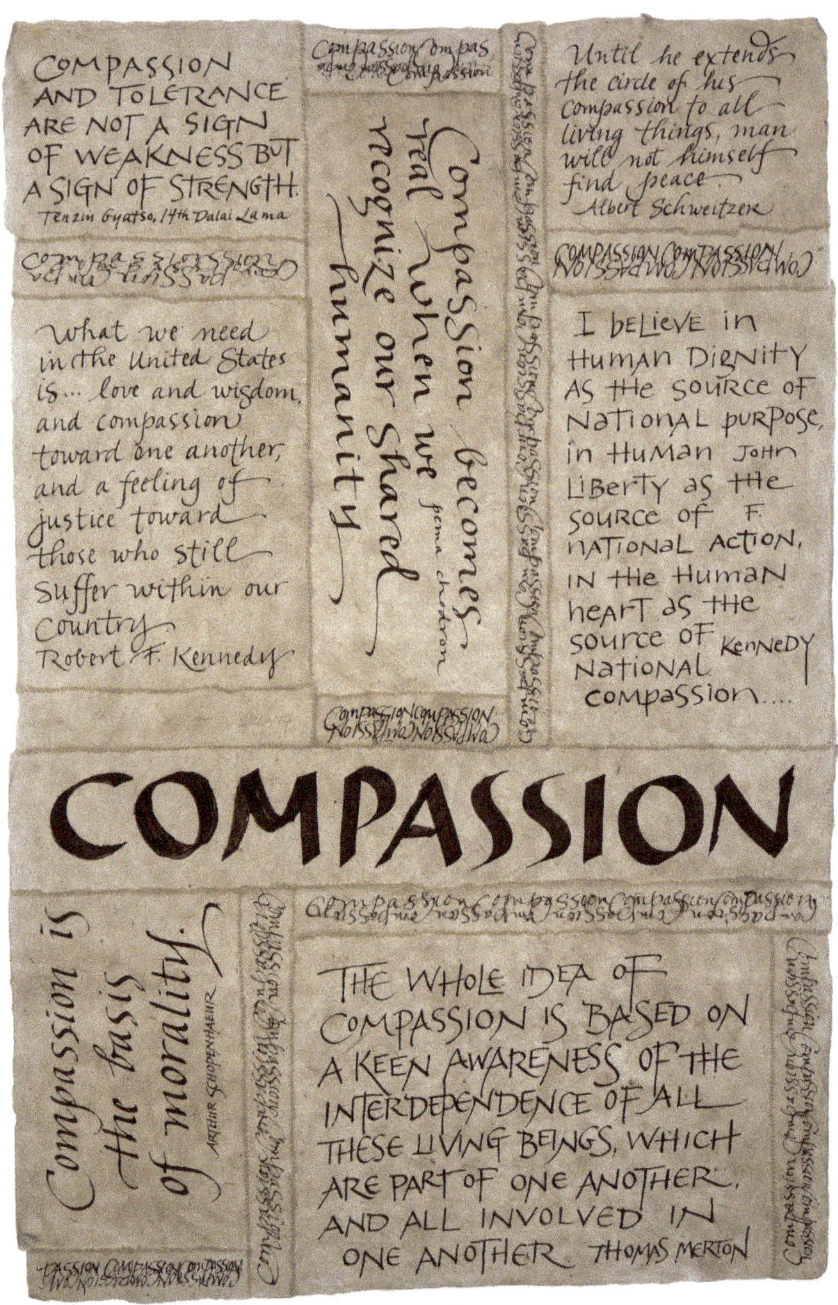

Words For Our Time is a series of eight works created in response to the 2016 election. Each one is based on a word—compassion, strength, justice, peace, love, courage, truth, hope—and made from one sheet of paper which was torn into pieces. They were lettered on and then sewn back together to make a mended and unified whole.

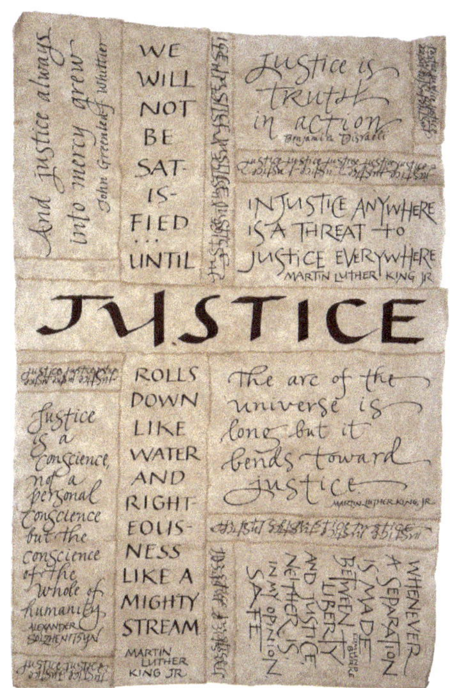

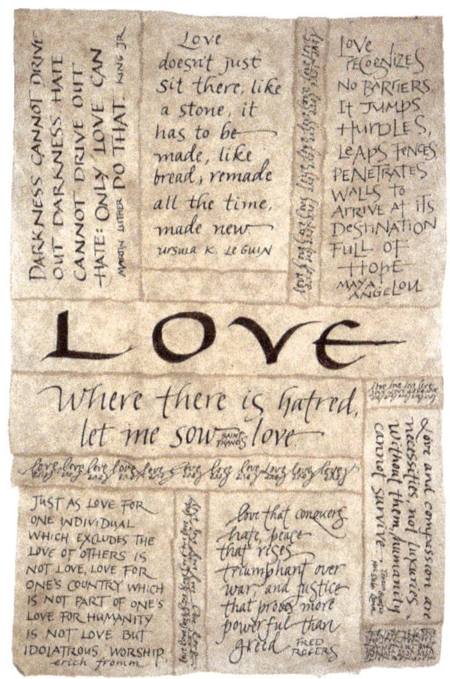

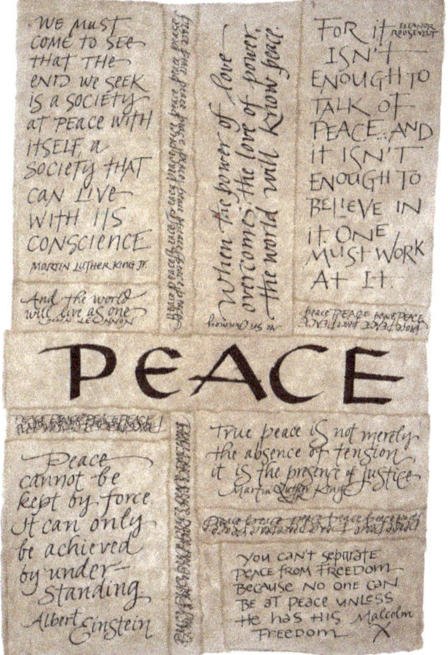

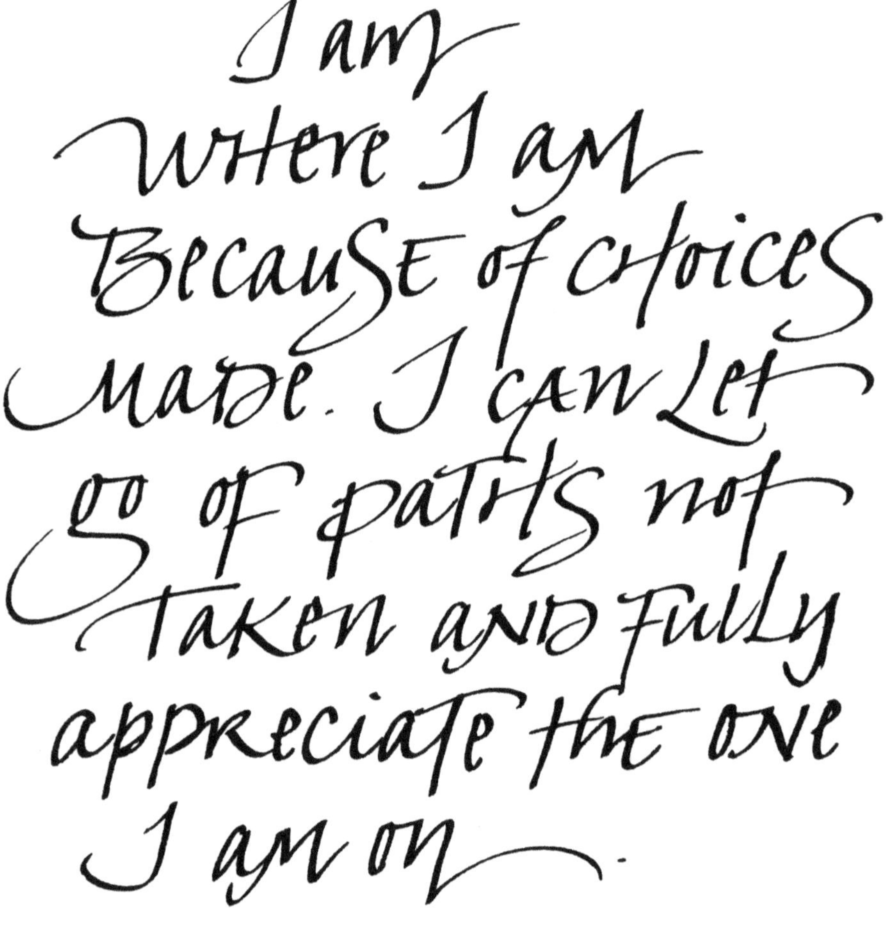

I am
where I am
because of choices
made. I can let
go of paths not
taken and fully
appreciate the one
I am on.

My current approach to calligraphy owes most to the organic process of the Spirit Books. I don't plan what style of lettering I will use until I start writing. The pen or brush, paper, words, and my state of mind decide for me. I try to let my calligraphic work unfold the way the Spirit Books do, with the work leading me rather than my leading it. I don't practice. I don't do exercises to try out ideas for their own sake. I only work with words and ideas that touch my heart.

I rarely make lines—only on the few occasions when I am making a longer original piece. If it is short and original, I'd rather do it multiple times than make lines. I think of Robert Henri's assertion that "every true work of art is the attainment of . . . a more than ordinary moment of existence." If I am doing work for reproduction (easier to post and share), I can make corrections in Photoshop. My most frequent problem is that the lines of writing go slightly higher on the right. I have been told that in handwriting analysis this is the sign of an optimistic personality.

There are two things in my relationship with calligraphy that have allowed me to develop this approach. One is that I do not teach. I feel no obligation to broaden my knowledge for the benefit of my students. Two is that I do no commercial or commissioned work. I can be completely personal in my focus. Of course, that means there are things I cannot do. I am where I am because of choices made. I can let go of paths not taken and fully appreciate the one I am on.

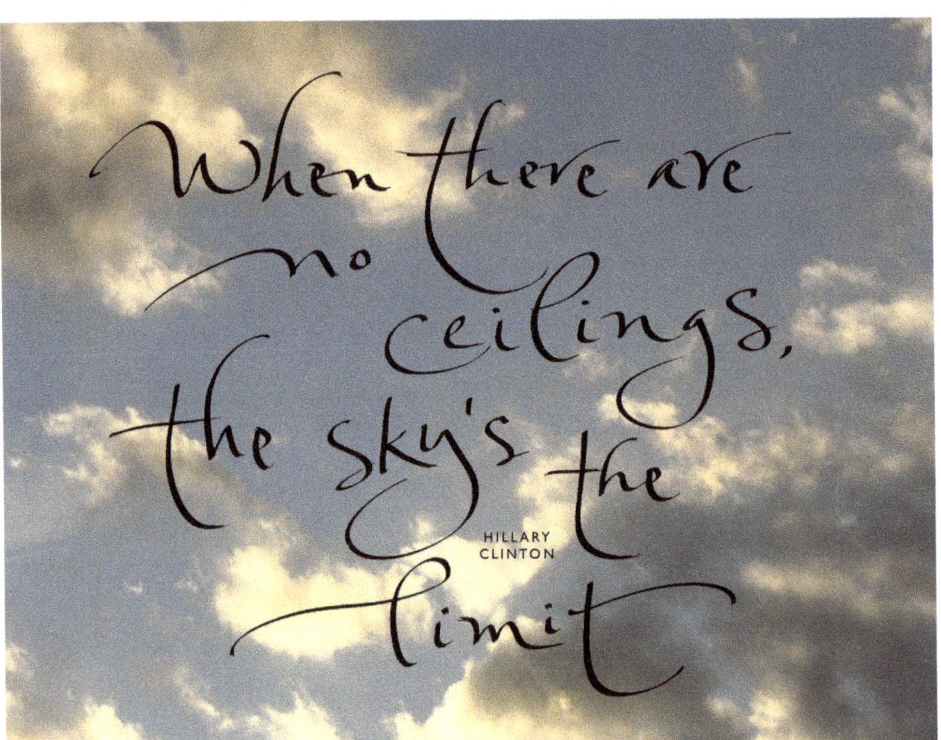

Above: Dr. Martin's Bleedproof White with Speedball C nib on charcoal paper. Below: Higgins Eternal Ink with Speedball C nib scanned and placed on photograph of clouds in Photoshop. Written and shared after the 2016 Democratic National Convention.

When I dare to be powerful, to use my strength in the service of my vision, it becomes less and less important whether I am afraid.

AUDRE LORDE

Lock up your libraries if you like; but there is no gate, no lock, no bolt that you can set upon the freedom of my mind.

VIRGINIA WOOLF

Both written with Pilot Parallel Pen. Above: Written for booklet made and shared at the Women's March in 2017. Below: Written and shared for International Women's Day.

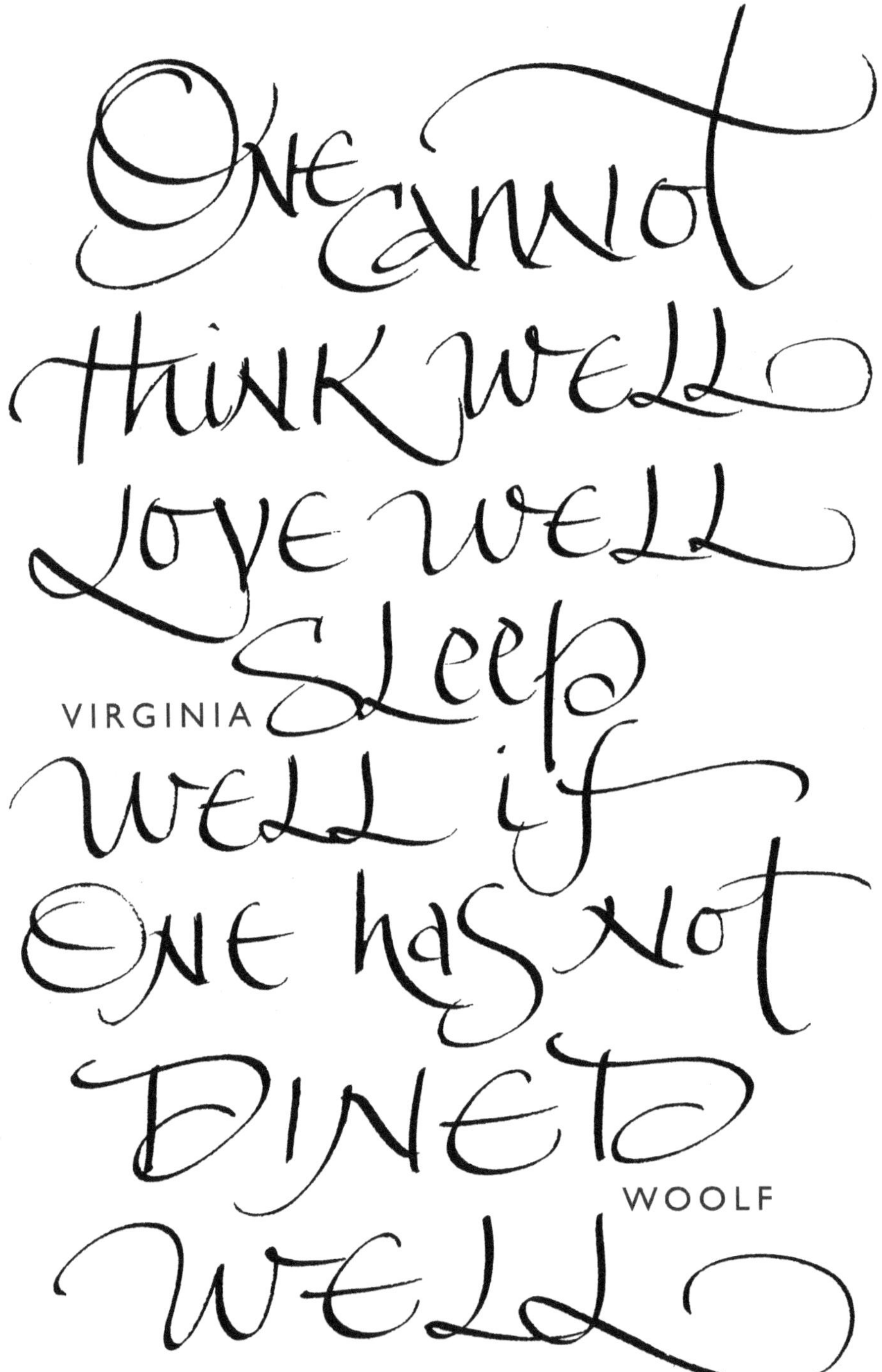

Above: Lettering with Speedball C nib and Higgins Eternal Ink. Opposite Page: Clockwise: Roses: Written with edge of automatic pen. Breathe: Written with automatic pen and duplicated and combined in Photoshop. Design: Written with Pilot Parallel Pen.

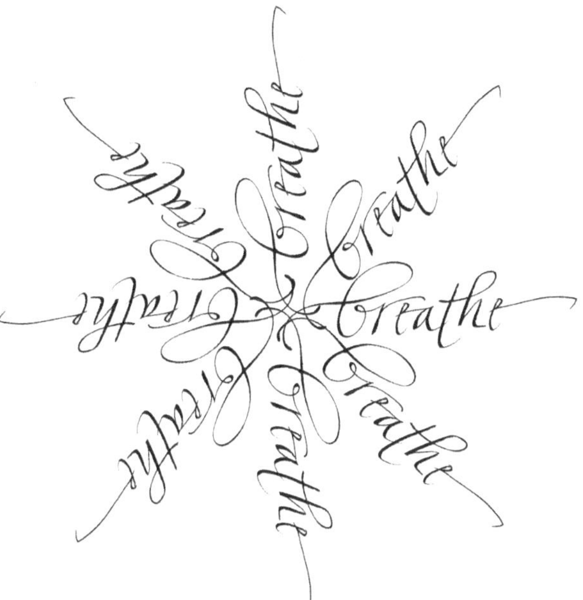

give us
BREAD
but give
us
ROSES
too

YOU DO NOT
WORK
AT DESIGN.
you PLAY
AT IT.

JONATHAN
HALE

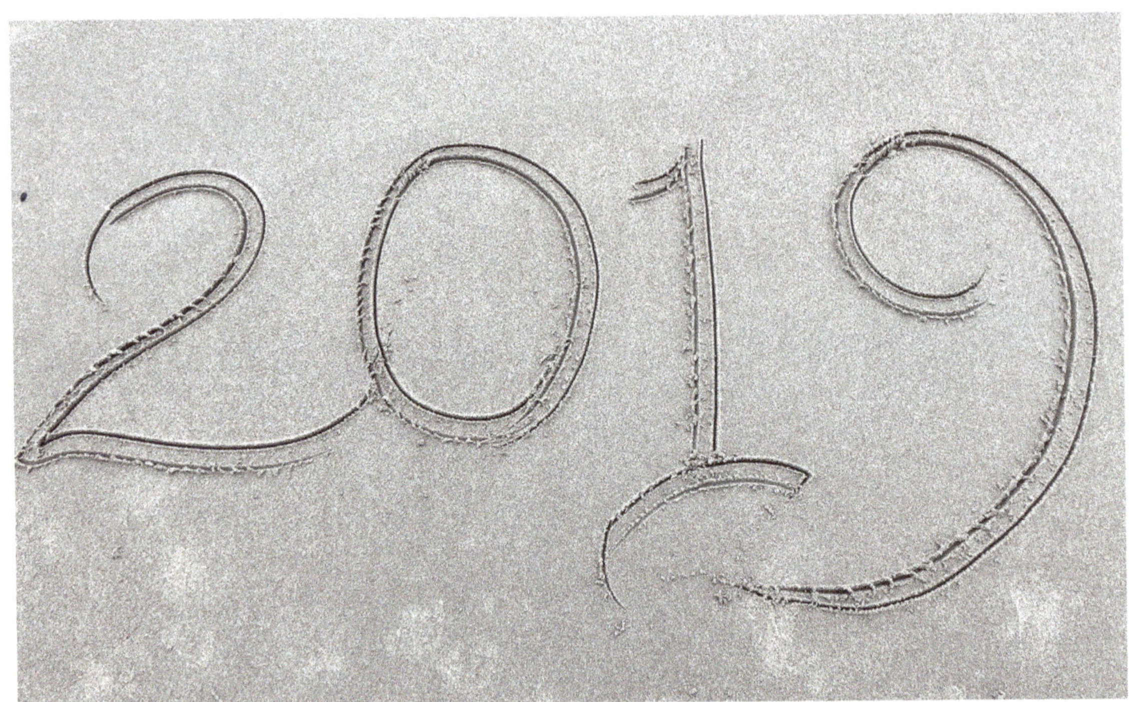

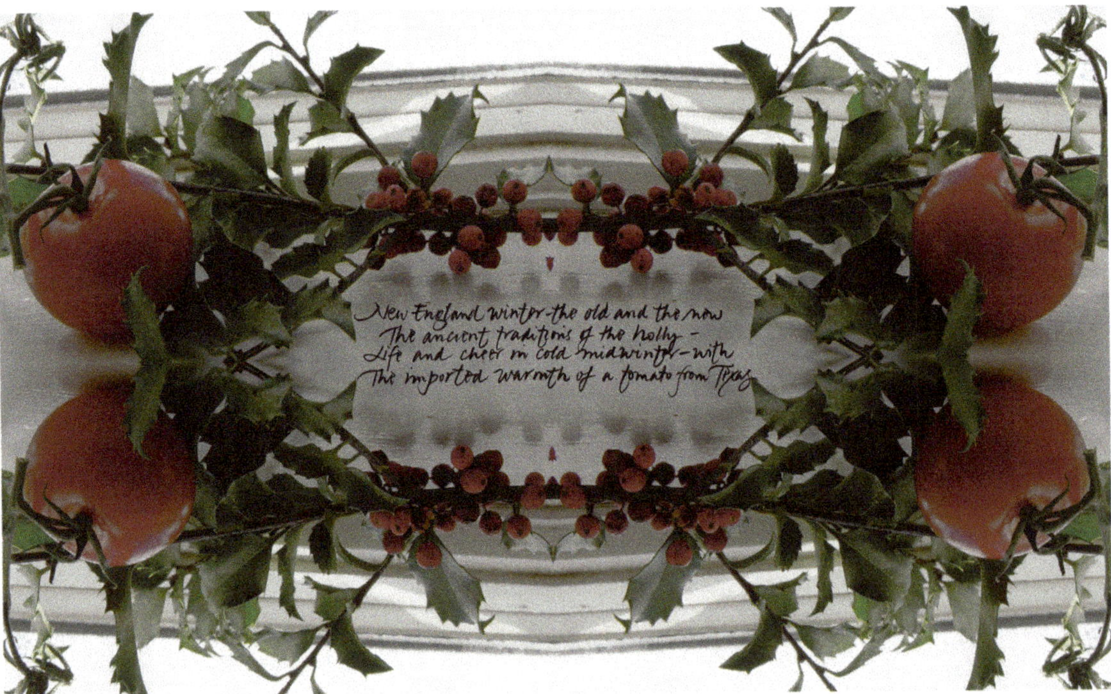

Above: Written with a stick in sand at Good Harbor Beach in Gloucester, Massachusetts. Below: Lettering done with Pentel brush pen, scanned and combined with photograph in Photoshop.

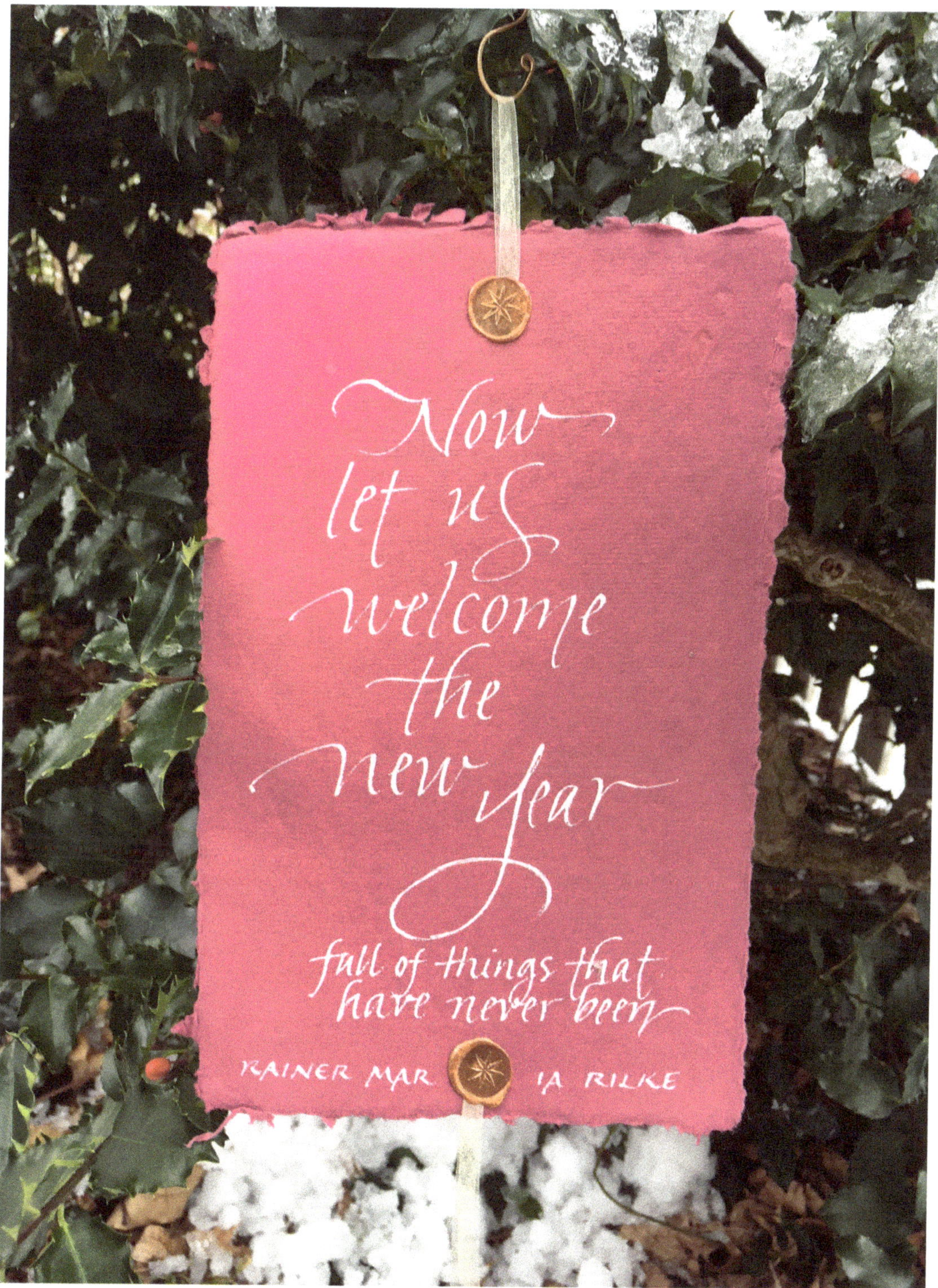

Lettering done with Dr. Martin's Bleedproof White and Speedball C nib on handmade Shizen paper from India.

Lettering done with ruling pen and sumi ink.

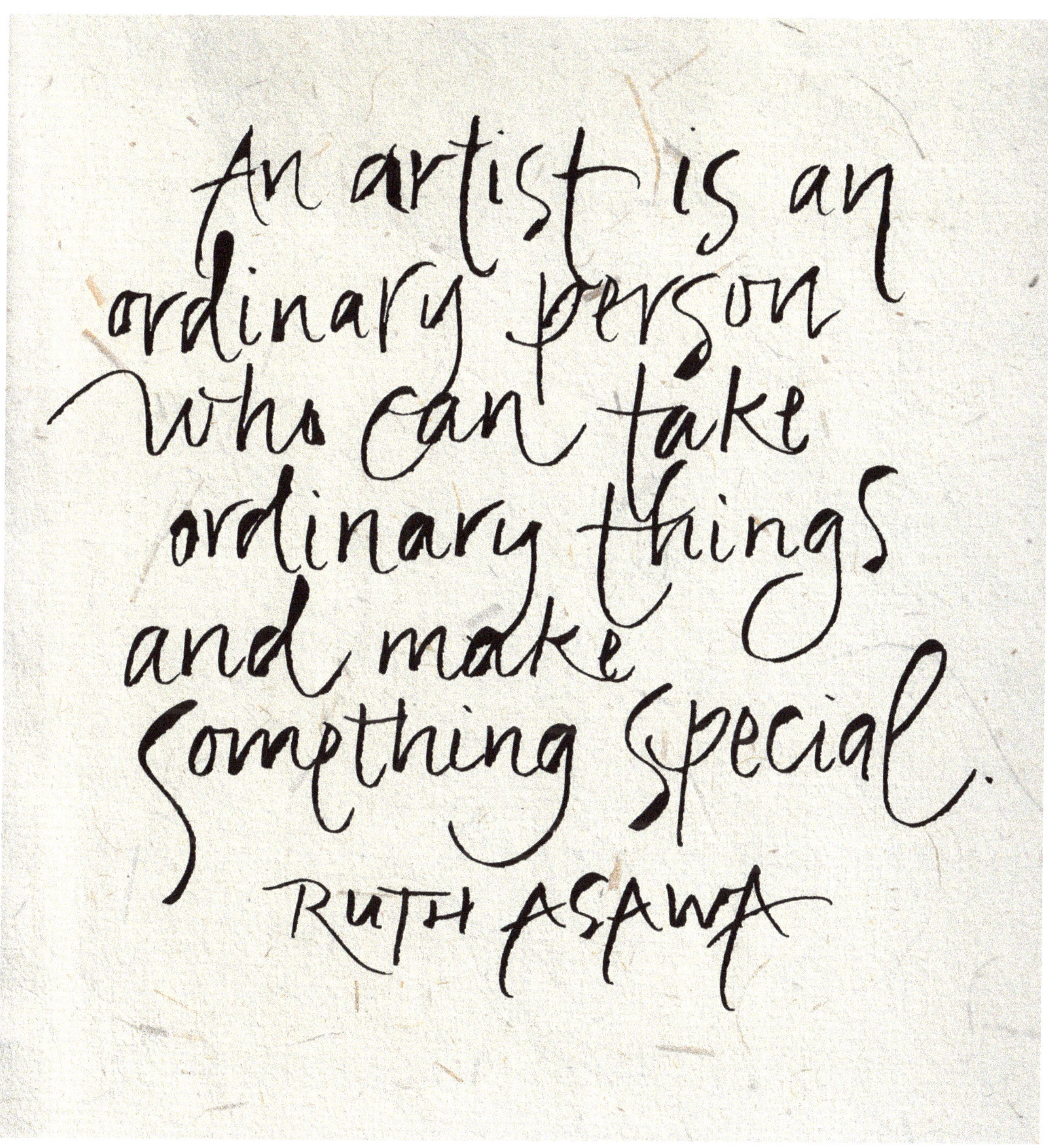

Lettering done with folded pen made in Masscribes workshop with Carol DuBosch.

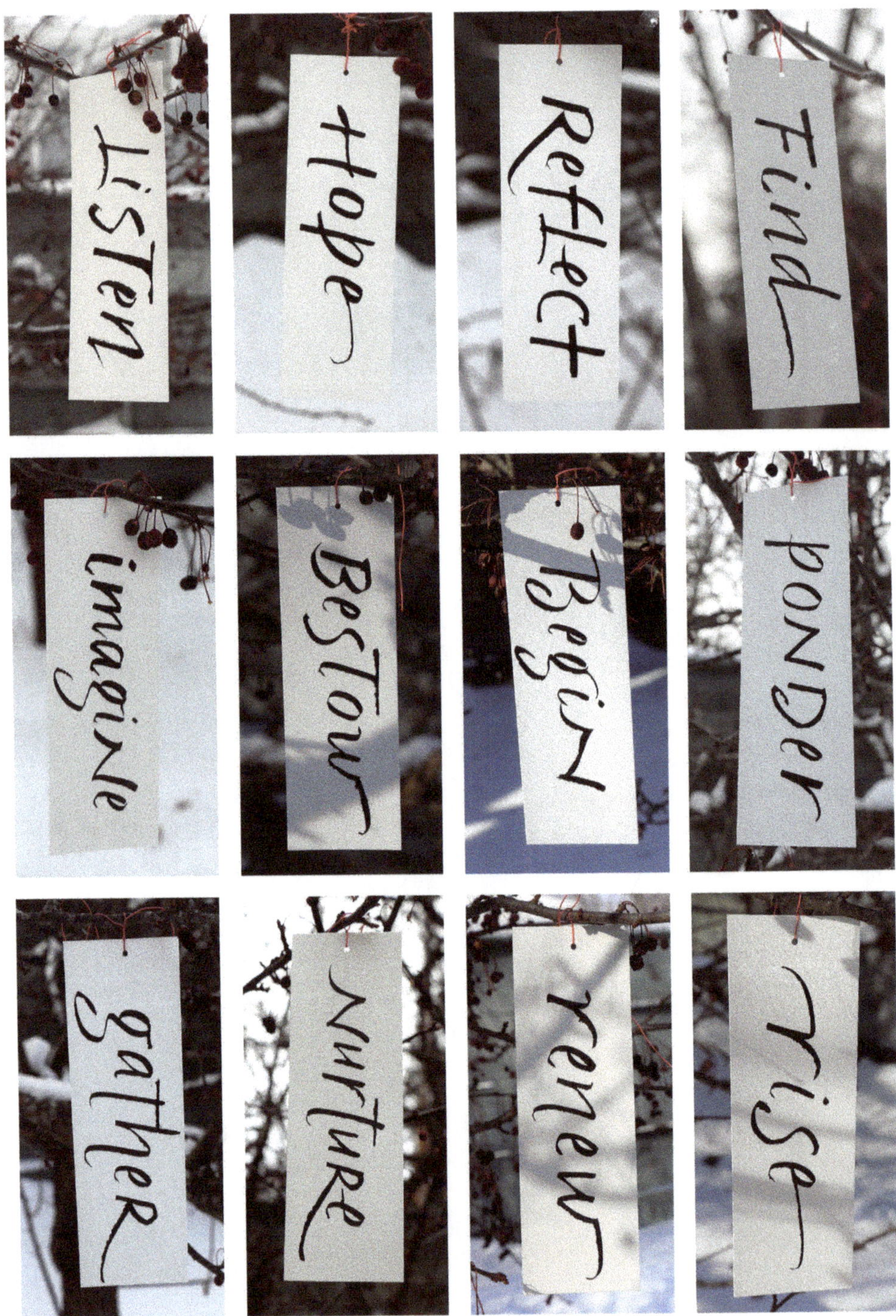

Above: Strips of words written on watercolor paper with folded pen and sumi ink, one for each of the Twelve Days of Christmas, hung on the crabapple tree in the garden. Opposite Page: Written with Speedball C nibs and Higgins Eternal Ink for Croning Ceremony in May 2018.

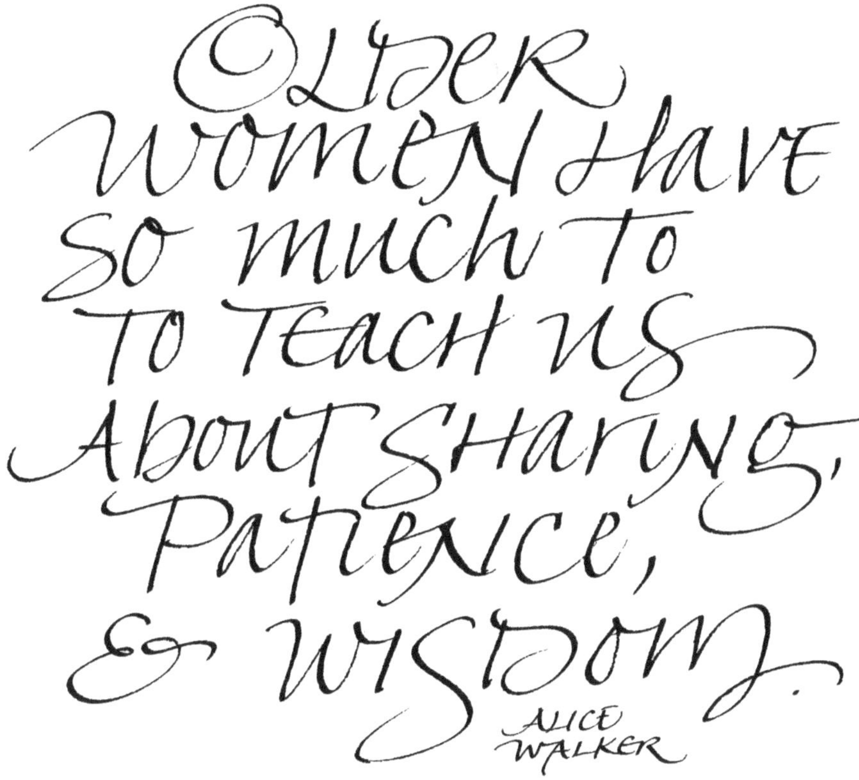

Older women have so much to to teach us about sharing, patience, & wisdom.

— Alice Walker

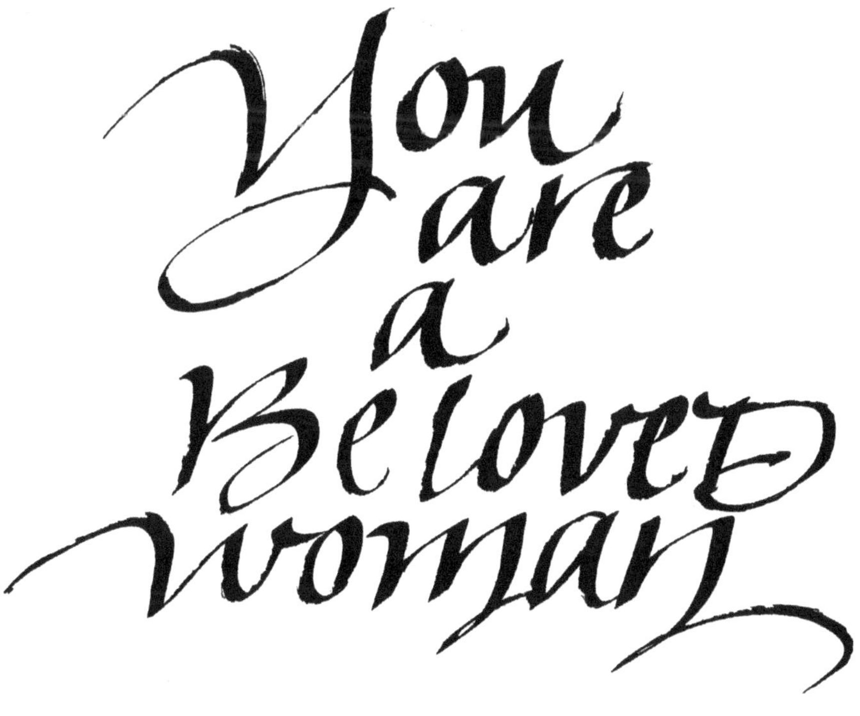

You are a Beloved woman

May I live this day
Compassionate of heart,
Clear in work,
Gracious in awareness,
Courageous in thought,
Generous in love.

JOHN O'DONOHUE

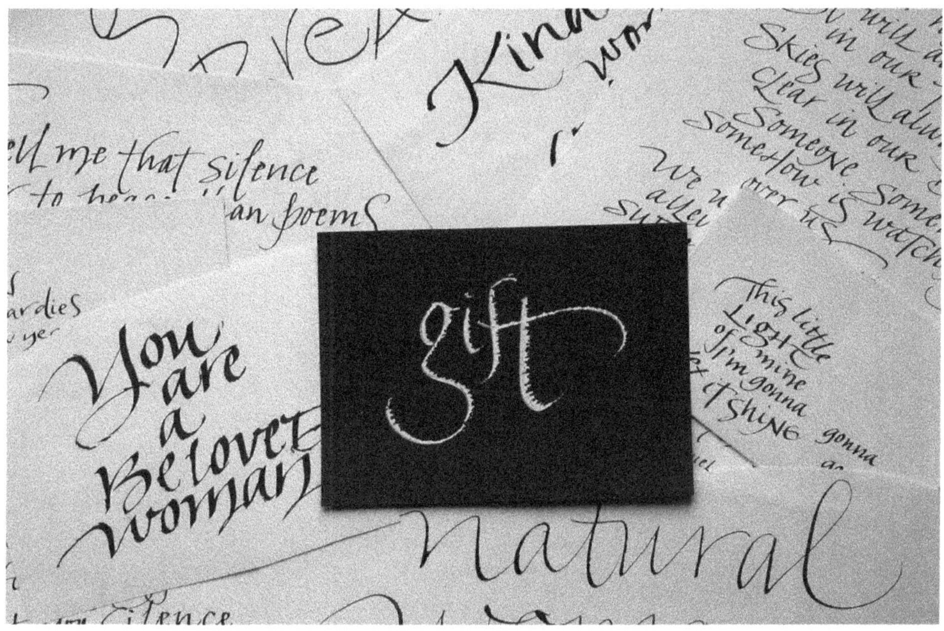

Forty years ago calligraphy came to me as a gift. It was a demanding gift that required work and discipline. It awakened my creativity as well as my insecurities and doubts. The joy of working with words that I loved and the twenty-six letters that I learned to love kept me going until they didn't. After years of focusing on making books, I slowly brought calligraphy back into my life.

Now the gift has changed. While I had been experimenting with freer letters for many years, they weren't free in my heart. They were still in a semi-constant state of comparison and often came up short. Now I take them as they are, a spontaneous expression of the moment, drawing on my history and hard work, opening myself fully to the joy of pen and paper and ink.

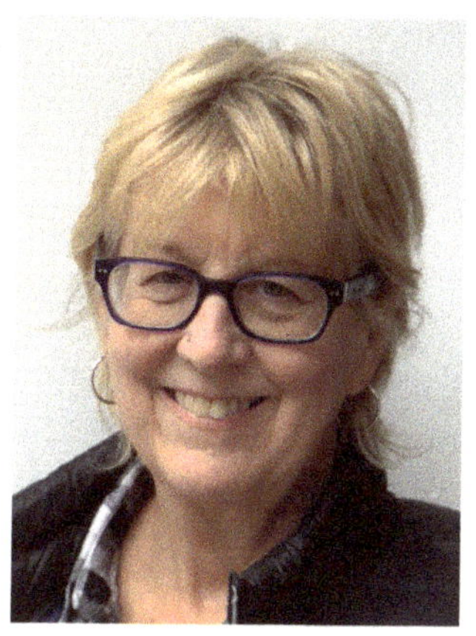

Susan's involvement in the arts includes roles as artist, teacher, speaker, writer, designer, and publisher. Her artists' books are in the library collections of the Museum of Modern Art, Wellesley College, Yale University, and Bowdoin College and have been exhibited across the U.S. and Canada and in Korea. She is the author of the independently published *Art Lessons: Reflections From An Artist's Life*, *The Spirit Books* catalog, and *Handmade Books For A Healthy Planet*, and *Multicultural Books To Make and Share*, *Hands-On History: The Middle Ages*, and *Super Pop-Up Reports For American History* from Scholastic Professional Books. Her work has been featured in magazines (*Somerset Studio*, *Fiberarts*, *Bound & Lettered*, and *Letter Arts Review*) and books (*500 Handmade Books*, *500 More Handmade Books*, *1,000 Artists' Books*, *Cover to Cover*, *The Art of the Handmade Book*, and *Handmade Books And Cards*). Susan is a seasoned presenter and currently lectures on the history of the book, calligraphy, the artist's life, and the intersection of art and commerce.